HISTORY
OF
SHELBY COUNTY, KENTUCKY

HISTORY of SHELBY COUNTY KENTUCKY

Written, Compiled and Edited by
George L. Willis, Sr.

Under the Auspices of the
SHELBY COUNTY GENEALOGICAL-HISTORICAL
SOCIETY'S COMMITTEE ON PRINTING

COMMITTEE
MRS. KATHERINE BRYANT SMITH, *(Genealogist) Chairman*
MRS. MARY MIDDELTON NICHOLAS, *(President) Member*
MRS. BELL WATSON BOTELER, *(Secretary) Member*
MISS ESTELLA ALLEN, *(Treasurer) Member*

HERITAGE BOOKS
2009

HERITAGE BOOKS
AN IMPRINT OF HERITAGE BOOKS, INC.

Books, CDs, and more—Worldwide

For our listing of thousands of titles see our website
at
www.HeritageBooks.com

A Facsimile Reprint
Published 2009 by
HERITAGE BOOKS, INC.
Publishing Division
100 Railroad Ave. #104
Westminster, Maryland 21157

Copyright © 1929 George L. Willis, Sr.

Index Copyright © 1999 Heritage Books, Inc.

— Publisher's Notice —
In reprints such as this, it is often not possible to remove blemishes from the original. We feel the contents of this book warrant its reissue despite these blemishes and hope you will agree and read it with pleasure.

International Standard Book Numbers
Paperbound: 978-0-7884-1178-6
Clothbound: 978-0-7884-8275-5

TO HER

Whose smile of approval, under the winter evening's lamp, inspired the effort and made the work a delight.

CONTENTS

PART I.

Shelby County—A Narrative

CHAPTER

	DEDICATION	5
	ILLUSTRATIONS	11
	PREFACE	13
	ACKNOWLEDGMENT	15
I.	GEOLOGY, TOPOGRAPHY, BOUNDARIES	19
II.	FIRST PERIOD OF GROWTH	27
III.	FIRST VISITORS AND SETTLERS	33
IV.	A CENTURY OF GROWTH	39

PART II.

Stations and Towns

I.	FIRST SETTLERS—STATIONS	45
II.	TOWNS AND VILLAGES	53

PART III.

Churches and Schools

I.	BAPTISTS IN SHELBY	65
II.	CHRISTIAN OR CHURCH OF DISCIPLES	77
III.	THE METHODISTS IN SHELBY	83
IV.	SHELBY COUNTY EPISCOPALIANS	89
V.	PRESBYTERIANS	93
VI.	CATHOLICS	99
VII.	FIRST SCHOOLS—*Stuart's, et al*	103

CONTENTS

CHAPTER
VIII. SCIENCE HILL 107
IX. OTHER PRIVATE AND PUBLIC SCHOOLS 109

PART IV.
Other County Institutions

I. COURT HOUSE AND COURTS 113
II. JAILS AND NOTED CRIMES 117
III. BLOCKHOUSE AND RAIDS 123
IV. COUNTY PRESS 127
V. FAIRS 131
VI. CEMETERY 133

PART V.
Pioneer Personages

I. SQUIRE BOONE 139
II. WILLIAM SHANNON 143
III. BLAND BALLARD 147
IV. COL. CHAS. S. TODD 153
V. WILLIAM LOGAN 155
VI. JOHN ALLEN 157
VII. COL. ABRAHAM OWEN 159
VIII. GOVERNOR JOHN POPE 163
IX. CAPT. JOHN SIMPSON 165
X. MOSES HALL 167
XI. DR. JOHN KNIGHT 169
XII. NICHOLAS MERRIWETHER 171
XIII. JOSEPH HORNSBY 173

PART VI.
Traditions and Reminiscence

I. WILCOX, STORY, LONG RUN MASSACRE 177

CONTENTS

CHAPTER
- II. JOHN W. WILLIAMSON'S REMINISCENCE 181
- III. CROSS KEYS INN 185
- IV. LINCOLN'S SHELBY ANCESTORS 195
- V. REMINISCENCES OF OLD ATTORNEY 201
- VI. THE SILVER MINE AGREEMENT 205

PART VII.
Official Statistics

- I. FIRST TAX LIST 209
- II. SENATORS AND REPRESENTATIVES 217
- III. CONSTITUTIONAL DELEGATES 219
- IV. COUNTY JUDGES—JUSTICES 221
- V. COUNTY CLERKS 223
- VI. CIRCUIT JUDGES AND CLERKS, ET AL 225
- VII. U. S. POSTMASTERS 227
- VIII. EARLY MARRIAGES 229
- IX. INDEX, FIRST WILL BOOK 241
- X. REVOLUTIONARY SOLDIERS IN SHELBY 243
- XI. FIRST IN PROFESSIONS, BUSINESS AND TRADES 249
- XII. EARLY BANK OFFICIALS 253
- XIII. PIONEER MILLS 257
- XIV. EARLY WEATHER RECORDS 259
- XV. SHELBY COUNTY MASONS 261
- XVI. GALLANT FIRST CITIZENS 265
- XVII. NOTED BURIAL GROUNDS 267

LIST OF ILLUSTRATIONS

THE BEN WASHBURN RESIDENCE BETWEEN SHELBYVILLE AND PLEASUREVILLE	19
SHELBYVILLE IN 1855	19
A MODEL, MODERN COUNTY ROAD	43
TREE ON EMINENCE ROAD, FRONT OF LAYSON HOME	45
TENANT HOUSE NEAR SITE OF BALLARD CABIN AND TYLER STATION	45
BUFFALO LICK CHURCH	65
MULBERRY CHURCH	65
"OLD BETHEL," ACROSS THE ROAD FROM "CROSS-KEYS"	83
SITE FROM WHICH "ANTIOCH," PIONEER CHRISTIAN CHURCH BUILDING WAS RAZED	83
"YE OLE STONE INN" AT SIMPSONVILLE	153
THE CHARLES TODD RESIDENCE FIVE MILES NORTH OF SHELBYVILLE	153
A LATE VIEW OF "CROSS-KEYS INN"	185
LONG RUN BAPTIST CHURCH	195
SURVEYOR'S CHARTS OF ABRAHAM LINCOLN'S ANCESTORS	197
SITE OF OLD LINCOLN CABIN	201
THIRTEEN MILES EAST OF SHELBYVILLE AT ABOUT WHERE TWO TRAILS OVER WHICH THE PIONEERS CAME NOW MEET	249
THE FLOYD MONUMENT, FIFTEEN MILES WEST OF SHELBYVILLE	249

PREFACE

Lord MacCauley: *"The best history of a country, is a record of the lives of its people."*

Longfellow: *"They who live in history only seem to walk the earth again."*

Voltaire: *"History is little else than a picture of human crimes and misfortunes."*

Lord Bolingbroke: *"I think that history is philosophy teaching by examples."*

Carlyle: *"History is the essence of innumerable biographies."*

The *biographies* of *pioneers* published herewith are not numerous but purposely of some *length*, because in these stories or sketches of men like Ballard, Boone, Allen, et al, is told *much of the* history of the county, that the casual reader may miss from other parts of the book, just as *so much* of the same sort of history is *incidentally* told in the *within* sketches of *Stations, Towns, Churches, Schools* and in *"papers of the period,"* and is not therefore *duplicated* in other parts where the reader might not unnaturally expect to find same.

For these reasons, *no reader can do* this book justice or judge as to its scope until he shall *have read it all.* Even then he will *not have found* reference to *every important* occurrence of the 150 *years* touched upon. Particularly, *this will be* found true *of the events of later years.* The *paramount purpose of the book is to preserve for posterity what was so rapidly fading into oblivion.* The older persons of the county can still tell and prove by the records, what their parents and grandparents told them. But *this book goes back of them,* and *when it is in the libraries of homes and schools,* will preserve for those to come the abstracts and facts from public and private records, that *could not be reproduced* were this county visited by the disastrous fires that have wiped out the court houses and other public buildings in other counties of the State.

There are *other reasons* why *histories* of the more important independent counties of the states, like the histories of the individual shires of England, are no longer novelties, but *necessities*. A World's Atlas cannot take the place of the county map. The general histories can no more take the place of the detailed record of a county than can the great metropolitan daily supplant the county weekly, with its peculiar field and mission. But in the history of a county like this there is so much to tell to the interested ones who have gone out to all parts of the world, and about those who have gone away to "that bourn from which no traveler returns," that it has been difficult to limit it to the proper territory and confine it to a reasonable volume.

We who *derive no revenue* from, nor reward for the labor expended upon it *will be content,* if it shall have served its purpose in salvaging for posterity, a record of the names and some of the deeds of those warm-hearted, stout-hearted pioneer men and women, who made Kentucky the Heart of the Nation and Shelby County, the Heart of Kentucky.

ACKNOWLEDGMENT

The man in the hold of the ship, the men behind the guns, the chemist, the modest engineer, laboratory employee, and others whose midnight oil and sweating brows are mainly responsible for the great achievements in the world, seldom get anything like their just share of the credit due. In years to come the nominal editor of this volume should not be accounted too mainly responsible for any merit it contains. His task has been like the task of most men, not only set for him, but made easier for him by the good women of his circle.

The tedium of writing and assembling the facts has not been all pleasure and ease. Neither was the work of those patriotic county women, the members of the Shelby County Genealogical-Historical Society, who through the years, garnered, with industry and commendably fine, meticulous care, their share of the facts dug from the soil and from the dusty, musty archives of this and other counties.

It seems somewhat the habit of Kentucky historians, little and big, to, in a manner, sneer at "Collins History," and then unconsciously to reveal that the most they know about the State has been learned not from the dependable court records, but from those whose work they would minimize. No real history of any Kentucky County has been or could be well written without drawing frequently and at length upon the work of Lewis Collins, and that of those no less valued Kentuckians, Richard Collins, Mann Butler and Humphrey Marshall.

In a lesser but no less appreciated degree, the author is indebted to Shaler, Smith, Durrett and the old newspaper work of the late Ed. D. Shinnick in his "Old Time History"; to his predecessors, and to letters and papers of such pioneers as Wilcox, Williamson, Ballard, Winlock, et al.; from all of whom he has appropriated liberal extracts. The Draper papers, and the courtesies of the Kentucky State Historical Society and the Filson Club have also been utilized in some degree.

PART I
Shelby County—A Narrative

The Ben Washburn residence between Shelbyville and Pleasureville, the oldest stone residence in Shelby County. Erected in 1791; has stood in two states, three counties and has housed three generations of Ben Washburns, never having been conveyed by deed.

Shelbyville in 1855—looking West over the Blockhouse that stood in the center of the public square. The third courthouse, "the little red building," had also taken the place of the log structures, and stood just to the right and front of the photographer.

A NARRATIVE
CHAPTER I
Geology and Geography

Shelby County is located on the Globe's surface, in all probability, about where it was when,

> "*He rounded out the new green Earth and flung,*
> *It out to roll the centuries away.*"

The waters which are said to now underlay it may have been underlain by it. The surface that it then had, may have been brushed away by the glaciers. The "eternal" rocks upon which it rests may be its comparatively new foundation, but it was probably then, as it is now, situate 2,310 miles South of the top of the world and 5,130 miles west of what later became Greenwich, England—in latitude 38.30 and longitude 85.30.

From the Silurian limestone capping its highest knobs down to the Eden shale that crops out along the Eastern boundary and the waters on its Southern line, it is, because of the meager exploratory boring and limited topographical surveys, still more or less a geological mystery. Its structural attitude is described by Dr. Jillson, the Geologist, as "monoclinal," the dip being pronouncedly to the Northwest "from a medial position on the Lexington dome of the Cincinnati arch. Minor flexures are recognizable at various points as anticlines and synclines, while in the vicinity of Jeptha Knob, Crypto-volcanic structure is responsible for a remarkable monadnock."

Of its soil, an amateur poet has said that here, we gaze on Shelby's beauty, as she stands on her native heather "where the Bluegrass touches the Beargrass, and they lie down in peace together." It is not generally known, however, that the highest point in the whole Bluegrass region is up Shelby's gentle rise to the top of Jeptha Knob, near Clayvillage, where the elevation is 1,163 feet above sea level. There are other high spots, literal and figurative, in Shelby County and it is upon some of these which this Part I of the volume seeks to touch.

Aside from its geology, topography and soil, Shelby County in Kentucky was for long the geographical center of the United States and for a longer period its center of population. In 1792, when Kentucky County, Virginia, had been made into a State of three Counties, one of which was Jefferson, Shelby County, named for the State's first Governor, was carved out of the latter, and was the third created after Kentucky was admitted into the Union. When Henry and part of Franklin, Oldham and Spencer were created from, and pared off of the original territory, and the exact boundary lines had been determined (by surveys of Commissioners, appointed by succeeding legislatures) it came to contain an area of 273,280 acres, 427 square miles, and remained and continues to be territorially one of the largest Counties in the State. From the beginning, throughout the one hundred and fifty years since its settlement by whites, it has been almost exclusively an agricultural county, whose Anglo-Saxon people have known practically no other vocation, and whose chief avocations from the beginning have been their churches, their schools and their politics.

With but little rugged, uncultivated territory even on its Northeast and Western boundaries, it slopes undulatingly and beautifully in two directions from the highest point already mentioned—the Northeast portion toward the Kentucky River Valley and the South and Western portion toward the Salt River and Ohio Valley. The streams of the Northeastern slope are Benson and Six Mile Creek, flowing into the Kentucky River; the streams of the much larger South and Western sheds are Clear Creek, Beech, Gist, Brashears, Bull Skin, Fox Run, Plum, Long Run and Floyds Fork, all joining and flowing into Salt River.

First Inhabitants

The ethnologists are demonstrating, convincingly to some, that, a few hundred thousand years ago a race of people crossed over from Asia by way of Siberia, the Diomede Islands and

Geology and Geography

Seward Peninsula, into Alaska, down through the costal plains and the Yukon and into North, and later South America. The Red man found by the first white visitors to Kentucky and Shelby County, they believe, was a descendant of these rather "old families."*

As to the first white visitors into what was then Shelby County there is considerable reason, in the writer's opinion, to believe that he was not Dr. Walker nor any of those who preceded Boone, into eastern Kentucky, but John Finley, adventurous woodsman and hunter, who in 1767 came out of North Carolina and entered not only eastern Kentucky but what is now known as the Bluegrass region.

Several historians agree he was the first white man to penetrate the Kentucky wilderness as far as the center of the State. Who were with him, where else they went, what they did, is not told on the printed page, but Finley went back and told Daniel Boone and their neighbors of the "wonderful land" with such eloquent enthusiasm as to inspire them with a determination to visit not only the Kentucky wilderness but what he even then called "God's Own Country." What became of Finley after his second visit with Boone is unrecorded, but it is reasonable to suppose that somewhere within the "stillness and sublime silence of the great forest to which he led the white man," the red man found him, took his life, and left him "as his shroud the leaves of the forest," and as his monument the mighty trees which stood sentinel through the ages over the genial and fertile soil of Central Kentucky.

At any rate, it was a Boone who began the settlement of Shelby County Territory; for most accredited historians agree

---

*Some think that these first arrivals on the continent may have come over "Atlantis" before it was an ocean and that they evolved, through the ages, into entirely separate races, with intermittent civilizations. The Indians who were found here two hundred years ago had some such theory themselves, for they claimed that their lands had been taken by them from the first occupants too long ago for history. Indian traditions say that the last great battle between the red men and the "long ago people" was fought near Louisville, and Col. Durrett in his "Centenary of Louisville" in 1880, says, Here and at Clarksville, on the opposite side of the river the first settlers found great quantities of human bones in the confusion in which the last struggle for life would naturally have left them, and the Indians claimed that these were the bones of the "long ago people," exterminated by their ancestors.

History of Shelby County

that the first of Shelby's peculiarly large number of Stations was that of the "Painted Stone," established in 1779, by Squire Boone, a younger brother of Daniel and that his and his associates' lives are those which etched in Shelby soil the first tragic traces of its start toward civilization. The Squire Boone Station is the first sketched in the sub-division of Part II of this volume, devoted to Shelby's Settlements and Stations.

Mostly Anglo-Saxon

The first settlers at the "Painted Stone" and at several other first Stations of the County seem to have been largely of pure Anglo-Saxon blood. Kentuckians generally, in the Mountains as well as the lowlands, are so largely of pure English stock, because it was principally the Virginia Anglicans who found their way to Cumberland Gap through which most of the Kentucky Stations' settlers first came. The people of other races who early landed on the Atlantic coast, were either far North or South of the Jamestown settlers and when they migrated they went, because of the mountains, far to the North and far to the South of us, and settled in the direction they took. This theory is true of the first settlers in Shelby County and it was some time before even the Ohio River brought its scattering quota from among Pennsylvania's and New England's sturdy Dutch and other races. Even those of the English who had left the Jamestown section for either North Virginia or North Carolina, when they came to Kentucky, frequently came on down to, or up to the "Gap," through it and up along the Wilderness road.

The first Kentucky forebear of whom the writer knows went from Culpeper Court House all the way to Carolina for his bride (also once a Jamestown-Virginian) and then back up to, and through the gap and on down into what was to become the original County of Shelby; and which at that time comprised no small part of "God's Own Country"—of which some of the other predecessors of Boone may have had a glimpse, but about

Geology and Geography

which Finley was the first to tell Boone. So doubtless was the story of many from Virginia and the Carolinas who made up the little heroic bands who were first into the forts and stations from which this County grew.

When the Hives Swarmed

The population of the several Stations grew as large villages and towns grow. They were hives that soon began to "swarm," and the individual bees, among whom there were no drones, began, each with his own queen bee, to find fields of sweet clover and to build hives of their own. By 1790, or ten years after the settling of the first of these stations, and after the massacre of Long Run there were in the County's broad expanse, and where Shelbyville the County seat now is, a population all told of possibly two thousand people. Agitation began for a County, a Government of their own, for a Court House and most of all for somewhere that churches, schools and more homes could be built. The year 1792, was big with important events for Shelby as for Kentucky itself. History-making events trod one upon the other's heels so fast they did follow. First the county was created, cutting off from the County of Jefferson the whole of the territory that is now contained in Shelby and Henry and in parts of Carroll, Franklin, Owen and Spencer. The creation of the County was by the little body of Legislators meeting in the old first Capitol, at Lexington. The baby county was named for brand-new Kentucky's brand-new first Governor, Isaac Shelby, of "Traveler's Rest," then and now in Lincoln County. He signed the act, creating the County and naming commissioners, on June 28, 1792, and on the same day appointed David Standiford (afterward Senator) Sheriff. It was a large-sized baby, and like most of the newly born a little helpless at the start. It had so much more territory than people. Several times the size it now is, it contained as already indicated not more than two thousand population, and these continued to be for the most part within a few miles of the several old stations and the point where the County seat was that year located.

Locating a Courthouse

The first road or trail was off to the North and East of where the great trans-continental Midland Trail, formerly called the "Old State Road," now runs. Probably for that reason the first stations, that Squire Boone settled in 1779, and Tyler settled three years later, were both North of where the main highway later and now approaches Clear Creek at Shelbyville. Also, that is the reason many wanted the new Court House Building at or near the sign of the "Painted Stone," the Squire Boone Station (changed the next year to "Lynch's" Station) which would have located the town of Shelbyville two and one-half miles North of where it now is. It was the legislature of 1792, as said, which enacted a law appointing a Commission to lay off the town of Shelbyville and under the Chapter in the portion of this work devoted to Towns and Villages the names of the Commissioners and patriots and the details concerning the birth and growth of Shelbyville and other municipalities will be found.

County's First Decade

It is difficult to say how many "farms" had been "cleared," how many farm cabins had been built and how much population the big County contained in 1793. The total was probably still less than two thousand, for in that year it was made the law that every male over 16 years of age was a "tithable" and the total number of such males found in the County that year were 519, and in 1794 there were 620. However, the new "hives" and honey making were not all built and begun immediately near the town and were probably not all known to the tax gatherers as "tithable." Older people remember, that fifty or sixty years ago, and even on the farms ten or twelve miles distant from the County seat, there were in the fields "black spots" where the corn, wheat and tobacco grew more rankly than elsewhere; and in which could be found many

Geology and Geography

evidences that a human habitation had stood there; and not far away frequently could be found strangely shaped stones that had undoubtedly marked the graves of pioneers, all trace of whose lives are lost. The number of these spots and the signs of former burying places all went to show beyond doubt that there were many settlers' homes and cultivated spots far removed from the county seat, long before, and when the log Court House and hewn log residences of the town were also new.* In other words that swarm of the station hives began early and the people then and for years after multiplied more rapidly than they do now.

The town and the County by the middle nineties had begun to take on the air of civilization. The first civilization a people learn after proper attention to their religion, and education is to submit to taxation. And taxes paid according to the property owned and ability to pay are, so long as public funds are indispensable, the proper method and should be the prevailing ways and means of supplying not only governmental expenditures, but for sustaining our churches, our ministers, our charities, and all public enterprises. These "tithable" males of over 16 years of age grew in a few years to more than a thousand. Not only had they begun to be taxed, they had begun to be compensated in the only way we still soothe the taxpayer, viz.: by allowing him to talk politics. They early had an election of some kind, for in 1793, the next year after the birth of the County, they sent to the House of Representatives at Lexington, William Shannon, who, it will be later learned donated an acre, the land for the county seat and otherwise showed his public-spirited patriotism. They were also represented in the State Senate from 1793 until 1796, by David Staniford, recorded to have been the first Senator to represent the District then containing Shelby County only. Their names and the names of all their successors in the legislature, for a hundred

---

*The Lincoln paper published in Part VI shows that President Lincoln's grandfather was granted land in the Long Run-Floyds Fork neighborhood in 1784 and that the nearby station was several years older.

and thirty-six years of the County's existence, are to be found in the list published in Part VII of this volume. The growth of the new town and the incorporation of other towns and villages, the erection of churches and schools also are told about all in more detail under the Classified Parts and Chapters hereinafter devoted to them.

CHAPTER II.

First Period of Growth

And so with building and planning in the towns, with sowing and planting, reaping and harvesting on the little plantations in the fertile uplands and rich creek bottoms, and with the sound of the flail in the rude barns and the looms in the little homes; with the log-raisings of the new school and church houses, and with endless industry, piety and quenchless hope, they, like the Boy, Jesus, "increased in wisdom and stature and in favor with God and man," until a new century dawned. And in 1800, Shelby was a county of law abiding, pious, educated people; and Shelbyville, already a town of hundreds.

A "big State Road" ran from Maysville, via Lexington, Frankfort and on down a little North of where it does now, to Shelbyville and on to the Falls of the Ohio. The villages, now large towns, were settlements in those days, and as a rule did not become incorporated for several decades. The roads were bound to have been busy, for hotels, or taverns, sometimes called Inns—two log room affairs—had sprung up, not only at the County seat and out at Cross Keys, five miles east of town, where Adam Middleton came as early as 1800; but at where Simpsonville now stands, eight miles in the other direction enroute to the Falls. There were necessarily numerous guests in the way of wagons, horses, and men, else these taverns could not have survived at the prices, which the law, itself, required them then to charge—twenty cents for a meal, eight cents for a night's lodging, five cents for a drink, or thirty-seven and one-half cents for a gallon of whiskey. It is true that the tavern keeper bought what he fed the horses and men, from the farmers at what the farmer that day, like the farmer of every day since then, considered "ruinously low prices." But for what he bought outside he paid, because of the distance and methods of reaching him, figures that no sort of Congress-made tariff did or ever could have piled on.* The roads were busy not only with the wagons, which had taken pork and tobacco to the Baltimore market, bringing back modern furniture, whiskey, sugar and salt, but with some of our own wagons and crops, and we had even begun to be sufficiently advanced in wealth and civilization (?) to bring in and own a few negro slaves;** because of whom the activities on the farms increased, as did the time for the political talk in the towns and at the stores and at the shops where the paths became roads and began to cross and men began to gather.

It has been complained that there is too much history, but a man of thought knows that he has forgotten much more than he remembers. Likewise the annals of any quiet neighborhood if known and appropriately told make stories of human interest unlimited; but the annals of many of the neighborhoods of 150 years ago are lost, and this is true of many communities that made up Shelby County, between the years of 1780 and 1812.

The stories of those brave hearts, their loves, joys and griefs, their holidays, their "Thanksgivings," their Christmas trees, their school entertainments, court days, speakings, horse shows, militia drills, their religious revivals, their superstitions, their tragic fear of plagues and epidemics, their frightened nights with skies alight with the savage-set fires of burning cabins and forests—all these—big events in those small lives, for the first twenty years of the county's life, must be largely left to the imagination of the individual reader. They are his forebear's history—*his*-story.

---

*In a house, torn down a few feet west of where the Federal building now stands in Shelbyville, built in 1793 in the then suburbs of the town (the "city limits" at that time ran from what is Third Street to the present Seventh Street) was found an old account book, dated later, or in 1833, and which showed the current prices at that time. White flannel sold at 75 cents per yard; bar-lead at 10 cents per pound; calico, 27½ cents; checked muslin, 50 cents; bed ticking, 25 cents per yard; tea, $1.50 per pound; saltpetre, 25 cents; cut nails, 10 cents; wrought nails, 25 cents; shoe-thread, 37½ cents per pound; spool thread, 12½ cents; paper of pins, 12½ cents, and one dozen needles, 6¼ cents. Among other charges was one for a gallon of whiskey, 37½ cents, and a jug to put it in, 25 cents.

**The Shelby County tax list at Frankfort for 1852, showed 6,704 slaves, valued at $3,253,825. Very much more than any other item of taxation except the land itself.

First Period of Growth

How the Earliest Settlers Lived

And the conditions under which the pioneers themselves lived are little realized by the people of this later day. Theirs were rude beginnings. But for tradition and legend, it would be difficult for the children of this day to realize how rude. The first "residences" were no better than the pictures and reassembled Lincoln and Fort Harrod cabins, now on exhibition. Some of them were but three-sided log huts, little better than a substantial shelter for swine. One log room cabins with one window and door each, were among the best. The furniture consisted of improvised puncheon board beds, and dining table, not infrequently on solid earth floors. The wooden spoons, forks and noggins and pails and plates were made in this country, and the ovens and case knives of iron had been brought at great labor and expense from abroad. The rifle, the powder-horn, the bullet-bag, the tomahawk, and the hunting knife were parts of the furniture and usually occupied the most conspicuous places on a rack made of wood or the horns of a deer.

The men hunted the game, cleared the land, raised the crop, pounded the grain, fought the Indians and did the outdoor work in general. The women milked the cows, spun the yarn, wove the cloth, knit the socks, made the garments, cooked the meals and attended to all household work. If a new house was to be raised in the neighborhood, all the men joined to help, and if a new quilt was to be made, all the women assisted in the stitching. The hunting-shirt, a kind of blouse reaching from the neck to the knees, with large sleeves, hanging cape, and a belt to fasten it around the waist, was worn by all the men. Breeches made of buckskin or linsey, a cap of raccoon skin, leggins and moccasins made of deer skin, and a shirt of such cotton or linen as could be gotten, completed the dress of the men. The women wore linen sunbonnets, linsey dresses, woolen stockings, cotton handkerchiefs, and home-made shoes; and if now and then a ruffle or a buckle appeared, it was a relic of olden times brought from the mother country. Wool hats were a rarity to the men, and straw bonnets only worn by ladies who could afford something better than the home-made hood. The food of all was the game of the forest, milk, butter, cheese, cornbread, hominy, mush, the wild nuts and the wild fruits of the country.

Frontier Hardships

Except for the names and numbers authentically told as to the massacre of the Squire Boone Settlers and the ambuscade of Col. Floyd's men there is little known of how much real loss of life from Indian raids there was in Shelby County in those years. Also, there is little told by early historians or in the records about the loss of life by plagues or epidemics during the years from that awful first winter of 1779-1780,* up to the great earthquake of 1811, and the cholera epidemic of 1833. But the plow shares of the farmers of fifty or sixty years ago turned up many old buried stones and other evidences of many graves that must have been dug about the same time; and the children of that day were told in awed, whispered tones that these buried rocks were once the head stones of many early settlers who died in the days before the birth of the county in an epidemic of cholera, black vomit, smallpox, meningitis or "spotted fever," as the case might be; or the imagination of the relator dictated. That there were such epidemics of disease, in those days when little was known about sanitation (and the facts about which will never be learned) is believed by many who in their researches have learned how easily all traces of what were important events have been entirely lost or rendered entirely worthless to a conscientious chronicler of facts.

Wars and rumors of war were not the greatest woes of those late "nineties" of the eighteenth or those first years of the nine-

---

*The frightful winter of 1779-80 must have come upon the new settlers at the station of "Painted Stone," without expectation or warning, and it is described as not unlike our winter of 1917-18, one hundred and thirty-six years later. From the middle of November till near the first of March the ground was covered with snow with almost daily snow storms accompanied by piercing northwest winds. The ponds, creeks and larger streams were frozen to their bottoms and the rivers were solid roadways and paths. No rain fell and water for all purposes was procured only from melted ice. The wild animals of the woods came to the settlements to shelter behind the cabins from the freezing storms. Whole herds of buffalo and deer were found frozen to death and the wild turkeys and birds dropped from the trees in which they had gone to roost.

First Period of Growth

teenth centuries in Shelby—these were few and only that of 1812, took away any of Shelby's sturdy yeomanry or many of the young cabinet makers, wagon builders, or other artisans who were too few to be spared. As each home had to make nearly all its own manufactures, so what the home did not furnish the county did, with its own wheelwrights, cabinet (or coffin) makers, rope-walk experts, wagon builders, blacksmiths and millers. And soon came also the itinerant preacher, the journeyman printer, the peddler and the pedagogue.

Churches and Schools

Early there was in the county and particularly Shelbyville a peculiarly large interest in the subject of churches and schools, and as will be noted in perusing the parts of this volume devoted to those subjects. Several of the schools founded more than one hundred years ago grew to have a Statewide and even nationwide importance, and one great institution of learning for girls has withstood and still withstands the mutations of more than a century of time.*

In no other one of the first counties of the State was religion, theology, denominational contentions and differences, or the struggles for their existence more zealously fought out, than among those primitive churches and congregations described in later chapters.

And so the industrial, the educational, religious, and social warp and woof of those early years were woven with the hand of time into a fabric worn by many generations of a later day; and the county for the first forty years of its home life and public annals was not unlike that of others of the first counties, although always just a bit in the lead in the matter of morals, religion, education and the material rewards that come of special industry and enterprise.

---

*A democracy comes up from the home and hamlet—not down to them, from any imaginary great fountain head of government. Neither the Federal Constitution nor Federal Government makes any provision for the creation of homes, churches and schools or a public press. These four basic rocks of society, originate with society, itself. The fact that the first settlers in Shelby seemed from the beginning passionately determined to have homes, churches, schools and, finally, a county press, may explain the excellent high standard maintained by all four of these institutions, and why the county and its people have always led in the things a bit higher than the purely material.

CHAPTER III

Rapid Early Growth

The rapid increase in the County's population during its first years, already referred to, was intensified between 1810 and 1820; and in the latter year the total population, it will astonish many to know, had increased to the largest the county has or has ever had. The great falling off in its population between 1820 and 1830 was of course, largely due to the cutting off of the territory that went into parts of Oldham and Spencer Counties; but for forty years afterwards without any changes in the territory the population instead of increasing decreased nearly twenty per cent. The adventurous, ambitious spirit of the sons of the first homes in the county added to the large number of those who sought the fields of larger activities in the East, and especially to those who joined the wagon-trains of '49 and with the Star of Empire took up their Westward way, may partly explain that decrease. The census beginning with 1840 and continuing for eighty years was as follows: 1840, 17,768; 1850, 17,095; 1860, 16,435; 1870, 15,733; 1880, 16,603; 1890, 16,521; 1900, 18,340. A slight gain started with the new century.

The total for 1910 was 18,004 which increased during the next ten years to 18,532.

Agriculture Chief Industry

For a hundred years, and for reasons already given, agriculture was the pursuit of the settlers and their descendants, while the colleges and the professions were their ambition for their children. In such a great expanse of rich soil it seems strange enough that Shelby County in particular and Kentucky in general followed not Virginia's example in the matter of tobacco growing so early a chief industry of the mother state. It did little tobacco raising for a hundred years after its creation, or not until 1880 when the era of Burley growing brought to the County a new industry—and also some of its most serious social problems, in the way of tobacco tenants, who, succeeding the freed and scattered slaves, had their share in the distressing era of night riding, plant bed raiding, and other woes that were bearable only because so short lived. But preceding the tobacco growing era for many years and in Shelby particularly, the hemp growing industry helped enrich many farmers, and also, like tobacco, to impoverish the soil of many farms. Its growing, however, had begun to be abandoned because of the scarcity of the sort of labor, so necessary in what is known as an all-year-crop, even before so costly a product was driven from profitable markets by the "untariffed" jute, and other fibres, imported from foreign countries and islands, and substituted for the higher quality and higher priced Kentucky product. The mainstays of the county after the pioneers ceased to raise their own flax for the little three legged spinning wheels, and other trifling small crops like patches of buckwheat, sage, millet and sorghum cane, were and continued for a hundred years to be her hogs, cattle, sheep, her wheat, her corn, her oats and hay; and, with advanced thought in all lines peculiar to the county, several incursions were made by ambitious farmers into the field of finer live stock; as in the era when the best shorthorn cattle in the country and the later period when the finest herds of Jerseys in the world were to be found within the County's borders. It should be added that the county has in later years furnished also to the world famous sires as well as milch cows of the Hereford and the Holstein breeds; and up until the time of the World War was contributing to the East the cream of the fancy saddle and harness horses of the State.

County's Chief "Product"

But Shelby's chief product through all these years was the splendid sons and daughters she reared, educated and sent out into all parts of both the civilized and heathen world, and also

Rapid Early Growth

the young men and boys who were brought here from other counties and states, and educated in her old schools; while daughters of some of the first families in every state in the Union came here and were educated at Shelby's seats of learning and under the church spires that everywhere have always surrounded or stood nearby her schools. During those years, the fruits of which we have just been detailing, there were periods of social and financial upheavals and of epidemics and plagues to which we have already referred. The cholera epidemic of 1833 is not dwelled upon much in the records of this particular county, though men and women of advanced years remember that as little children they were shown long rows of limerock "headstones" peeping above the ground in the pastures and on deserted hillsides, and were told they marked the graves of those who died in that epidemic. However, exaggerated, or however authentic these neighborhood legends were we are at a loss to know. But from the War of 1812 down to the Mexican War in 1846-48, nothing, not even excepting "when the stars fell,"* so shook the foundation of their happiness or the excellent morale of the people of Shelby and the State, as that scourge of 1833.

Sad, Bitter Years

And then after the Mexican War, came those long distressing years preceding, during and succeeding the War Be-

---

*Up until the Civil War many old residents dated all happenings from "the night the stars fell." The meteoric shower which so startled all the people of this section and the State at large and so terrorized not alone the superstitious and uninformed, occurred in 1831. The old fashion blacks left over from the Civil War, when in care of the juvenile whites wound up their grave yard stories around the kitchen fireplace in the late evenings with tales of the "night the stars fell." Mr. L. C. Willis, the veteran lawyer, during the famous campaign of 1896 when all the "fixed" stars of democracy seemed "slipping" used to refer to the Carlisle's, Lindsay's, et al, as the "Pleiades," and then tell the story of the mountaineer, who on the "night the stars fell," rushed out in his night clothes, found his wife on her knees in front of their little cabin, and after viewing the awful phenomenon called to her, "Pray Ol' Woman, pray hard. I'll step around back, and if the seven stars has slipped, we're gone to hell, shore." That the phenomenon was general throughout the State is further evidenced by a story that Judge Lawrence Anderson, of Graves County, quotes his grandfather, a county physician as telling. The latter said he was returning from a night sick call, when the rain of meteors began, and the skies literally snowed stars. He says his faithful riding horse instantly fell upon his knees. The old doctor used to go on to say, "I concluded that the horse had more sense than I did, and I, too, got off, and down on my knees." The horse was quaking with fright, and the doctor says he never knew how he got him home and into the stall, where he left him shaking as with a chill.

tween the States. Like those who die so many times because of their fear of death, that War and its woes were lived over many times by the people of this section, because of the many long years during which it was threatened. Shelby County was peculiarly like to Kentucky and the Nation in the even way in which its people, brother against brother, father against son, and neighbor against neighbor—were divided and pitted against one another. It, in a smaller way, suffered all the woes of the great and growing nation, and of the proud and prosperous State which, with advancing step and proud bearing, seemed the "heir of all the ages in the foremost files of time," but, that in a few short years was so rent and torn and worn by the most tragic, the bloodiest, internecine strife the world has ever known. With its sons fighting on both sides in all the great battles of the early Sixties, its people were in the valley and shadow, passing through the sorrow and travail that only the birth of a nation can entail. The children who were born during that struggle and have borne some of the marks of those sad times all their lives may only imagine what the parents and the adults of that day themselves bore. They, from the beginning, had taken their politics seriously—more as a duty and business without realizing that it was really one of the chief sources of their entertainment. They were warmly enough interested in all the contests* for President in those early historic times of "Old Hickory," and his bitter fights with Clay, and through the succeeding quadrennial contests of Clay, Polk, Van Buren and Harrison, *et al.*

---

*There have been thirty such quadrennial contests and in each one of them Shelby County has been typical territory—its people just as enthusiastic and sometimes just as bitter and excited for the candidates of their choice, and just as smilingly reconciled and peaceful immediately after the decisive vote; if we except the exciting events following the presidential elections of 1860 and 1876, when they were again merely typical of the balance of the country. One such entertainment was a debate between Henry Clay and John Jordan Crittenden, noted orators and statesmen of that day. The occasion was a great barbecue held about 1840, in the forest now known as Guthrie's Wood, just north of Shelbyville. Bland Ballard appeared in his pioneer dress and arms, entertaining the gathering by showing his skill with the long rifle and in throwing the tomahawk. This event was described to a great-granddaughter of John J. Crittenden's, Mrs. Bell W. Boteler, by a great-granddaughter of Brackett Owen's, Mrs. Julia Owen Cochran, who personally witnessed it.

Rapid Early Growth

Social and Political Divisions

But not until the close of the Civil War was there a readjustment, complete realignment and wiping out of the old Whig and other parties that were succeeded in the county by the new Republican party and the new Democratic party, with their bitter talk and feeling. The Democrats early knew the Republicans as the "Black Abolitionist," and the Republican party knew and called all Democrats "Secesh Rebels," and when one was not listening the other sometimes thought up worse names. Because of the preponderance of southern sympathy in the county, the Democrats were then and ever after largely in the majority notwithstanding a rather large colored population that voted and was always permitted to vote solidly with the Republican party. The Democrats were so decidedly in the majority and because old enmities engendered by the war were so bitter, for many years a call of the list of the county and city officers was like a muster roll of ex-Confederate soldiers, and there were at times hardly enough qualified white Republicans of sufficient political activity, from whom to pick post masters, during the long years the Federal Government and the Post Office Department at Washington were under that party's control.

Other institutions in Shelby were more completely rent and torn by the awful conflict, and more evenly divided. This was true of the membership of at least two religious denominations, who each separated into two churches—the "North" and the "South," and were for more than fifty years as widely divided as the politicians continue to be.

Rapid Reconstruction

But the days of reconstruction were less long in Shelby and in Kentucky than further South. The only secret organization for the preservation of law and order that was ever even partly justified, (made up of really intelligent, high minded citizens), officiated and needed to be active, but for a short time. Shelby's surviving soldiers who fought on both sides, left many dead comrades behind, but the survivors promptly returned from war and as promptly began work helping rebuild the material prosperity and social structures that existed before the outbreak.

By 1870 Shelby was back on the road to the prosperity that came of peaceful industry, self-reliance and hope.

Hard Times

But as an aftermath of the war and for other reasons, came the dark days of '73, the financial disaster, the panic of that year, and the period of low prices, of failing banks, and bankrupt farms. These hard times or money panics, under our early imperfect financial system, seem to have come like the locust at fixed periods, though not so regularly. One happened again in 1893 and one in 1907, and it is believed would have ended there, with a more perfect financial system, had not the great World War come and again so sadly affected the agricultural industry, and lands of counties like Shelby. With her farm boys by the hundreds in camp; lack of farm labor and implements, a sudden unprecedented inflation of prices of farm products started an unheard of boom in farm lands in Shelby. Farms, little and big, all over the county were bought and sold and re-sold three or four times within as many months, with the prices per acre, ranging from double to four times any sum they had ever brought before. The oil-boomed counties in the hills and the Bluegrass counties to the East, suddenly grown affluent themselves, sent new residents to Shelby, some of whom spent their all to pay cash first payments amounting to about one-half or one-third the price they bound themselves to pay in a few years. The forced-sale price of such farms dropped to where it was less than the total of these deferred payments, and the last purchasers lost their all. The hard times that the farm industry of Shelbyville had known or knew for the ten years succeeding the World War were not all due to it, but were mostly due to this unnatural, abnormal inflation of farm land prices during the years of the War.

CHAPTER IV

Public Improvements

Something should be said in this general outline of the County's history about its roads and railroads, and here, too, is an instance of how incidentally the story of a county or country may be told in the records of its industries as well as in those of the lives of its people. A detailed history of the roads and railroads for one hundred and fifty years, were one practical, would be a history of the county itself. Its first "big dirt road" was that from Maysville by way of Lexington, Frankfort, Cross Keys Inn and on to Shelbyville and Louisville; and this was, likewise, fifty years later or in 1825, its first big macadamized or stage coach road—and Kentucky's first. It is likewise the same road that for twenty-three miles through the heart of Shelby was the State's first black-topped, modern motor vehicle thoroughfare; and for long the most traveled of any in the State.

Early in 1800, the other "big dirt roads" began to be plowed and spaded out in the direction of other county seats; to the outlying churches and schools, the cross-road blacksmith shops, stores and post offices. Shelby once had a greater mileage of these than any neighboring county, not excepting Jefferson. In the years following, private individuals and enterprising companies began to acquire and macadamize these roads and to maintain them with money collected not exactly at the "turnpikes," but at the toll-gates, where a pole took the place of the "pike," and where prices were charged sufficient not only to maintain the roads moderately well, but in many instances to enrich their owners. And then came the toll gate raids of the late eighties and the new law permitting the counties to buy the roads and when all that era was ended Shelby had on her hands nearly five hundred miles of macadam roads without means, methods or money with which to maintain them.

But she did maintain them to a point where the Commonwealth was willing when it went in the highway business to take some of them off her hands and make them fit for the marvelous, sudden development of the motor craze, and the motor vehicle traffic. Such development would have been impossible, or else the road problem in a County like Shelby would have been impossible of solution, had not the State gone into the business of highway construction at the time it did and had not the County and its officials taken the lead in the industry and enterprise that led to better roads, of their own.

Railroads' Rapid Growth

The railroad development of Shelby was long secondary to its vehicle roads and promises to fast become so again. The extension in the middle of the century of the State's first railroad from Frankfort to Louisville kept around to the east and north of Shelby County, along the high points between the Kentucky River Valley and the Ohio, and on to Louisville. For many years, Christianburg, nine miles to the east, and Anchorage, eighteen miles to the west were its closest to contact with the county seat and center of Shelby. It was in the 1870's that the enterprising Shelby Railroad Company built the road from Anchorage, the straight way, to Shelbyville, and which many years later became a part of the L. & N. System. It was not until 1895 that the air line was taken nine miles on to Christianburg and thereby made a through, fast route from the State's metropolis to its capital and all points east, for two great railway companies.

Meanwhile a great north and south road through Henry County from the north and across the county at Shelbyville and into Spencer was projected, and in part built (with the "Cumberland & Ohio Railroad Company bonds" so long a contention among the taxpayers of Shelby). Only one small link of this road was ever completed and that was from Shelbyville to Taylorsville, which link was later absorbed by the L. & N. system, to whom it became the same baby white elephant, that the whole project had proved to Shelby County.

The Southern railway from Louisville to Lexington and Danville built in 1887-88 and at first a local proposition, made, finally through Shelbyville, another great north, south and west trunk line, and, with the coming of the electric or interurban from Louisville to Shelbyville in 1910, combined with the others mentioned, in giving to the County of Shelby the finest transportation facilities for passenger and freight that any county in the State then enjoyed.

The Motor Vehicle Craze

But these seem going like the great livery stables that for many years occupied the best buildings on the main streets of the county seat and the county towns, and every vestige of which, along with the horse-shoers and the harness shops, have disappeared from the face of the earth. The electric lines and the railroad too, seem to have fallen on evil days; the motor craze has swept the country as none other has ever done.

Farmers and farm hands live in town; carpenters, painters, dressmakers, clerks all own motors and ride to their work, and to their pleasures on wheels. The amount of capital invested in motor vehicles and in their maintenance, whatever the result may be in the future, would ere this have resulted in country-wide business disaster, but for the better system of laws concerning finances that now apply to the whole country. Meanwhile the chief problem and task of the taxpayer and the State and county officials has come to be the building and maintenance of such a network of smooth, travelable highways as will something like meet the demand and clamor of this army of travel-mad motorists, to which every citizen seems to belong.

The Future?

At this point the historian might turn the microphone over to the prophet. Maybe he could tell you how soon these roads will be grass-grown or useless except over which to haul live stock to market; that the farmer and town man everywhere will be caught overstocked with motor vehicles of every kind, unpaid-for, and useless because unfit for those real "highways" of the crowded, uncharted lanes of the air.

A model, modern county road near where the "Painted Stone" settlers made their first trail.

Tree on Eminence road, front of Layson home under which the settlers from "Painted Stone" rested the morning of their flight before going on to their fate at Long Run.

Tenant house near site of Ballard cabin and Tyler Station, where Ballard massacre occurred August, 1788.

PART II
Stations, Towns and Villages

CHAPTER I

Boone's Station

If, as Macauley said, the best history of a Country is a record of the lives of its people, then also are the records of the stations, churches, and schools and towns, the best history of a county's people themselves.

What tomes of romantic stories of absorbing human interest could be written around and about the lives of those who lived in every one of the first stations—of those who participated in the activities of each and all of the primitive churches and schools—and about most of whom we really know so little!

This year of 1929, is the sesqui-centennial anniversary of Shelby County's settlement by the whites—of the best authenticated important event of its early past—the establishment of the "Painted Stone Station" by Squire Boone in 1779. The story of Boone's interesting arrival and first years in the State is told in the sketch of his life, in Part III.* It was the first Station situated near Shelbyville in the center of what was later Shelby County and was for nearly two years the only station between Harrodsburg and the Falls of the Ohio, and because of the tragic fate of many of its settlers and for other reasons the history of Boone's Station or the station at the "Painted Stone" is better known to the general public than any other in that section.

Squire Boone arrived there with his party and began the erection of the little log fort or cabins in the late summer of 1779. Besides his own family and those of Evan Hinton and Peter Paul, who arrived in the early autumn, Alex Bryan, John Buckles, Richard Cates, Chas. Doleman, John and Joseph

---
*To avoid duplications, the sketches of pioneers, with important papers, reminiscences, etc., will be found in other portions of the book and the reader disposed to criticize the brevity and seeming omissions is once again advised that he will find the data that he misses under some other head considered more appropriate for it. The sketch of the wonderful life of Bland Ballard, tells of the Long Run and Tyler Station massacres, as does the John Williamson and Wilcox papers.

45

Eastwood, Jere Harris, John Hinton, Abraham Holt, Morgan Hughes, John McFadden, John Nichols, John Stapleton, Robert Tyler, Abraham Vanmeter, James Wright, Adam, Jacob and Peter Wickersham and Geo. Hunt are known to have been in the company that followed the dread winter of 1779-80, and undaunted, pursued the work begun in the previous fall. The population of the station had grown continuously for a year and was reasonably happy and prosperous when its inhabitants in September, 1781, were "flushed" by Bland Ballard's news of Indian uprisings and suffered the loss of some forty or fifty men, women and children slaughtered by the Indians just west of the western line of the county on their flight to Lynn's Station and the other larger stations near the Falls of the Ohio and Beargrass Creek.

The terror of the survivors was added to by the fate of Col. John Floyd and his men, who hearing of this disaster started in pursuit of the Indians and were next day ambushed a mile further west where what is known as the Eastwood monument marks the spot near where fourteen of his men were slain. (He himself was fatally wounded by Indians two years later).

It is not known how soon again Squire Boone and his family and a few of those who had not left the station were rejoined by the surviving ones who had taken their flight, but the fort was not really reoccupied until about Christmas of that year, 1781. For some reason, probably because Squire Boone was unwilling during his absence at Richmond as a member of the Virginia Legislature to leave his family in so exposed a location, he disposed of his interest in and his proprietorship of the station in 1783 to a Col. Lynch and thereafter the station was known as Lynch's Station. Bland Ballard was not one of the first settlers of Boone Station as will be observed in the sketch of his life to be found elsewhere in this volume. And the fact that his name has been confused with those of the Boone Station pioneers had to do with his being the "Paul Revere" who rode through the night to warn the Boone Station settlers of the near approach of Indians and because among the slain were some of those near to him.

Daniel Boone was a frequent visitor to the "Painted Stone" during its first years, and his brother, Squire Boone, and the other settlers there were advised and guided by him in the conduct of their affairs and the precautions necessary to their safety.

Tyler Station

Tyler Station on "Tick Creek," four miles east of the city of Shelbyville and perhaps two miles east of the Boone Station was established in 1783, (about the time the name of Boone Station was changed) by Capt. Robert Tyler, one of the pioneers of Boone's, and by his friend and relative, Bland Ballard, of the Lynn Station near Louisville. This station was north of what is now known as the Midland Trail or U. S. Highway No. 60, but not a great distance from the marker which stands on the roadside five miles east of Shelbyville, and not far from the site of the Ballard Massacre, told of in the sketch of life of Bland Ballard, in Part V.

The list of those from Central Kentucky and from the Boone Station and from the stations on Beargrass and at the Falls, who joined Tyler and Ballard at the new station are not recorded in the manuscripts and histories concerning the county's first stations. Ballard remained there and later represented the county, as will be noted in the sketch of his life, in the State Legislature.

Brackett Owen Station

Of the Brackett Owen Station, the best authenticated legend and records indicate that it might have been built only a year or two later than Tyler's, by Brackett Owen, father of the gallant Col. Abraham Owen who fell at the battle of Tippecanoe in 1811, and a sketch of whom appears under the head of "Pioneers."* That Brackett Owen owned a great stretch of territory just south of the site of the city of Shelbyville and that his station was located on part of the farm now owned by Robert Courtney, to the south of the town and to the east of Grove Hill Cemetery, is very well known. (He also owned the western portion of Shelbyville, beginning with Seventh Street, that was at first called Owen.) It was in the house near this fort on what was earlier known as the J. W. Goodman farm that the first court was held in 1792—one of the historic events that helped to make the name of Owen Station and of Brackett Owen of importance in all historical mentions of Shelby County.

Some Less Known Stations **

Capt. Samuel Well's Station was one of several other small stations that first sprang up under the enterprise of the daring population that came from the first three named and from out of the other parts of Kentucky and from the forts or stations "where the hives" had begun to swarm. This station was located three and one-half miles northwest of Shelbyville in what was long known as the Harrington Mill section of the County.

Whitaker's Station, sometimes known as the "Red Orchard" was founded by the Rev. John Whitaker on a spot that the late John T. Ballard said was many times pointed out to him by Col. James Whitaker, son of the founder, and was built just south of the town of Shelbyville on what was long known as the Carrither's Farm across Clear Creek from Shelbyville and not far east of Zaring's Mill. It was told of the wife of the Rev. Whitaker, the founder of the station, that she was as expert as her husband with the rifle and killed not one, but several Indians, with the weapon she carried and with which

---
*Brackett Owen's biographers put him in Shelby as early as 1782, but those of his son, Abraham, say the latter reached Shelbyville in 1785. The author does not find any authentic record indicating that either Brackett Owen or his son reached the county before 1785.
**For much of the data as to stations we are indebted to the research of Miss Estella Allen.

First Settlers

she guarded the field while her husband plowed the corn. Rev. Whitaker had early planted an orchard which produced what was then an unheard of generous crop of great red apples and it was from these that the other name of "Red Orchard" came to be used.

Little is known of the details or the names of the inhabitants of the Van Cleave Station which was located to the west and south of Shelbyville on what was later known as Bull Skin Creek. Spencer's History of the Baptists in Volume I, Page 209, speaks of a baptist preacher, William Ford, who remained, he says, a short while in "Van Cleave's Station" on Bull Skin in Shelby County.

It is said that a station called "Newlands Station" was located in the southeast part of the county or in what is known in later years as the Olive Branch Neighborhood, but there is no record of which this writer ever has seen that there was such a station though there were a number of families of that name at one time in that section of the county.

It is of but recent years through the enterprising efforts of Mr. R. C. Ballard Thruston, President of the Filson Club that it became known just where the cabin of Abraham Lincoln, the grandfather of the president stood or that the spring used by the grandfather of A. Lincoln is just over the Shelbyville County line from Jefferson and about twenty miles east of Louisville.*

Hume's Station

Established in 1784 seems certainly to have been just east of the Shelby-Jefferson County line and nearby the trans-continental Highway U. S. No. 60. John Hume's grave and nearby the house, the eastern end of which is on where Hume Station stood are located on the Midland Trail just within the County at the western boundary line.

Collins History speaks of an ancient fortification situated

---
*See paper from "Kentucky Highways," Chapter IV., Part VI.

six miles east of Shelbyville and has caused some to confuse it with an early station. The outlines of this "fortification" can still be seen on one of the principal knobs 200 feet above the surrounding county, but it is of age far antedating any Shelby County Station and was doubtless the work of Indians many generations older than those first found by the white settlers. In form it is circular with a double line of earthwork four to eight feet high and enclosing about three acres well overgrown with trees; a supply of water overflows from the interior. A few graves and Indian relics were found nearby, and it was perhaps these that a few years ago started the very improbable theory that the knobs of Shelby were themselves only Indian mounds.*

*The Low Dutch Colony****

The Low Dutch colony came mainly from Mercer County, Kentucky, and located in and around the site where Pleasureville is now situated. The colonists purchased about 10,000 acres in 1784, from Squire Boone, the famous pioneer. This section of Kentucky was then all forest and inhabited by Indians. It is as remarkable, as true, that some of the descendants of this colony now reside on and own a portion of the original purchase. The Bantas, Bergens and Shucks still own the land of their ancestors, together with many old relics and papers which they value highly. The land was not held separately, but the company had a trustee whose duty it was to look after the estate. There were thirty or more families and they all resided in a fort built of logs and stones. The hostilities of the Indians once compelled them to retire for a short time, part going back to Mercer and part to Clark Counties, but they returned in 1786.

*Col. Bennett H. Young indicates in his books, particularly in the "Prehistoric Men of Kentucky," a rather firm belief in the theories and alleged discoveries of Rafinesque, who would have us believe that nearly all the territory in which we live is underlain by ancient villages, dead ditched towns, walls and fortifications, burial grounds and endless numbers of the works of the mound-builders and "Long Ago People."

**Written some years ago, by the late Richard H. Shuck, whose forefathers crossed the waters with the original stock and followed the colony through all its migrations.

First Settlers

Papers show that 34 lots of land were purchased by the company varying in size, but ranging from 200 acres upward, and paid for in pounds, shillings and pence. The following statement shows how the tracts were awarded in the division; that is to say, to whom and the prices paid:

No.		L. S. P.
1.	Jno. Comingore, transferred to Jasmond	24-11-01
2.	David Vories	52-17-00
	Same	48-17-11
3.	Andrew Shuck	70-11-11
4.	Albert Banta	50-10-03
5.	Albert Voras	26-08-07
6.	John Banta	62-17-03
7.	Abraham Banta	52-17-03
8.	Simon Vanisdal	24-11-08
9.	Henry Banta	66-03-03
10.	Samuel Demaree	52-17-03
11.	David Bank	59-03-03
12.	Bennett Montfort, transferred to Mason	52-17-03
13.	Ben Spade	62-26-06
14.	Daniel Banta	52-17-03
15.	Heirs Cornelius Cozine	19-19-11
17.	Samuel Banta	43-19-11
18.	Francis Cosart	43-19-11
20.	Aaron Jno. Montfort	52-17-11
23.	Blue John Voras	21-16-07
24.	Lucas Vanosdal and Jacob Smock	21-16-07
26.	Peter Banta	12-19-04
27.	Jacob Banta	32-18-03
29.	Wm. Shuck and Big John Vories	52-17-03
30.	Peter Banta	59-19-03
31.	Abraham Brewer	17-04-11
32.	Cornelius and Peter Banta	62-16-09
33.	Peter Banta	56-03-09
34.	Coptrea Voris	29-11-09

Some of the members were missing but there were at least thirty-four tracts. All of this land was managed by Abraham Banta before it was settled up, and then it was transferred to George Bergen as trustee, whose duty it was to look after all the estate. The land was resurveyed in 1833 and found to contain a large surplus, which was sold and the money divided among the members of the company.

About this time the "Low Dutch Colony," swarmed again and quite a number settled in Johnston County, Indiana, and another colony in Switzerland County, same state.

The company members worked together, some standing guard while others labored. At night they went into the fort for protection against the Indians—closing the doors and pulling the latch string inside. The old spring that supplied the company with water is still in use. These good old people cleared the Indian from the country and the wild animals from the forest. They also cleared the heavy timber from the land and built houses for themselves, and it was long years before they could safely leave a latch string outside at night.

Verily we are enjoying the fruits of their labor. An uncle of the writer, Cornelius Banta, built the first house in North Pleasureville which was then called Bantatown. Then New Pleasureville began in 1850. The bones of the pioneers are resting in Pleasureville Cemetery.

CHAPTER II

Towns and Villages

The location of the town of Shelbyville was really determined at the session of the first Court held in Shelby County at the house of Brackett Owen in what was Owen's Station just south of town, on October 15, 1792, because it was at that session of the court and on the second day thereof that the subject of fixing a place for the location of public buildings came up and it was decided that where the "main road leading from Frankfort to the Falls of the Ohio crossed Clear Creek between the mouth of Mulberry Creek and the mouth of the first branch west of the mouth of Mulberry," should be chosen for this purpose.

William Shannon, the owner of the land being present, agreed to donate one acre of land to the County and to lay off fifty acres adjoining into convenient streets and lots. It was ordered by the court that Mr. Shannon's proposition be accepted, and this action settled the rather long and bitter contention about where the town should be located. Trustees, to lay off a town at Shelby Court House, had been appointed by the act of the General Assembly of Kentucky, in 1792; and on January 15, 1793, the trustees laid off 50 acres of land, "around and adjacent to the place whereon the public buildings were to be erected, into suitable lots and streets." The "gentlemen trustees" as they are styled in the record, among their first acts, passed the following resolution, indicating, very clearly, the plainness and simplicity of the style of building of our ancestors: "Ordered, that every purchaser or purchasers of lots in the town of Shelbyville, shall build thereon a hued log house, with a brick or stone chimney not less than one story and a half high, otherwise the lot or lots shall be forfeited for the use of the town." These trustees were David Standiford, Joseph Winlock and Abraham Owen. As those who favored the site of Boone's Station had lost their contention, finally, also those who wanted the public buildings erected on the hill, one-half mile west of where the court house now stands were compelled to abandon their preference.

The town as laid off after the acceptance of the Shannon proposition extended from what is now Third Street to the east side of what is now Seventh Street; Third Street then being called Scott; Fourth Street, Simpson; Fifth Street, Allen; Sixth Street, Logan, and Seventh Street, Owen. Washington and Clay Streets, paralleling Main, were not named until long after and were known as North and South back streets.

The Justices of the "Quarter Sessions," as what then corresponded to our present magistrates, were called, appointed Phillip Whitaker, Bland Ballard and Peter Belia to "view and mark" out the best road from where it had been agreed Shelbyville was to be located, to the Falls of the Ohio. Their selection was what is now Main Street, east of Third, as well as what was then designated as Main Street, west of Third. The road between Third Street and the creek on the east was marsh land and that the trees which fell on the new building lots were used in making of it a corduroy road, is evidenced by the excavation of some of these old logs considerably below the present surface of Main Street years after they were first laid down.

The acre donated for public buildings by Shannon was through arrangements by him with the commissioners, located as near in the middle of the fifty-acre town as possible and while the new jail and court house were being erected thereon the other fifty acres were divided into blocks or lots of two acres each, criss-crossed by the Streets above referred to. The committee in charge of this work was composed of Joseph Winlock, David Standiford and Abraham Owen. Arrangements were also made by Mr. Shannon whereby the town officials were empowered to sell the lots and give deeds to them. The first deed was to the lot on which the Masonic Temple or Hall now stands and some 100 feet to the east, all fronting on the Southeastern city park or quarter of the original acre, and was to John Bradshaw, grandfather of the late B. B. Ross, and the price he paid therefor was twelve pounds and six shillings. A part of the property is still in possession of Mr. Bradshaw's direct heirs.

The lot just west of the court house corner of the one acre on which are now located four business houses was sold to John Felty for fifteen pounds. Forty fine two-story hewn log houses were put up under an ordinance or requirement that no other kind could be erected on the city lots and all forty of these buildings were said to have been "among the finest of their kind in the world." Every log was nicely hewn and fitted with the finest workmanship, and was of blue ash timber. Some of those first settlers, who are said to have built some of these first houses between 1794 and 1797, and on up to 1802, were Mrs. Carson, Joseph Glenn, William Glenn, J. McGauhey, and Moses Hall. Others were Steele, Bradshaw, Butler, Felty, A. Owen, B. Perry, Geo. Hansbrough, G. Cardwell, T. Redding, S. Wilson, H. McClelland, A. Bruner, James White, John Shannon, John McCochran, Stout, Lock and Denny. It should have been stated in the foregoing that the acre for public buildings is that which has the four "parks," one of which has long been occupied by the court house and the other three of which are now public parks.

The lots on which the jail and the jailer's residence are located were long afterwards bought by the County. The town's first pavements were ordered built by the trustees in 1808. Moses Hall, who owned all the property east of the town limits, and much to the south of both, built a bridge across Clear Creek on what is now known as the Mt. Eden pike, or Cemetery Road and donated to the town sufficient land for a road to Main Street. It is now known as Third Street. The land from that point to the Clear Creek bridge on the main road which is now a part of Main Street, had been previously donated to the town, and in 1814, we find that Moses Hall, was advertising for sale all the land east of the town lots of Shelbyville, or that bounded by Third Street, Main Street and Clear Creek.

The subsequent growth of Shelbyville, the lives of its pioneers and their descendants also would make a long interesting story, but the building of the town itself, its growth from a hamlet in the wilderness to a splendid little city with churches, schools and homes, already described as a pattern for those of other counties and states, are told in the chapters devoted to the County's churches, schools, courts and other institutions.

Some of the first influential citizens of Shelbyville, whose names are not mentioned in other parts of the volume include the first physicians. Doctors Knight and Pendigrass who were succeeded by Doctor Wardlow and Doctor Moore in 1800, and Doctor Willitt in about the same year.

The first taverns were kept by John McGaughey, John Felty, and George Hansborough. The first tragedy was when the innkeeper, Felty, had a difficulty with William Shannon, the surveyor who laid out and donated most of the site of the town on it. Shannon stabbed Felty (with a thrown dirk), and was struck by a rock thrown by Felty. Shannon's skull was fractured. Both men died of their wounds. Felty's tavern was located on the southwest corner of the public square. Daniel McClelland succeeded him as proprietor and married his widow. A Col. Tunstall succeeded McClelland and converted the old tavern into a brick, pretentious and imposing for that day and time.

The present day tendency toward voluminous law books and innumerable laws was to some degree prevalent early in the State's and County's history. Ordinances on the subject of taxes and many others were enacted by the first Board of Trustees of Shelbyville. One of these enacted as early as 1793 (then an order of the County Court instead of an ordinance) provided that tavern keepers in the County should charge no more nor less for whiskey than six shillings per gallon; that breakfast with tea or coffee was to cost one shilling, three pence; warm dinner, one shilling, six pence; cold dinner, one shilling; and lodging "with clean sheets," six pence. Twelve years later at the August term of court, the rates which tavern keepers were allowed to charge were fixed—regular meals, twenty cents; night's lodging, eight cents, whiskey, one-half pint, eight cents; hay and keeping a horse all night, seventeen cents; for corn and oats, eight cents per gallon.

The town limits were first enlarged in 1803, by an Act of the Legislature. The whole territory between what is now Third and Seventh Streets had been taken up, the territory added by the Act of the Legislature was divided into lots and sold privately and presumably at auction. The square between Eighth and Ninth Streets on the north side of Main sold for $175. The square further out between Ninth and Tenth on north Main brought $61.00, whereas, the block to the north of it between Ninth and Tenth at Washington and College sold for $42.00. Property from College Street north to the creek and between Eighth and Ninth Street on which the graded school building and numerous residences are located sold for $154.50. One of the principal lots between Eighth and Seventh Streets near to where the Government Building stands sold for $24.50.

In 1806, another order of the court allowed many claims presented for the scalps of wolves; twelve shillings being paid for those from old wolves and six shillings each for young wolves' scalps. The County Attorney was allowed forty-five pounds for his services that year. In 1808, there were three thousand, two hundred and ninety-nine tithers paying fifty cents each and as only males over sixteen years of age were tithable some idea of the very rapid growth of the County and town is gained. Two hundred and ninety dollars and fifty cents of that year's receipts were paid for building pavements around the court house and across the public square, but in that year, a flood washed away the bridges over Clear Creek on the Eminence and Frankfort Pikes, as well as other smaller bridges, and superfluous funds of the young County and town were quickly used.

In 1814, the town Board of Trustees were functioning and enacting ordinances or new laws with the same readiness that characterizes their descendants. One new ordinance provided a fine of $2.00 for laying hold of any article of merchandise in or out of the market house until after the same had been offered for sale, and parents of children or owners of slaves were held responsible for infractions, the parent being fined and the slave receiving ten lashes on his or her bare back, at the town whipping post. Another ordinance provided that no water from the public well or public springs of the town was to be used in watering horses or cattle and the "washing of clothes on the public square in water obtained from the public well" was ordered discontinued. Exhibitors of wax figures could operate within the town limits for two weeks upon the payment of $15.00 license. In that year stone was ordered to be put onto the dirt street on Main between Third and Sixth, the owners of the property along the street each paying his half of the expense.

In 1815, the town pump near Sixth and Main was ordered taken out and the spring filled up because of the growth of traffic at that point. The town tax in 1816, raised to $1.00 for each male, white or black, over sixteen years of age, and in 1817 and '18, the poll tax was reduced to sixty-two and one-half cents, but a small ad valorem tax on each one hundred dollars was assessed. Joshua D. Grant (whose widow afterwards married Robert Lawson, Sr., of the Clay Village neighborhood) and Company were publishers that year of the *Impartial Compiler*, which seems to have succeeded the *Kentuckian* as the County paper. In 1824, a stage line was established between Maysville and Louisville. It was in May, of 1825, that the visit of LaFayette along that route from Lexington to Louisville was made so notable. On the morning of the Twelfth of May, 1825, he, General LaFayette, was met by a committee of gentlemen between Simpsonville and Shelbyville and escorted to the principal tavern where he was entertained during the day and where a ball and banquet were given in the evening. The old newspaper files say that Miss Eliza Bullock, afterwards Mrs. Pettit, and Miss Jane Hardin, afterwards Mrs. Logan, mother of James M. Logan, were belles of a large company of "brave men and fair women."

In that year (1825), the property in the town of Shelbyville was valued at $231,300. There were 176 white and 111 black tithes and the tax on these for that year was seventy-five cents, while the property was taxed at fifteen cents on the one hundred dollars. The following year for some reason the property was assessed at nearly a thousand dollars less, but the tithes had increased by thirty and the poll tax had increased to $1.00 and the ad valorem tax was increased from fifteen to twenty cents on the hundred. A strange new ordinance in 1826, ordered that Sunday School for slaves be prohibited, and an order was made prohibiting the sale of any merchandise except that produced in this State or sold inside a house. By April, 1828, the question of streets had become paramount and the owners of property on Sixth Street and other cross streets from Third to Seventh were ordered to macadamize from the line of their property to the middle of the street and on some of the more thickly populated streets were ordered to make foot pavements. Two years later, or in 1830, the chief improvement to the town was the building of a second story to the market house, the rooms of which were rented out for the production of city revenues.

That year was a tragic one for the forty-year-old town. An epidemic of smallpox was followed by a drouth in town as well as all over the County, and the procurement of sufficient drinking water was a serious problem. Besides the drouth and the raging smallpox, mad dogs became more common than before or since. In 1831, more pavements were ordered built.

In 1832, February 22, the birthday anniversary of Washington was celebrated, and according to the files of the *Examiner* and *Recorder*, edited by William Knight, and which had succeeded the *Impartial Compiler*, the celebration turned out a tragedy in that J. M. Owen, the grandfather of the present merchants of that name and father of the late Mrs. Mary L. Moore, lost his left arm and Mr. Marius Hansbrough, the greatuncle of Rodman Hansbrough, lost his right arm in an accident with the cannon used in the celebration.

The *Shelby Sentinel* (then the *Shelby News*) was established as the principal newspaper of the town in 1842, and having been continuously published since then, its files give in detail the innumerable happenings since those years, many mentions of which excepting in the general way they have been treated, would make this record voluminous beyond all reason. The reader is again reminded that so many events in the history of the town and County are recorded in some one of the other many pages, chapters and parts of the book and have therefore been deleted from some of these articles, chapters and paragraphs in which he or she might reasonably expect to find them.

Villages

Simpsonville, long a small settlement, was laid out in 1816, and incorporated January 14, 1832. It was named for Capt. John Simpson, prominent lawyer of Shelbyville, sketch of whom is to be found in Part III. Simpsonville while a tavern town and a stage coach station, never grew to beyond a few hundred inhabitants, though surrounded by some of the first families and, like Shelbyville, always a school and church center.

Harrisonville was laid off in 1825, and was at that time Connorsville. Afterwards it was changed to Harrisonville, twenty-two years later, when on February 26, 1847, it was incorporated.

Towns and Villages

Clayvillage was first laid off in 1830, but was not incorporated until February 18, 1839; it was of course named for the "great Commoner" Henry Clay.

Hardinsburg (or ville), was incorporated December 18, 1850, and the name was changed to Graefenburg a number of years later by the Post Office Department, because of an already existing Post Office of similar name in the State.

Bagdad, Jacksonville, Waddy, a part of Pleasureville and Consolation (the latter now the smallest of all incorporated in 1860) have never grown beyond a few hundred inhabitants and are for the most part now unincorporated, though made up of happy, prosperous, cultured homes surrounding the churches and schools whose primitive beginnings are elsewhere detailed. The name "Bagdad" was taken, tradition says, from the afflicted little son of a local miller who could not talk, but who when a customer appeared could say "Bag-Dad."

Taylorsville, the present County Seat of Spencer County, was in Shelby County when it was laid off in 1799, on the lands of Richard Taylor, who was the proprietor of a grist mill and large tract of land at the mouth of Brashear's Creek and above the intersection with Salt River where the aforementioned town is located. About sixty acres were taken from Taylor's tract by the Shelbyville Court on motion of Taylor himself and the first trustees of the town born on the era of a new century were: George Cravinston, Wm. Bridgewater, Robert Jeffries, Elisha Prewitt and Isaac Ellis Gent.

PART III
Churches and Schools

Buffalo Lick.

Mulberry.

CHAPTER I

Shelby County Baptists

Coincident with the very first settlement in Shelby County was the organization of religious bodies and providing for places of worship. The predominance of the Baptist Church as to numbers has been in about the same proportion in the County as in the State and Nation. There seems little doubt that they, the Baptists, were also the first denomination to organize and have a place of worship in the County.*

Back in the last part of the first half of the Eighteenth Century, William Taylor, a native of New Jersey, was growing into manhood and soon became to the "regular Baptists" of the southern settlements what Louis Craig** was to the north. He not only collected the settlers together in the region immediately around him and preached to them, but like Paul, visited the little churches, preached, wrote to them and encouraged them.

The Mother Church

After various activities in Nelson and other surrounding counties, he, with John Whitaker, seems to have organized in 1785, the Brashear's Creek Church in Owen's Fort, where

---

*The history of the Baptist church in Kentucky by Spencer fills two large volumes of several hundred pages each. A really complete history of that denomination's activities in Shelby County for 140 years would easily fill a volume as large as this history of the entire county. The same is true of the material we have before us concerning the Christian and Methodist churches in this county, and is true in a smaller degree of the Presbyterian, the Episcopalians and the Catholic churches in the same territory. No one would be able to group and intelligently condense the history in a manner any way satisfactory to all concerned, until each denomination raised up some man capable of, and inclined to write its story, with proper records of each church in his particular denomination, in a county where its churches have ever led the hope of civilization.

**With Squire Boone, enough of a minister to perform marriage ceremonies, and other God-fearing men and women in the station, it is fair to presume that they early and often had religious services, but the first sermon known to have been preached in the County, was by the indefatigable Louis Craig, in the fall of 1782, at the Squire Boone Station of the Painted Stone. Craig was busy organizing new churches—one on Dick's (Dix) River near the mouth of Gilbert's Creek, in what is now Garrard County, Ky., and came down into Shelby to preach to, and pray with, the survivors of the Long Run massacre and the other hardships of those first years.

seven years later the County itself was born. It was constituted of eight members, seven of whom were: Martha Whitaker, Col. Aquila Whitaker and wife, Mary, Peggy Garrot, Nathan Garrot, Col. James Ballard and Rebecca, a colored woman.

The Indians kept its members from meeting for two years soon after their organization, and in 1787, at the time it joined the Salem Association it still contained only seven members, and the next records found of it, was in 1803, when it united with other churches in forming the Long Run Association at which time it had grown to 101 members.

William Hickman, its pioneer visiting minister was succeeded by Joshua Morris, and he, it is said, by James McQuade, Sr., and the church continued to grow for the following forty-five years until in 1843, when it had a membership of 123, changed its name to Clear Creek, after which the neighborhood churches and the large church at Shelbyville gradually absorbed its members until 1858, it ceased to exist. It was the mother church in this region of the State and from it sprang in some numbers the early churches of Shelby County.

Beech Creek

Beech Creek Church, of "Regular Old School Baptists" was organized in 1796. It was "constituted in the same faith as the Elkhorn Association and Salem Association constituted both in 1785. The church was located in the southeastern part of the County, two miles south of Waddy, and its activities for 130 years form no small part of the history of that section. It has had three different buildings during the years. Its first pastor was John Penny, its second, Warren Cash, who was succeeded in turn by Moses Scott, James McQuade, Abraham Cook, John Holland, Geo. Bristo, Caleb Guthrie, Garland William, W. D. Ball, John Knight, N. A. Humston, John F. Johnston, James E. Newkirk, J. W. Hardesty, and the late Elder P. W. Sawin.

Baptists

Salem (Beech Creek)

The church historians of the County have devoted more detail authentic work to Salem than to a Mother Church. It is regretted that all that has been written about it cannot be reproduced here. Salem was organized on January 19, 1811, by Moses Scott, pastor of Beech Creek Church, and by James McQuade, pioneer circuit writer at the home of Mrs. Sarah Dugan, in the old brick house formerly owned by John Hedden and later by James Radcliff and was temporarily called Beech Ridge, probably because the nineteen charter members were largely from the original Beech Creek Church. Their names were: James M. Leodocy, Mary P., Ann and John Holland, William, Mary and Lydia Collins, Samuel and Catharine Gray, Betsy, John, Jane and Edmon Graves, James M. Judith and Polly Burnett, and Mary Firguson.

Thomas Martin was the first pastor. There have been several separate buildings, the third or brick building having been destroyed by fire in 1894, when the present building was erected on the lot originally donated by the Slaughter heirs. The church and its great growth and wide usefulness celebrated its anniversary in 1911. John Holland, the charter member baptized by Rev. John Rice, said to have been the first preacher in Kentucky, was long the pastor of Salem and at his request his body was buried under the pulpit of the old church and a monument to him was unveiled at the centennial celebration mentioned above. He had been succeeded by Elder Geo. Bristol, in 1841; by Nimrod Beckham, from 1846-1851; W. G. Hobbs, 1851-1861; T. M. Vaughan, 1861-1870; V. M. Hungerford, 1870-1883; O. L. Haley, 1883-1884; J. B. Tharpe, 1885-1888; H. C. Davis, 1888-1901; W. S. Thomas, 1902-1904; A. J. Foster, 1904-1906; J. S. Wilson, 1906-1907; A. R. Willit, 1908-.

Buffalo Lick

Somewhere about 1804, Tarlton Lee and Martin Basket

donated each an acre of ground upon which to build a church at Buffalo Lick, where a church still stands and has so long been the center of the "Buffalo Lick neighborhood, between Peytona and Bagdad in the eastern portion of the County, taking its name from the lick, found at Peytona by the first settlers. The first meeting was held at the house of Thos. Basket, Sr., and the constituents were members given up by the "Tick Creek" Church and were: Phillip Weber, I. Underwood, Benj. Boyd, Martin Basket, Thos. Basket, Sr., Roderick Perry, John Yount and Chas. Michel. The first meeting in the new church was held on June 15, 1805, with the selection of Phillip Weber, as moderator and Chas. Michel, clerk and the adoption of the new name. They, like the Salem and Long Run Associations, agreed on the "Philadelphia Baptist Confession of Faith" excepting something contained in the third and fifth article, if construed so as to make God the author of sin, and also in the thirty-first article, laying hands on newly baptized persons that the using or non-using of that ceremony be no bar to fellowship, and that an oath before a magistrate be not considered a part of real worship as contained in the twenty-fourth article of the same." The membership rolls of this church early became one of the longest in the County because of the fertile territory surrounding it and the rapidity with which it was settled and peopled.

Buck Creek Church

The church of this name, still a historic spot and burial ground in the southwest section of the County, was organized in 1799, but for the first three years was called Plum Creek Church, when it became "Plum and Buck Creek Church" which name was four years later, or in 1807, contracted to simply "Buck Creek."

William Edmund Waller, the distinguished Virginian, who had already been a resident of Shelby for some ten years seems to have been the moving spirit in the organization of the church of which there were only eight charter members: John Patterson, Geo. Davis, Sarah Patterson, Johnston Patterson, Theodore Davis, Priscella May, Elizabeth Breedon and William Mocensen. Rev. Waller was pastor for four years when upon the death of his wife he returned to his home in Spottsylvania, Virginia, where a few years later he, too, died. His son, Geo. Waller, who married Mary Ware, a daughter of Ruben Ware, of that neighborhood succeeded his father as pastor for the almost record-breaking length of time of forty years, and at the end of that service in 1842, had helped to build up a membership of from eight to 342. It is said that for the nine years preceding 1842, an almost continuous revival was in progress and 289 members were added to the church. In 1849, there arose some trouble between the new pastor and the public which resulted in a strange dismemberment of the church. One hundred and forty adhered to the pastor while seventy-two formed a new organization, but the two factions continued to worship in the same building for more than ten years or until 1860, when they reunited and continued as Buck Creek Church.

The church was a plain substantial brick about a mile from the present town of Finchville until 1891, when it was razed and its material used in the erection of a handsome edifice which now stands near the center of the village itself.

Buck Creek Burial Ground

Just a little way from where the old church building stood, on a beautiful spot, was the "Burying Ground," and there rest many of those intrepid men and women who fought the arduous battles of the pioneer life, and assisted in building the sure and strong foundations of our present peace and quiet and prosperity.

The fence which once enclosed this hallowed spot has been removed and the cattle permitted to roam at will over the graves, and fell the stones and destroy them, until now it is not possible to know the names of those who were buried there. About the graves of the beloved pastor, the Rev. Geo. Waller and his family and kindred there has recently been placed a high and substantial wire fence which bids to protect them from intrusion for many years. Of the great number who appear to have been buried in these grounds, many graves are without stones and others so broken and mutilated as not to be read at all. Herewith is presented the epitaphs on those stones which have been preserved, in this once large city of the dead:

Eld. George Waller, B. Sept. 12, 1777; D. July 17, 1860.

Geo. W. Kenney, B. Dec. 25, 1794; D. Nov. 25, 1854.

Ann J., wife of Geo. W. Kenney, B. Oct. 7, 1800; D. March 21, 1872.

Douglas Cowherd, B. March 1, 1817; D. Dec. 13, 1892; aged 75 years, 9 months, 6 days.

Mariah, wife of Douglas Cowherd, B. April 28, 1818; D. April 5, 1870.

Sarah Catherine Cowherd, B. Oct. 21, 1839; D. July 20, 1841.

Lucinda, wife of Douglas Cowherd, B. April 15, 1807; D. Sept. 9, 1876.

Gertrude, Daughter of Waller and Mattie Cowherd, B. Dec. 11, 1890 and D. aged 11 years, 10 months, 13 days.

Ann Lucinda, daughter of D. C. and M. M. Cowherd, B. Sept. 12, 1849, D. Feb. 25, 1854.

Polly Waller, wife of Geo. Waller, B. Dec. 19, 1775; D. Oct. 24, 1849.

Sacred to the Memory of Wm. E. Waller, husband of Belle R. Waller, B. Nov. 17, 1845; D. Nov. 10, 1878.

Mary A., daughter of A. D. and G. Waller, B. Dec. 15, 1856; D. April 10, 1874.

Sarah D., daughter of A. D. and G. Waller, B. April 12, 1842; D. Feb. 5, 1874.

John Overton, son of A. D. and G. Waller, B. Sept. 6, 1843; D. Dec. 22, 1853.

BAPTISTS

Mary G., daughter of A. D. and G. Waller, B. Feb. 28; D. April 6, 1855.

Kate A., daughter of A. D. and G. Waller, B. Sept. 28, 1854; D. Oct. 5, 1856.

These names which follow are outside of the enclosure.

Frances M. Allen, B. July 4, 1817; D. Jan. 2, 1837.

Hiram Melone, B. Feb. 9, 1803; D. May 4, 1838.

Catherine, wife of A. D. Waller, Sr., B. —; D. April 17, 1891, aged 76 years, 5 days.

Sarah Brashears White, D. June 15, 1849; aged 33 years, 11 months, 20 days.

Fox Run

The church by the name of "Fox Run" was organized also by John Whitaker and Joshua Morris at the house of James Hogland, January 26, 1794, with the following persons charter members: Jesse Buzan, Eliza Buzan, James Hogland, Mary Hogland, William Metcalfe, Hester Metcalfe, James Metcalfe, Thomas Metcalfe, Mary Teague, Milly Long, Robert and Jane London, Joseph and Margaret Ervin and one other. William Marshall was the first pastor of the church. He preached "Eternal Justification" and refused to preach the gospel to sinners. The church would not receive this doctrine and this irritated him, bitter differences ensued and Spencer, the Baptist Historian says, that this minister "who had been so wonderfully successful in Virginia was excluded from fellowship and remained out of the church until his death."

This church, it is thought, joined the Salem Association the same year it was constituted and remained therein until it entered into "the Constitution of Long Run Association of 1803." Its membership of twenty-seven at that time had increased to sixty-five in 1812, and to one hundred and fifty-three in 1826 or '27, when as Spencer describes "during the Campbellite disturbance* reduced from one hundred and fifty-three to about ninety" (as explained in the history of the Christian Church in Shelby County the many members left churches like the Fox Run Baptist Church to become members of the new "reform" or "Campbellite church" during the several years of revival beginning with 1823).

Fox Run in 1839, joined the Sulphur Fork Association to which it reported a membership of seventy-eight. This membership was slowly increased up to 1880, when it reported one hundred and fifty-six members. The church for some reason was removed to Eminence, in Henry County, a good many years ago. William Ford, a member and deacon of Fox Run Church was one of the early settlers of what is now Henry County.

John Penny was the first pastor, but Warren Cash, a member, developing a gift for preaching was called and in 1799, was ordained their pastor. A revival started under his ministry and a large number were baptized, and the handful of members under him increased in four years to one hundred and fifty-one, then the largest membership in the Long Run Association.

In 1817, it took a letter and united with the Franklin Association; it continued prosperous until 1836, when it went into the Constitution of the Middle District Association where it remained for some years and then joined Mt. Pleasant Association of Anti-Missionary Baptists and, in the language of Spencer, has "of course since been withering away."

"Pin Hook" or Chestnut Grove**

The Pin Hook Church, about eight miles north of Shelbyville, at the intersection of the Christianburg-Ballardsville Road with the Smithfield Road, was organized about 1846, and held its meetings in a store room previously occupied by

---

*Mr. Spencer (J. H.) the Baptist historian quoted above frequently in his writings permitted it to creep out that his prejudice was as strong against the anti-missionary Baptist as it was against those to whom he contemptuously referred always as "Campbellites" and it is to be assumed that he believed that they, as much as the "reformers" injured the "Regular Baptist" of this and other counties.

**Information gathered and contributed by Miss Lyle Booker.

Thomas Denny, who sold general merchandise. This store was a hundred yards or more west of the church building in a small grove of chestnut trees. (Hence the name, Chestnut Grove, by which name also a Christian Church located several miles nearer Shelbyville was known in more recent years.) The church held meetings in this storeroom for six or seven years during which period it prospered so that it was decided to build a new house of worship. The new church was built in the angle of the cross roads near the creek. The logs from which the lumber was sawed to build the new church house were cut from the old Williams farm and sawed in the old mill on the creek just back of the Williams' barn. A historian writes that, "Henry Williams helped to haul the lumber from the mill to the church site, where Tommie Williams and Garland Williams superintended the construction of the building."

Elder Caleb Guthrie and wife deeded the land on which the church was built. The Articles of Faith and rules of decorum were in accord with the London Confession of Faith published in 1628. The charter members were: Gilson Yates and wife, Micajah Williams and wife, Martha and Jane Williams, Elijah Woods and wife, James Baskett, Nathaniel Dowden and wife, Elder Caleb Guthrie and wife, Hiram Morton and wife, William Royster and wife, Allen Kinkead and wife, Garland Williams and wife, Jonathan Woods and wife, John Tinsley and wife (parents of Dr. Tinsley). Elder Guthrie was the first pastor, Garland Williams was the first clerk and served in this capacity until his ordination to the work of the ministry about the year 1850. He served as pastor from his ordination until broken in health early in the seventies. He was followed by Elder Gardner Berry, he by W. W. Foree. He in turn by Doctor I. N. Porter, who was succeeded by Elder John Freeman, the last regular pastor of the church to its dissolution about 1878. John Robinson was the last clerk.

After the dissolution of the church, the members cast their

lots with the Dover, Smithfield, and Eminence Baptist Churches. The old church building stood idle a number of years being used occasionally for a school entertainment.

Horace Hopkins bought the old church, tore it down and used the lumber for building a barn about 1886.

Tick Creek—Bethel Church

Bethel Church so frequently referred to as Old Bethel and formerly called Tick Creek was originally located on a small stream, from which it derived its old name, five miles from Shelbyville and not far from where Tyler's Station was first settled. It, too, seems to have been organized or "gathered" by Joshua Morris or James Dupuy and was constructed in 1797. It first united with Elkhorn Association to which it reported a membership of 16. In 1799, it joined the Salem Association with twenty-four members, and in the division of the latter fraternity in 1803, it fell into Long Run Association with 107 members. Five years later when the famous Geo. Waller became the pastor, it had dropped again to forty-five members, but during the twenty-three years under his pastorship was trebled in number of members.

About this time the split on account of the Missionary and Anti-Missionary divided not only the congregation, but the ministers, Rev. Holland having temporarily succeeded Waller in the pastorship. Out of the two hundred and fifty-nine members a large majority of the missionary party withdrew and went to Clay Village nearby and built a church, whereas the old, greatly reduced membership which advocated the Anti-Missionary idea remained in charge of the old building which for many years has been only a building and burial ground.

The fact that it was the place of worship and burying ground for the Cross Keys families and many distinguished early families of that section has added to the fame of Old Bethel.

Baptists

Shelbyville Baptist Church

The Baptist people of Shelby County instead of originating at the largest center and multiplying therefrom into the County reversed the procedure and the first organization in, and worshiping at the County Seat appear, not to have been by those alone from the town but from seed planted in the rural early churches.

The first church building of any kind in Shelbyville was undenominational. It was erected in 1814, and was called the Shelbyville "meeting house," being used by all three of the then existing Protestant denominations.

It was the property of the Methodists and the meetings of the other denominations were not allowed to conflict with those of the owners. The Shelbyville Baptists used it until 1819, when their new church on the corner of Eighth and Clay Streets was complete. It was used also by the Presbyterians until 1820. The new church was occupied by the Baptists until the year before the outbreak of the Civil War or for more than forty years when a newer, more imposing structure, used until recent years, was erected facing the southwestern part or quarter of the old Shannon acre of public grounds.

Other Organizations

Early Baptist organizations of no less historic interest, perhaps, but about whom the records furnish less data were: Long Run, 1796; Indian Fork Church, organized as early, it is believed, as 1806. Six-Mile Church, not far from Christianburg, organized in 1799. Blue Stone Church near the south line of Shelby County, in 1805, Simpsonville and Mt. Pleasant.

CHAPTER II

Christian Churches

While not the next largest denomination in the County, the Christian Church, also known as the Church of the Disciples, the Church of Christ and formerly more often called the "Campbellite" or the "Reform Church" has been prominently in the forefront of the County's civilization for one hundred years.

As is generally known it was largely the offspring of the Baptist and Presbyterian denominations. Alexander Campbell was himself first a Presbyterian and then a Baptist. He was a native of Ireland, the son of a Presbyterian Minister and was educated at the University of Glasgow. He came to the U. S. in 1809, and was a minister in good standing in the Pennsylvania Presbyteries, but soon announced that his faith in creeds was shaken and after much debate joined the Baptist Church. At that time he lived near Bethany, Virginia, (later West Virginia), where he farmed and taught school. In 1823, he began the publication of a paper called the "Christian Baptist." It had a wide circulation and influence. In 1827, an extensive religious revival was begun in that section and throughout Central Kentucky, including Shelby County, which lasted three years and "greatly favored the reformation" viz.: That is the forming of a church or denomination with "no creed but the Bible."

Into New Faith

Baptist churches which belonged in the Long Run Association, lost numerous members who united with the new denomination and included such men as Phillip Fall, Zachius Carpenter, and Benj. Allen among their leaders. Sixteen hundred and seventy-eight people were baptized "into the Christian Church" this first year in Shelby, and already more than ten thousand in Kentucky followed Elder Campbell, who spoke many times in Shelby County. In 1830, a congregation was formed in Shelbyville, of which Major James Whitaker's family, the families of William Standiford, William Smith, Doctor G. W. Nuchols, Travis Wilson, Achilles Chinn, Thomas Chiles, Hamilton Frazier, Thomas B. Caldwell and a number of others were members from the beginning. Several years later, Joseph L. Fore, sold to the congregation a lot on which to build the church. The lot was fifty feet square and fronted on Fourth Street, the southern side of the lot running with the alley between Fourth and Fifth Streets and Main and Clay. At the corner of Fourth and Main and between the church and Main Street Abraham Smith owned a lot fifty by twenty-five feet on which he conducted a gunsmith business. There was a vacant lot immediately west of the lot purchased for the church, and the lot owned by Mr. Smith. On this lot fifty feet square, which is covered by a part of the present Christian Church, was built the first church, which was called in those days the Campbellite, the Reform, and the Church of the Disciples of Christ.

It was a brick church and fronted on Fourth Street. It was back from Main Street fifty feet, and Smith's gun shop was on the corner and between it and Main Street. It was necessary to climb several steps to get to the main floor. There were two doors fronting Fourth Street and the pulpit was between those doors, making it necessary for those who had occasion to go to the farthest end of the building to walk down the aisle with their backs to the pulpit. This was the first Christian Church in Shelbyville or Shelby County, and it served the purpose for which it was constructed for over thirty years.

Still Another New Church

The church prospered, the membership grew in numbers, and in 1863, there being a number of wealthy citizens affiliated with the congregation, it was determined to build a larger and more attractive edifice.

In December, of that year, the lot belonging to Mr. Smith was purchased and a few months later, the vacant lot adjoining. This gave the congregation a lot fronting Main Street sixty-seven feet, and extending from Main Street to the alley, a distance of 100 feet.

During 1864, the plans were agreed on and contracts were let. James McCarthy built the foundation; "Big Frank" McMahon and "Bob" Rogers did the brick work; Herman Deiss did the cut stone work; and R. M. and Jeptha Layson were the carpenters. The church was completed in 1865. The first service conducted in the church was the funeral of Richard Whitaker, a son of Major James Whitaker. The dedicatory sermon was preached the next day, after Mr. Whitaker's funeral. The church was later enlarged by the addition of an annex, which connects with the main auditorium.

Clear Creek

Two other churches of this denomination were organized in Shelby County, only a few years after the church in Shelbyville had been built. These were Clear Creek Church, in 1835, and Antioch, in 1839. Many left Fox Run Baptist Church and joined these congregations. Among them were Jeptha and Emma Bright, James H. and Nancy Drane, Oswald and Mary Thomas, and these, with John, Preston, Lindsay and Wilson Thomas, William Crawford, Pauline Crawford, (nee Thomas), and John Donaldson and wife, joined the Clear Creek Church. For a time the members met at the house of Harvey Stone, one of the progenitors of the Helm, Maddox and Bright families. Clear Creek Church was built on a lot donated by Lindsay Thomas, near the headwaters of Clear Creek. Two of the first preachers of Clear Creek were "Billy" Crawford and Robert Rice. On May 5, 1844, a church was organized one mile east of Eminence, in Henry

County, called "Congregation of Christ at Macedonia," twenty-five members of Clear Creek joining that church. Among those who changed their membership, at that time, were the Brights, Dranes, Hopkins, McCarms, Donaldsons, Yates, Allisons, Fords, Joneses and Sadlers. Other members of Clear Creek changed their membership to Cropper or Shelbyville, and services were discontinued at Clear Creek.

Antioch

In 1839, Gilbert Jarvis donated a small tract of land two miles north of Simpsonville, on which to build a church which was called Antioch. That piece of land is on the corner of a farm later owned by Miller Wilhoit and his successors. The charter members of Antioch, were thirteen in number. Robert Long and wife,* James Young and wife, John Crosby and wife, Robert Elkin and wife, Nancy Brown, Frances Whitington, Margaret Long, and Mr. and Mrs. James L. Long. Shortly after the organization of the church, J. S. Willis, a young minister, from Madison County, married Mary J. Long, a youthful member of Antioch and came to the County to live. When the log church was remodeled in 1848, he became the pastor and remained such for many years. He preached the dedicatory sermon, and the last services in the church on January 21, 1883, were his funeral services. He, several of his family, a few strangers, and a host of the Long, Jarvis, Campbell, Crosby, and other families and relatives of the first members are buried there in the neatly kept little cemetery that overruns the site of where the old church stood. The church was torn away shortly after Elder Willis' death. A cemetery company was formed, money from the sale of the

---

*The Robert Long was a first cousin of J. L. and S. C. Long, and of Mrs. J. S. Willis. His brother, Saml., later, was one of the deacons of the church for many years following its organization and was a prosperous farmer of the neighborhood, interested in all public enterprises, and reared a large family of reputable, useful citizens. One noted among these was Robert A. Long, the lumber magnate, who was baptized into this church of his fathers, several years before he left to become a citizen of Kansas City; from which point, in later years he was the first known citizen of the United States to give as much as a million dollars to a church of one denomination at one time. And that gift has been but one of his nation-wide activities on behalf of the Church of the Disciples.

CHRISTIANS

church and from several small bequests was constituted into a fund, the interest of which is used in keeping up the burial grounds, the land of which may never be sold.

"Flat Rock," on the edge of the County, near both Oldham and Jefferson, one of the pioneer churches in which Elder Willis and a long line of successors preached is still standing, though abandoned; and the Masonic Lodge at Simpsonville, where the congregation of that name early worshipped, remains a land-mark of that section. Reverend Willis and other pioneers of this church preached a number of years at "Plum Creek," a little church supported by the Bairds, Beards, et al., on the edge of Spencer County, until the building was moved to the town of Waterford, where it became a dwelling, after being superseded by a larger building.

"Old Bethel," across the road from "Cross-Keys."

Site from which "Antioch," pioneer Christian Church building was razed nearly fifty years ago.

CHAPTER III

Methodist Church

In the spring of 1790, was held the first annual conference of the Methodist Church in Kentucky. The conference commenced at Masterson's Station, about five miles northwest of Lexington, where the first Methodist Church, in Kentucky, was erected.

The first mention of Salt River Circuit found is in 1791. It included Jefferson, Nelson and Shelby Counties, and all the settlements from the Kentucky River to the mouth of Salt River. It is probable that Barnabus McHenry, who served the Danville and Madison circuits, in 1789 and 1790, was the first Methodist minister who ever preached the gospel in Shelby County, and this prepared the way for the Salt River circuit in 1791.

At the conference of 1796, the Shelby Circuit was formed, but the appointment of preachers was still made at times to "Salt River and Shelby" combined. In 1796, Jeremiah Dawson was in charge. In 1797, William Kavanaugh, the father of the later celebrated Bishop Kavanaugh, was pastor.

First Shelby Church*

The first Methodist Church in Shelby County was organized in the Cardwell neighborhood, on what was then known as the Fielding Neel farm on the Rockbridge pike. It used a log house, and was given the name of Rockbridge by some of the charter members, who came from Rockbridge County, Virginia. The charter members included: Samuel Ratcliffe, Mrs. Susan Ratcliffe, James Figg, Susan Figg, Lemuel McCormick, Sarah McCormick, Joseph Hite, Sarah McCormick Wright and John McCormick.

*From paper by Mrs. Edwin H. Davis.

Shelbyville Methodists

About 1804, a Brick Chapel was erected (and this was said to have been the first brick church for Methodists in Kentucky); it was located about four miles northeast of Shelbyville and about one fourth of a mile east of the Walker Daniel farm.

The Methodist people who lived in Shelbyville held their membership at the "Brick Chapel" and worshipped there, with an occasional service in the court house, and in private residences, where prayer and class-meetings were also held.

Own the "Meeting House"*

The Methodists built probably the first place of worship in Shelbyville, on a lot given them by John Bradshaw, on the back corner of what then was Lot 9, and would now be the rear of a lot facing south on Washington Street and east on Fourth. This was somewhere about 1810 or '12. They soon turned over this building to colored people; for in 1816, they bought parts of Lots 10 and 11 (about midway between Fourth and Fifth on North side of Washington) from John Bradshaw and Jos. Willett, and built a church that was called "the meeting house," and, while owned by the Methodists, was used for a time by all Protestant denominations. As elsewhere told, the Baptist Church held services in this building until they erected a house of worship on the corner of Eighth and Clay Streets, where the colored Baptist Church now stands, and the Presbyterians, until 1820, when their church was built. The name of "Meeting House" was then changed to the Methodist Church. Richard Corwine was pastor, from 1823 to 1824. In 1824, the Kentucky Conference, presided over by Bishops McKendree and Roberts, met in Shelbyville and in that year the church building was enlarged. Shelbyville and Brick Chapel were

---

*Mr. Camden W. Ballard, to whom the author is indebted for other courtesies, has among his wealth of historic data, the maps, plats, etc., of the lots mentioned and abstracts of title for all that section. These are the authority for the locations given and the dates fixed as to these buildings.

METHODISTS

detached from the circuit and for a number of years united as one charge, and were served by ministers whose names are prominent in church history; from 1824-25, by Richard Neal; 1825-27, by John Tevis; 1827-28, by George C. Light; 1828-29, by Edward Stevenson; 1830-32, by Johnathan Stamper.

As officers in the church, the records name William Owen, George Robinson, John Bradshaw, Isaac Pomeroy, William Cardwell, Jacob Cardwell, Robert Bull, Edward Talbot, Nathaniel Talbot, Hardin Magruder, Adam Winlock, Richard Waters, and Robert McGrath, at whose house for many years services were held every Christmas morning at five o'clock.

Another New Building

In 1857, during the pastorate of Rev. J. W. Cunningham, a new church was erected on the site where the present now stands at the corner of Fifth and Main Streets. The church built in 1817-18, was torn down in 1859, after having been used for two years as a school house by Professor J. W. Dodd. The first board of stewards in the church of which this takes the place, was composed of William Winlock, Jacob Owen, John Robinson, John R. Beckley, Fielding Neel, Daniel Polk, and Doctor B. P. Tevis, Judge Thomas Wilson, T. B. Cochran, Doctor Robt. Winlock and Judge Martin D. McHenry, son of Rev. Barnabas McHenry.

The present church was erected in 1897, when Doctor W. T. Taylor was pastor.

Olive Branch*

For nearly a century there stood a little frame building on the banks of Brashears Creek, about nine miles south of Shelbyville and two miles from Finchville, on a branch road of the Finchville and Taylorsville turnpike. It was used as a place of worship by members of the Methodist-Episcopal church.

---

*Data furnished by Mrs. Reuben Smith.

It was built on the land of Mrs. Barriger, a short distance from a big spring from which flowed a stream, that divided into two branches, running on either side of the little church building and so nearly surrounding it by water that, taking the story of the Dove and the Ark, and the branch from the stream itself, the church was christened "Olive Branch."

It is said, that a meeting held in the open near that church in 1860, and then called a "Woods meeting" was the first camp meeting held in the County, and that it resulted in a very large number of new members for the church. A large colony of relatives of the Figgs, Boswells, and Taylors had come from Culpeper Court House, in 1800, and had settled around and near the little church. Many of them were charter members, and a descendant, Warren T. Figg, a wealthy landowner, when the little church became old and dilapidated, donated an acre in a more desirable location two miles nearer the County Seat, on the Zaring Mill pike and gave liberally toward the building of the new church. His wife Lucinda Taylor, also was a descendant of those who came in the first colony, and their large and prosperous family helped fill the church membership, and offices, as well as its coffers, for many years. Descendants of others of that first colony burned the brick and built the building that was at that day considered a beautiful bit of architecture. John and Younger Ford were the contractors for the wood or frame work, and the building begun in 1861, was completed in 1862.

Taylor Boswell, who helped burn the brick and build the church had three sons, Chas., Everett, and Geo. W., who became consecrated ministers and served many Methodist Churches in the Kentucky conference. The largest membership of any county church known at that time, was acquired by Olive Branch, in 1885, with a total of several hundred members. The charter members of the church were: William Taylor, Mary Taylor, Mary Taylor, Jr., Zurilduer Taylor, Doctor Taylor, James Taylor, Martha Taylor, Stokeley Law-

METHODISTS

son, Sarah Snyder, Absolom Campbell, Sallie Campbell, Doctor Blankenbaker, John Clark, Bell Clark, John Clark, John Boswell, Doctor Boswell and Wife, James Boswell, Madison T. Boswell, George G. Boswell, Warren Figg, Lucinda Figg, Bushrod Figg, James Figg, Margaret Figg, Jennie Boswell, Georgia Doyle, Bettie Jessie, James Harrison, Eleanor Harrison, Thomas Smith, Bettie Smith, Edwin Dorsey, Eliza Dorsey, D. O. Fisher, Angeline Fisher, Doctor Alexandria, Doctor William Wilson, and John Spangler.

Many of the church's ablest ministers have served this church, among them: Revs. J. E. Strother, Minor, W. H. Winter, Robert Hiner, W. F. Vaughn, J. A. Henderson, D. B. Cooper, T. B. Cooke, T. J. McIntyre, George Frok, J. J. Johnson, T. J. Godbey, W. S. Grinstead, T. W. Barker, T. Chandler, J. W. Simpson, E. K. Pike, P. J. Ross, J. E. Wright, C. H. Caswell, and R. R. Rose.

Stanley Smith, E. V. Dorsey, and Marvin Figg (grandson of Warren T. Figg, who donated land for church) were stewards as late at 1923.

CHAPTER IV

Episcopalians in Shelby

In his History of Kentucky Baptists, J. H. Spencer, in Volume I, says:

"In 1810, there was one Episcopal Church in Kentucky. It was organized in Lexington in 1794, and was under the pastoral charge of James Moore, who was its first rector."

The first register of St. James Church was not found, but the present register gives the date of organizing as 1858. Before the erection of the present church, the Episcopalians held their services in the Chapel of the Episcopal Theological Seminary, then on College Street, between Eighth and Ninth Streets, now a city school.

At this time they had a large congregation and baptism in the chapel with confirmations by Bishop Smith, in the Masonic Building when they held their services there. The only record of service held there is a "Certificate of Baptism of Julia Bonney, April 1, 1866," A. F. Freeman, Rector.

In the Court Records is a letter of "Association" as follows: "The undersigned Wardens and Vestry of St. James Church, Shelbyville, Kentucky, of the Protestant Episcopal of the United States, hereby, voluntarily associate together for the purpose of maintaining and erecting a place of public worship for said Church and, to perform such other duties as may be assigned to us, and our successors as Wardens and Vestry of said Church by the Cannons of the convention of the Diocese of the State of Kentucky. The conditions of membership of the said Vestry, shall be, the election of its members according to the Cannons of the convention of the State of Kentucky, and shall do all other things and exercise all the rights and privileges belonging to the Wardens and Vestry of a Church in said Diocese.

"J. M. Bullock, G. W.,
"S. H. Ellenwood, Jr. W.,
"J. Baker,
$1.00 U. S. S.   "Geo. Rowden."

Kentucky, Shelby County:

I, John T. Ballard, Clerk of the County Court of the County aforesaid, do certify that this letter of association between the members of the Protestant Episcopal Church of St. James, at Shelbyville, was this day filed in my office by S. H. Ellenwood, stamped with a one dollar United States revenue stamp and recorded at his request. Given under my hand this Twenty-second day of March, 1865.

J. T. Ballard, Clerk,
Shelby County Court.
Deed to Lot No. 163.

An Old Deed

E. H. Tubman, to Vestry of St. James Church. "Know all men, that E. H. Tubman, of the city of Augusta, and the state of Georgia, for and in consideration of five hundred dollars, cash in hand paid, hath sold, and by these presents doth convey unto S. H. Ellenwood, J. Baker, M. C. Taylor, G. M. Bright, H. H. Malone, and A. Hollenback, Wardens and Vestry of St. James Church, Shelbyville, Kentucky, and their successors, heirs and assigns, the following described real estate, to-wit:

"Part of Lot No. 163, situated on Main Street, Shelbyville, Kentucky. Beginning at the northwest corner of said lot, and running east sixty feet, south one hundred feet, west sixty feet, north one hundred feet to the beginning, together with the privilege and appurtenances to the same belonging, to have and to hold unto the said grantees and their successors, heirs

EPISCOPALIANS

and assigns forever; and the said grantor hereby covenants with the said grantees and their successors, heir and assigns that she being seized of an estate in fee simple in said premises, that her title thereto is unencumbered and that she will warrant and defend them the same against all claim payment of part of the purchase money. Witness the hand of the grantor this Twenty-first day of September, 1867.

E. H. Tubman.

(50 cents U. S. S.
E. H. T.
Sept. 21st., 1867).

Mrs. Emily H. Tubman, the above grantor, was a sister of Mrs. Whitaker and Mrs. Standiford, (of the Christian church).

Rectors of St. James Church from 1865 to 1923, were: A. F. Freeman, 1865; Doctor Chapman, Doctor George McCready, Doctor Flowers, M. M. Benton, Milton Worsham, April, 1908-1909; Clinton Quinn, November 1, 1909-March 1, 1911; Middleton Barnwell, June 21, 1908; Edw. C. McAllister, May 1, 1911-May 9, 1915; Frances M. Adams, May 16, 1915-December 1, 1916; Edw. C. McAllister, May 1, 1919-March 13, 1921; George Dow, April, 1921.

St. James Church was built in 1867, or 1868, the members at that time were: George Bright, Miss Minnie Bright, Miss Hannah Bright, Mr. Graham Bright, Horatio Bright, Judge James M. Bullock and Mrs. Bullock, Sam H. Ellenwood, Doctor J. Baker, H. C. Malone and Mrs. Emma Bonney Malone, Mrs. Thos. Todd, M. C. Taylor, Miss Julia Bonney, Charles Kinkle and Mrs. Kinkle, Mr. and Mrs. Albert Hollenbach, Mr. George Rowden and family, Mr. Pierce Noland.

CHAPTER V

Presbyterians in Shelby County

In a yellowed, musty old "Deacon's Record," the property of Mr. J. A. Logan, of Christiansburg, the cover of which bears dates of 1796, 1819 and 1839, under the head of "A Sketch of Presbyterian Church History in Shelby County," is the following:*

"In the spring of A. D. 1796, Archibald Cameron received a call from a people who wished to be congregated and enjoy the regular ministry of the gospel, both in the counties of Shelby and Nelson—two-thirds of his time in Shelby and the other part to be at the Big Spring meeting house in Nelson County. The friends of the Presbyterian Church were scattered in different directions around Shelbyville; but most of them were living on Bull Skin and Tick Creek and of course their first places of meeting were on these creeks and that summer the preacher, whom they called being only a licentiate, was ordained and installed among them. The first administration of the Lord's Supper was in the fall of 1796, and all the communicants were about thirty-five. The great part of them were received upon examination and not by certificate. Mr. Cameron soon found it expedient to disengage himself from the people of the Big Spring congregation in Nelson County and confined his ministry wholly to the people of Shelby. In a short process of time the communicants increased to nearly a hundred and it was thought proper upon consultation for convenience of assembling together to change the place of meeting. A people in this Presbyterian connection called the low Dutch congregation suffered considerable diminution by dereliction to the Shakers and removals to the Indiana State.

"The congregation of Tick Creek by deaths and removals of families and individuals to the Indiana and Ohio States

---
*Records contributed by Mrs. Mary Middelton Nicholas.

was reduced likewise to a few. It was found then expedient for them and the remaining part of the 'low Dutch,' to build a meeting house on the head of Mulberry Creek, which place lies between the two settlements. The stated preaching was then established at the Mulberry meeting house and the name of the church was changed from that of Tick Creek to Mulberry. Preaching was occasionally continued among the low Dutch at a commodious school house until they had a good meeting house called the Six Mile Meeting House, but the communicants were still few owing to the opening which the rising families have for the obtainment of lands in the Indiana State and consequently the occasion which it gives for a change of situation.

"The Presbyterian connection in the vicinity of Shelbyville had then a general place of meeting for preaching and public worship on Fox Run. The people up Bull Skin above that agreeing to hold meetings there for the sake of general convenience—after some time it was thought proper by the same general connection of Presbyterians to establish a part of the public service of the gospel at Shelbyville. The main places of public and stated assembling for the service of the Sabbaths among the connected Presbyterians were Mulberry, Shelbyville and Fox Run. In the meantime the Presbytery of Transylvania, presuming that congregations, whether single or being several and united, were entitled to a representation or an elder as member of Presbytery only when they were able and willing to support a preacher required of all the congregations to make an exhibit in Presbytery which would give evidence of that fact. In compliance with the requisition of Presbytery the congregations mentioned of Shelbyville, Mulberry and Fox Run made their representation to Presbytery by a written instrument in which they recognized the Reverend Archibald Cameron as their regular pastor which had formerly been installed at his ordination and in consequence of which their Elder was received to membership. Thus continued these people under the ministry of the Reverend Archibald Cameron, and though different vicissitudes took place as we have seen above peace and harmony prevailed between them and their minister from the beginning.

"It may indeed be remarked that individuals at different times endeavored to create discord, but their efforts never had much effect.

"Presbytery thought proper to dissolve the connections between the congregations of Fox Run and the Shelbyville Church in October, 1819. The vicinity of Fox Run meeting house at that time afforded a more numerous population attached to the Presbyterian Church than any other part of Shelby County. They were freed from the interference of other denominations and growing families were in steadier habits of regular attention to public worship. The plan of constructing two meeting houses within three miles of one another which took place among this people seems not to have been rightly considered. Had they been at greater distance they would embrace a larger number of people who would frequent them, but as it is one central place of meeting would serve as well for the whole.

"The old Transylvania Presbytery was not in the habit of calling up and examining sessional records. This may be assigned as some reason why we were not particular in keeping a full register of our church transactions. Though we had occasion to inflict church censure in some few instances there never were any complaints or appeals made to Presbytery respecting our decision, and we at this distance of time think it not expedient to trouble the new Presbytery of Louisville with reviews of all our ancient transactions committed to record.

"In April, 1807, our list of names who were in the full communion of our church belonging to the congregation of Tick Creek (now Mulberry), Shelbyville, including also Six Mile, were the following numbers:

Tick Creek 52
Shelbyville 25
Six Mile 18
                                                                            —
    Total 95

"Of this number there remain only at the present time (viz. October, 1827), 37 persons, some have removed to Indiana State and some to the State of the dead."
A. D. 1828.

"From this time forward we keep an account of the State and doings of Mulberry Creek Church separate from Shelbyville and Six Mile congregation."

The indistinctly written names of the members of the Shelbyville part of the joint churches in 1819, are given in the same book as follows:

Robert, Deborah, Anne, Jane Allen, Singleton, Wilson, Mr. Cull, Mrs. Cull, Mr. Montgomery, Mrs. Montgomery, Mrs. Scott, John Reily, Mrs. Reily, Mrs. Middleton, Mrs. Knose, Betsy Hardin, Mrs. Killpatrick, Mrs. Steele, Mrs. Bullock, Robert Brooky, Sam Harbison, John McCampbell, Mrs. McCampbell, Mrs. Hall, Moses Hall, Rebecca ————, Mrs. McDavid, Mr. Craig, Mrs. Craig, Mr. Long, Polly Paterson, Annie King, Arthur Paterson, Mrs. J. Venable, Alexander Logan, Mrs. Logan, Elson Wilson, Wm. Allen, W. Boyd, Mrs. Boyd, Nancy Logan, Mr. Lemam.

Mulberry Creek Church

Thom King, Ann King, William Graham, Patsy Graham, James Graham, Caleb Shilidray, Charles Baird, Caty Baird, Caty Shiliday, Wm. Johnstone, Mrs. Johnson, Mrs. D. Swearnger, James Venable, Betsy Venable, Sam Graham, George Pearcy, Margaret Smith, John Demaree, Nancy Demaree, David Harbison, Mr. Miles, Mr. George Smith, Mrs. Smith, Mrs. Edward Smith.

PRESBYTERIANS

Six Mile Creek Church

Peter Banta, Albert Voz-His, Andrew Carnine, Mrs. Mitchell, Leah Voz-His, Caty Voz-His, Poly Shugh, Isaac Voz-His, Mr. Shugh, Mrs. Cameron, George Lyst, Poly Polyne, Mr. Polyne, Massy Voz-His, Anne Voz-His, Polly Turchum, Tunis Voz-His, Sam. Demaree, George King, Nelly King, Rachael Demaree, Polly Bip, another woman, Mip Carnine, Peter Banta.

To Mulberry and Shelbyville Added

Mr. Muelin, Mrs. Bowen, David Van Cleave, Rachael Van Cleave, Mr. Moore, Mrs. Graham from the creek, Patsy Harbison, Mrs. Thomson, Mrs. Hannah Steele, Moses Hall, Betsy Hate, Betsy Vetch, one black woman.

Shelbyville Church

The Shelbyville congregation separated from and worshipped, until 1820, in the Shelbyville "meeting house," which was used for a time by all the congregations of the town and in that year built a church on the rear half of the lot where the old grave yard and library now are.

This church was blown down a few years later during a severe storm and temporarily rebuilt at the same place and used until 1846, when a brick church was built on the lot at Seventh and Main Streets, and remained the worshipping place for the Shelbyville congregation until 1888, when remodeled into the more commodious building now used there. In the meantime the war had caused in this church and congregation the same sort of schism that afflicted the Methodist and other Presbyterian churches in Kentucky, and a pretentious new building was erected two blocks further west on Main Street, and was used for many years by the "Northern" Church, and until the congregation was reunited about the beginning of the Twentieth century.

Shiloh—Olivet Church

The churches jointly known as the Fox Run-Shiloh and Bull Skin-Olivet seem to have been organized in 1815 or '16, with the Rev. A. Cameron preaching for both for about five years. The records show that on November 5, 1819, the two united to support a pastor, Rev. John F. Crow and Jacob Fullenwider and James Allen, Alex Logan, Aaron Van Cleave, John Van Cleave, James White, ruling Elders, and ninety-four members. Two years later Rev. Henry L. Price became pastor and succeeding him in 1825, was James L. Marshall. 1828*, witnessed a great revival in which seventy-seven persons were added and twenty-nine baptized. Then came not only in this church, but in all the churches of this denomination in the County what seems to have been a season of strangely rigid discipline, where men and women, including blacks, were tried for every known crime or sin and the records of whose trials on these minute books all over the County furnish unique examples of the weaknesses of the flesh and the intolerance of those who sat in high places. In four years in the little congregation under description there were eighty-five members dismissed from the church and in the next two years thirty more were dismissed. In 1833, the name of the church was changed to Shiloh and Olivet, and Rev. D. S. Russell succeeded Rev. Marshall, deceased, as pastor. Successive pastors were: D. T. Stuart, pastor for sixteen years following 1837, and Rev. James H. Densmore, G. L. Reid, J. P. McMillan, who served until 1867, when the pastoral relations of Shiloh and Olivet Church dissolved.

William Crawford, of Augusta County, Virginia, who married Margaret Dean, came to Shelby County in 1806. He settled in Olivet neighborhood and is buried in the old church yard at that place. He was a Revolutionary Soldier and had a grant of land for service.

---
*From data contributed by Mrs. William Fitch.

CHAPTER VI

Catholics in Shelby

In his History of Kentucky Baptists, J. H. Spencer, in Volume I, says:

"Two Roman Catholic families, those of Doctor Hart and William Coomes, settled in Harrodsburg in 1775, where Doctor Hart began at once to practice medicine, and Mrs. Coomes to teach school. After a few years, these, with other Catholic families, settled near Bardstown. In 1785, a large colony of Catholics from Maryland, settled on Pottengers Creek in Nelson County. By 1787, there were about fifty Catholic families in Kentucky. During this year, Mr. Whelan, an Irish priest, came to the new Country and ministered to the Catholics about three years. Mr. Baden, who came out in 1793, was their next priest. At this date, the number of Catholic families in the State was estimated at 300. From that time we have no estimate of their number until 1846, when there was supposed to be 6,000 families."

This substantiates, in part, the generally believed contention, that the first Catholic Diocese west of the Alleghenies was in Kentucky, but that church, however, with all its growth and power for good was slow in taking root in Shelby, where the only church it has ever had was only a mission up until the year 1860.

The Church of the Annunciation was the first and is the only Catholic Church ever in Shelby. It was built and dedicated in 1860, and while the members of the first churches of other denominations built in the County suffered many privations and encountered many obstacles in getting the funds necessary to construct their houses of worship, none labored harder or had so much to contend with as the handful of Catholics.

The first Catholic priest in Shelbyville, was Father James Quinn, 1842. He came at the request of Mrs. James Mc-

Laughlin to give spiritual advice to her husband who had been brought to Shelbyville for trial on a charge of murder.

Pat Higgins was the first Catholic in Shelbyville and Wm. Shinnick, who came to this country in 1849, was the next.

In 1853, Bishop Spaulding, of the diocese (afterwards Arch Bishop of Baltimore) went to Europe to obtain more priests for Kentucky. He succeeded in getting five, one of whom was Rev. John H. Bekkers, a native of Holland. To him is due the establishment of a church in Shelbyville.

In 1855, he made his first trip to Shelbyville. His presence soon became known to the handful of Catholics here and the next morning after his arrival the first mass ever celebrated in Shelbyville was celebrated at the home of Mr. and Mrs. Shinnick.

Subscriptions for the establishment of a Catholic Church was headed by Mr. John Tevis for two hundred dollars, signed by Lud Fore, Marion C. Taylor, G. A. Armstrong, Culvin Fore, each giving one hundred dollars. Other donations from non-Catholics put the sum total up to nine hundred dollars. This with several hundred accumulated among the few Catholics themselves, encouraged Father Bekkers in his ambition to build a church here.

Mrs. Jane Campbell donated the lot on which to build the church. Prior to her first marriage, Mrs. Campbell was a Catholic and lived in Baltimore. She married Mr. Peter Crapster and the grandfather of the former assistant postmaster. After Mr. Crapster's death she married William F. Campbell, also a Protestant.

The lot was located on east Main Street, corner of First. The deed from W. F. Campbell's wife, Jane, was dated December, 1859. The lot was seventy-eight by two hundred and twenty-four feet.

Excavation for the foundation was made in the spring of 1860. The brick for the building were made by Ed. and John Brady. The foundation was laid under the direction of James McCarthy and he was assisted by Peter Lee, David Boyle, Thomas Fox, Thos. Gernert, John and Michael Harris, Joseph McGann, Will McFadden and John Lyons, for which work they received no pay. Carpenterman's work was done by Watts and Wells; the bricklaying by a man named Campion; plastering by Nolan, and stone work by Herman Deiss and Michael Brown.

The Church of the Annunciation was dedicated by Rt. Rev. M. J. Spaulding. Two years later a rectory was built and then the priest (who had lived in a boarding house) had a home of his own. After Father Bekkers, Father Lawrence Bax and Polydore Fermont, a missionary priest, attended the spiritual wants of the congregation until 1861, when Rev. M. D. Lawler was appointed regular pastor. Rev. D. F. Crane, afterward Chaplin St. Mary and Elizabeth Hospital, came in 1868.

In the early '60's a pipe organ was purchased and given by Mrs. Chas. Harwood. The first organist was Miss Lizzie Deiss, then came Miss Maggie McQuillan, Miss Mary Shinnick, Alyce Dubourg, W. S. Kaltenbacher, Miss Mary Meade and Mrs. Ed. Shinnick. The first marriage ceremony in the church was that of Michael Brown and Miss Kate O'Connor, on January 8, 1861.

CHAPTER VII
Shelby County Schools

The very first "place of learning," of which tradition tells, in Shelby County, was a little school located on Clear Creek, two miles south of Shelbyville on land owned by William Shannon, and on what was later the farm of Doctor Elliott. The teacher's name was Dillon. He was succeeded by Moses Cook, and they taught for short terms intermittently, between the arrival of the first settlers and the early nineties of 1700. The second school of which any record is found, was taught in a Presbyterian Church, built in 1798, on Dry Run, the teacher being Godfrey Ragsdale. Among his pupils were the children of Benj. Logan, later General Logan, James Shannon, John Williamson, Dan Colgan, Bland Ballard, Aquilla Whitaker and Samuel Shannon.

The church in which the school was taught was three miles southwest of the town and near what was later known as the Samuel Henderson farm. After the school taught by Professor Ragsdale, at Dry Run, possibly the next was taught by David Lock, at the west end of Shelbyville and antidated the one to the north of the town.

Some of the patrons that sent pupils to this school bore the family names of: Cull, Wilson, Lively, Bruner, Bullock, Craig, Glenn, Shipman, Elam, Thrusby, McGaughey, Perkins, Carson, Hall, Collier, Whitaker, A. Owens, Joseph Owens, McCurham, Boyd, Maddox, Williamson, Steele.

About the same time there was taught a school one mile east of Shelbyville by James Herndon. The patrons of this school were: the Scott, Wells, George Carr, Trudle, Parker, Guinn families.

First Shelbyville School

The first school in Shelbyville was taught on the lower floor of the building known as the Masons' lodge, erected and owned by Solomon Lodge F. and A. M. No. 5, for many years the pioneer Masonic building and organization in this section of the State. The lodge building then adjoined the Rogers home on Washington Street, between Sixth and Seventh, and the lower portion was used as the school until the Shelbyville Academy was built, one block west, in 1798. The first trustees of the Shelbyville academy were: Joseph Hornsby, Benj. Logan, Bland Ballard, Ben Roberts, Thos. Guin, Simon Adams, James Logan, John Allen, Jos. Winlock, John Pope, Nicholas Merriweather, Dan McClelland, Aquilla Whitaker. The modest beginnings of the Shelbyville Academy remained such for many years, and it was not until 1816, that the academy had as many as fifty pupils and two teachers. By 1821, it had grown gratifyingly and in the County's next to the first newspaper, *The Impartial Compiler,* printed in 1821, on March 17, was a notice by the trustees of Shelbyville Academy that the "Senior Annual Examinations of the pupils of this Institution will take place on Friday, the Thirtieth instant," and that the "parents and guardians of the pupils and the friends of literature are requested to attend and that, the summer season will start on Monday the Twenty-second of April and will continue without any vacation until the first of August." The Shelbyville Academy, through lotteries and other enterprises, grew sufficiently to move a block farther northwest, on the site of what is now the graded school building of the town, and which from the Shelbyville Academy (afterward Shelbyville College) was changed to the St. James (Episcopal) School.

Schools less old than Science Hill and the Shelbyville Academy, but well nigh as well known in the history of the town and County as they were: St. James College, opened in 1842, with Rev. R. B. Drane as president and Joseph Sweet and W. F. Roe, teachers. This college was really the successor of Shelbyville Academy and Shelbyville College and built the splendid building located on the block

First Schools

between Eighth and Ninth Streets north of College and occupied it until 1871. The cupola upon the top of what was then one of the finest buildings in Central Kentucky, was erected, and the telescope (through which distinguished astronomers viewed the eclipse of 1869; and other astronomical phenomenons), was brought from a distance by the early officers of St. James College.

In 1846, Samuel V. Womack began the teaching of a classical and mathematical school which lived for several years and along about the same time, Professor Knott taught a private school, which like all the others drew largely from the surrounding counties and states, and enjoyed wide influence and reputation beyond the bounds of the County for many years.

Stuart's College

It was about the same time that Professor Hill opened his school in the big new brick building that so long stood between Seventh and Eighth on Main Street, and was later known as "Stuart's Female College." The latter was for many years a real, if friendly rival, except for a much shorter life, of famous old Science Hill.

The purchase of the building and good will of Professor Hill, was by a syndicate of Shelbyville men, who importuned the Reverend Doctor David Todd Stuart, then a young Presbyterian minister in charge of Olivet and Shiloh Churches, to take charge. He did so; finally became the owner of the property and changed the name to "Stuart's Female College", and successfully conducted it until his death in 1868. A little later his widow called their son, Winchester Hall Stuart* to be the principal, and he was in charge until he sold the property

---

*Mrs. Stuart, the wife of Prof. W. H. Stuart, and the mother of the large family of fine young men and women they sent out into the world was Miss Martinette Chiner, a descendant of Benj. Logan, a progenitor of the Bells, Hardins, Logans and other families of distinction, and who is referred to in different chapters of the book, particularly in the sketch of his son, William Logan, in Part V.

in 1890. It became nationally known as "Stuart's Female College," acquiescing in the Presbyterian name attached to it in the minds and conversations of all who knew of it. It drew girls from the first families of many states in the south, and reunions of its alumnae, of comparatively recent years, drew charming women of advanced years from many sections of the west and the south.

The school continued and prospered under the Stuarts for more than a half century but in the 1890's, passed into the hands of Professor J. E. Nunn, a minister of the Baptist Church. He continued it for some years as a girls' school, under the auspices of the Baptist denomination, but he finally sold the property to Mrs. L. C. Willis, in 1912; and she in turn, to the Federal Government, who had the old building torn away and the Federal Post Office erected thereon. Doctor Hill, it seems, continued to teach school for years after parting with the old school to the Stuarts, there being a record to the effect that he bought and rebuilt the burned building of Doctor Broaddus' Baptist Female College, at Second and Main Streets, in 1850.

CHAPTER VIII
Science Hill

Science Hill School which celebrated its hundredth anniversary in 1925, and with the exception of the Shelby Fair, is the only institution that lived and flourished throughout even war times, has a history that is as familiar to Shelbyians, and to many in other states as is the history of the County itself. As elsewhere mentioned it was founded in 1825, by Mrs. Julia A. Tevis, the wife of Rev. John Tevis, a Methodist minister, with whom she had come, as a bride to Shelby County, from Tennessee, though she was a native of Clark County, Ky.

The life of Mrs. Tevis (and in a measure that of her husband), is of as much general interest throughout the southern states as in Shelby County alone, for Science Hill has never been an exclusively local institution, having drawn from the beginning upon most of the states in the Union and particularly the south for its patronage.

At the end of the first fifty years of the school's existence under Mrs. Tevis' management (1875), the semi-centennial anniversary was celebrated by a reunion of its former pupils, and it is told that even that early in its history, nearly all states of the south were represented and in some instances as many as three generations in one family returned as former pupils. Mrs. Tevis' control and management of the school continued until her death in 1880, at which time the school became the property of the late Doctor W. T. Poynter of the Methodist-Episcopalian Church, and, since his death in 1896, has been not only kept up to its former fine standard, but annually improved by his widow, Mrs. Clara M. Poynter, and his daughters, Misses Julia and Harriett Poynter, sending out to the best institutions of higher education throughout the Union, not only many Shelby County girls, but daughters of practically all the states in the Union.

There are in the local public and private libraries volumes written by Mrs. Tevis and others, that go as much into the details of the history of Science Hill and its proprietors as it is possible to do, into those of the whole County in this book.

Mrs. Tevis' book "Sixty Years in a School Room," a volume of five hundred pages, is not only an interesting intimate story of her life and of Science Hill for its first sixty years, but is prefaced by an autobiography of her husband, Reverend John Tevis, and with much relating to the whole Tevis family and so vitally connected with the County's first years.

At the first session of the Science Hill School in March, 1825, the pupils enrolled were:

Elizabeth Hall, Maria Rouse, Agnes Bradshaw, Harriett Ann Tennison, America Pomeroy, Lucinda Johnson, Margaret Smith, Margaret Waters, Priscilla Logan, Mary Hardin, Louisa Adams, Amanda McGaughey, Lucinda Shelburn, Susan Taylor, Sarah Ann Davis, Jane A. Logan, Sarah Crawford, Anna Craig, Martha Jane Edwards, Miss Fields.

Pupils enrolled at the second session:

Priscilla Jane Logan, Margaret Lynch, Margaret Waters, Margaret Hall, Juliet Crawford, Matilda Smith, Lucinda Johnson, Margaret Gorley, Susan Taylor, Mary Hardin, Louisa Adams, Maria Rouse, Agnes Bradshaw, Lucinda Fullenwider, Elizabeth Fullenwider, America Greathouse, Susan Ashby, Eliza Dalton, Carolina Rankin, Pamelia Cheek, Martha I. Hanna, Maria Good, Joany Bean, Camilla Brashear, Lydia A. E. Wickliffe, Elizabeth Anderson, Margaret Sproole.

CHAPTER IX

Other Private and Public Schools

The long list of institutions like "Professor Dodd's school," Professor Fulton's, the later institutions taught by Professor Russell B. McCreary, by Professors Geo. Sampson, and Geo. Scearce and other men of learning and character, were probably short-lived because of the large program of the public school system in which enterprise Kentucky was a pioneer.

A complete, exhaustive history of the schools of the County would include those of Professor John W. Adams, near Simpsonville in the 1850's; the "East Cedar Hill" school for girls by Mrs. Cleo. Clark Coon, near Clark's Station in 1860-70-80, "Jordans" Fairview Academy at Simpsonville, between 1868 and 1880, and other early substitutions for high schools, at Bagdad, Waddy, Mt. Eden and Finchville.

There is an unauthenticated legend to the effect that Theodore O'Hara taught a small school in Shelby County for a time; and the story of the Red Brick School in the Finchville neighborhood where the pupils of the name of all the pioneer families of that section were taught flourished long and of much later years.

A school that flourished and is yet of historic interest in the western portion of the County was Woodland Seminary, founded in 1847, near Simpsonville, at the homestead of Leonidus Webb, and his ancestors.

The first teachers were, in turn: Miss Selia A. Bell, who later became Mrs. John Scott and was succeeded by Mrs. Mary L. Ferris, Miss Rucker, Miss Ewing, Miss Lizzie McCormick, V. A. Dale, and G. A. Webb. Among the roster of pupils for the first four or five years is to be found the names of nearly every family that lived in that part of the County during the Nineteenth century, including, Allen, Cowherd, Dedman,

Finley, Newland, Pemberton, Waller, Webb, Wilson, Stout, Young, Hope, Shouse, Melone, Collins, Kirk, Dugan, Botts, Fisher and Pearce.

Public Schools

Shelby County's public schools have taken a lead among the rural county schools of the State in much the same proportion and manner as her churches, her press and her political leaders have done. There has hardly ever been a time in the past century when there has not been a high school and graded school in Shelbyville, which grew in strength and excellence until early in the Twentieth century they began to spread to new and larger buildings, one of which is now one of the boasted ornaments of the County Seat.

In the outlying towns of Waddy, Bagdad, Finchville, Clayvillage and Simpsonville are also excellent high schools, the outgrowth and upgrowth of the little one-room school houses that early dotted the County at every cross road and under the shadow of every prosperous county church.

These, too, with the coming of the motor bus concentrated into the model consolidated schools and where whole countrysides of school children of all ages are taught in grades and prepared for higher education in the high schools and colleges.

PART IV
COURTS AND OTHER INSTITUTIONS

CHAPTER I

Court House and Courts

All the several buildings used as Court Houses in Shelby, since the first court was held in the Bracket Owen house south of town on October 15, 1792, have been located on the northwestern quarter of the one acre donated by Shannon to the town and County for public buildings. At the term of court just mentioned, preliminary steps for the erection of the court house were taken. On January 15, 1793, the final necessary order was made and the contract for erecting a building that cost but fifteen pounds was let to William Shannon who had donated the land. The new "temple of justice" was built of logs and from the amount of cost was bound to have been an unpretentious affair. However, it like a jail erected at the same time and elsewhere referred to, served its purpose for several years.

At the session of court, which under the first constitution was composed of four justices, held on May 18, 1796, a new court house was ordered "to be of brick forty by thirty-six feet from out to out," the lower story to be fourteen feet in height in the clear and the upper story ten feet with a sufficient number of windows and three doors; a square roof with a spire and a neat pediment front, with "conveniences becoming a court house," and all to be done in a "good workmanlike manner."

The specifications were drawn up and the erection of the building supervised by John Allen, Benjamin Logan, Adam Steele, Martin Daniel and Isham Talbot, commissioners. Before the building was erected, at the next term of court in August an order changing the dimensions making it forty-foot square was entered and on October 18, the commissioners again changed their minds and accepted plans of a Mr. Hunter for building a thirty-six by forty-two feet in the clear with a steeple and a bell spire and weather cock "in proportion to the house." A great many other details as to the erection of this latter building were gone into. The final plans and specifications made public at the succeeding term of court resulted in a contract being awarded to the lowest bidders, Josiah Bullock and Wingfield Bullock who agreed to do the work for eleven hundred and seventy-six pounds and who gave bond in the sum of two thousand three hundred and fifty-two pounds with Benjamine Roberts, Martin Daniel and Nathan Crawford as sureties, for faithful performance of the contract.

Not much is told in the old records about the erection eighteen years later of a building in the place of this condemned building and which later was built with a "hip roof and a belfry in the center."

In 1844, the corner stone of a new court house was laid and the building completed in 1847, stood and was known as the little red brick with belfrey tower and clock on top, for more than sixty-five years. It was not replaced until by the stately, luxurious stone building erected at the cost of several hundred thousand dollars in 1912.*

First Courts

It is assumed that the court held at Brackett Owen's house on October 15, 1792, was presided over by the four judges or justices provided for under the first constitution. The records show that the first judges at least to preside in the new fifteen-pound courthouse were: Authur McGaughey, Alex. Reid, James Logan and Judge Davage, all of whom continued to preside up to the altering of the constitution. The first lawyers mentioned in the records were John Allen, John Simpson, William Logan, John Logan, Isham Talbot, Blackburn and Roberts. The first clerk of the court was James Craig,

---

*At the term of court in 1796 when it was ordered that a new courthouse be built, Alexander Reid, the sheriff, protested against the indisposition of the court to do anything toward enlarging or repairing the jail, which, he said, was insufficient and insanitary, and that a county that could jump in four years from a fifteen-pound courthouse to a twelve hundred-pound building should look more favorably on his request. It is of record that he was censured for his "talk" which "bordered on contempt," but he disclaimed any intentional offense and was dismissed with a reprimand.

who seems to have been succeeded in 1799, by Plumer Thurston, then by Jack Newland, he by James S. Whittaker, in 1812. The other clerks up to the long regime of John T. Ballard and John F. Davis, as well as their successors are given in Part VII. The office of the clerk was not in the first court house buildings used along about 1815. It was decided that the room for that purpose was too dark and inconvenient and the court appointed Joseph Simrall, Thos. Mitchell and Samuel White, to procure a clerk's office. These commissioners rented a room for a year for seventy dollars. At the next term of court, Robert Allen, Thos. Mitchell, James Young, Joseph Simrall and Thos. Wells were appointed commissioners to procure a lot and erect an office thereon, and a three thousand dollar office building was erected in the park in front of what is now the Methodist Church, and was used for this purpose for many years.

Early Trials

Some of the early trials in which the extreme penalty was given in cases of what would now be petty larceny are mentioned in the Chapter under Jails and Celebrated Crimes. The records indicate that these trials by jury for small offenses were in vogue as late as 1807.

At the September term, 1807, Polly Carr was indicted for feloniously stealing and carrying away one flatiron, the property of George Corn. The crime was alleged to have been committed more than a year before. When the case was called for trial, a long time was spent in arguing a motion by her attorney to quash the indictment, as it did not state the exact time and place, when the said flatiron was stolen. The court after mature deliberation, decided to overrule the motion, and it was ordered that the trial proceed. Three days were spent in hearing the testimony and arguments, but the jury acquitted her, whereupon the records show that her attorney was commended and complimented upon the "masterful" manner in which he conducted the case.

In the early days in this County, some of the people must have been profane, or the courts were determined to punish those who were addicted to the habit of swearing. This was evidenced by the number of indictments that were returned by the grand juries, charging from eight to a dozen each term with "profane cursing." There were several indicted on that account and intemperance by nearly every one of the grand juries in the first fifteen years of the last century. On February 13, 1807, among others who were indicted for "profane cursing" was the Commonwealth's Attorney, and he, like the rest, was compelled to pay a fine of five dollars.*

---
*The list of judges, magistrates, lawyers and other officials of all the old courts are to be found not only in the statistics published in Part VII, but incidentally in Judge Willis' and other interesting papers in Part VI.

CHAPTER II

Jails and Noted Crimes

The records are cloudy as to the first building occupied as a jail, though trials for crimes began soon after October 15, 1792, when the first court convened in the house of Bracket Owen, just south of the present site of Shelbyville. On the third day of court, Sheriff David Standiford applied for a jail and was informed that the best that could be done for the time being was for him to confine any prisoner in his charge in the manner that seemed to him the safest. An order that a jail for the County be built was soon afterwards made and provided that it be a stone house fifteen feet square, the walls to be three feet thick and well put together with lime and sand, the foundation to start three feet below the surface of the earth, and the walls to be raised until they were eight and one-half feet above the ground. The floor to be laid with flagstones of brick, and overhead on top of the walls, pieces of hewn timber one foot square were to be laid and pinned together. One door and two windows, to be secured with iron bars were added. A fence was to surround the one-fourth of an acre on which this old jail stood, for a pound in which to keep stray animals.

Joseph Winlock, the great-grandfather of Mr. Camden W. Ballard, who is the great-grandfather of the present youngest generation of Ballards, was the justice of the peace who was assigned to award the contract for the old jail house. How long this old stone cell of a jail stood and just where it stood is not definitely known, but it was succeeded in 1847, by a more pretentious building erected by Edward Sain, on a new site and about where the present County "bastile" stands. The papers of the late E. D. Shinnick, show that the first jail was where the colored Methodist Church later stood, and was the one in which McGlaughlin committed suicide; that after his death the superstitious claimed that it was haunted and the negro prisoners and others "would not remain in it." This second jail did service until 1864, when it was declared insanitary and the County Court ordered a second story made of brick and iron. There were many escapes made from the old jail; the most notable was that of Edward Terrill, the guerrilla chief, who with his lieutenant, Harry Thompson, made a hole in the northwest corner of the building, during the night, and was safely out of town before his absence was discovered. He and Thompson were charged with the murder of Johnston, a stock trader who was boarding at the same house with them, located about where First and Main Streets are, and it was charged that he had a large amount of money on his person, that Terrill and Thompson decoyed him to a lonely spot down the creek, shot him, tied strings around the lower part of his trousers, loaded his clothes with stones and threw his body into the water where it was found by Tom Fox, an elderly fisherman. Thompson was never apprehended. Terrill, with another companion, Baker by name, rode into town one night, "shot up" certain sections and took charge of the old Armstrong Hotel. Citizens on the outside armed themselves and determined to take the desperadoes, dead or alive. When they came out of the hotel a surrender was demanded and a fierce battle ensued. Merritt Redding, proprietor of the Redding Hotel, located mid-way between Sixth and Seventh Streets on the southern side of Main, was fatally wounded and died a few days later. Several other citizens were slightly wounded or grazed, Baker was shot many times and died near by, Terrill was wounded and after long suffering in the Louisville jail was permitted to return to near Harrisonville where he died.

Among other escapes from the old jail was that of Simon Bryant, charged with incest, who was captured in Tennessee and sent to the penitentiary. Rogan and Beaver, safe blowers, escaped in the eighties and Beaver was recaptured and sent

JAILS AND NOTED CRIMES

to the penitentiary. A new jail was built in 1891, by McDonald Brothers of Louisville, and while there have been few escapes therefrom, at least two lynchings, one of them a triple affair, disgraceful to the community, and which helped to hasten the days of prohibition, have occurred.

Other threatened affairs of the same kind have been perhaps prevented through the caution of officials and the incarceration of certain criminals in stronger protected prisons.

Only a few crimes that resulted in capital punishment have occurred in the County's history of one hundred and fifty years. In 1803, a "free negro" called Ned, lived four miles north of town, killed Miss Betty Bean, returning from a neighbor's where she had been visiting, and threw her body into a hog pen where it was discovered torn and mangled almost beyond recognition. The father of Miss Bean, a few days previous had ordered the negro off his premises and the latter threatened at that time to "get even" with him for the "insult." Miss Bean, as stated, had visited a neighbor where she remained all night. Early in the morning she passed through the yard of a Methodist minister, Reverend Talbert, near where the Daniel Farm on Mulberry Pike is now located, and was not seen alive again by anyone except her murderer, to whom the crime was clearly traced, and who, after his arrest confessed.

Tradition says that the negro while in jail awaiting execution sold his body to some youthful students of medicine and spent the money for delicacies that he could eat until he was hung. It is said the purchasers were not satisfied with the body and skeleton of the negro but had the former "flayed" by a tanner named Dillo, then living in Shelbyville who tanned the skin, and made razor straps from it. The hanging of the negro Ned, in 1803, was on a scaffold where the Benson Turnpike now intersects the Midland Trail just east of Shelbyville.

The second execution in the history of the County was that of Jeff King, a white man, who was convicted in 1823, of the murder of a negro in September, 1820. He was hanged as early as October 1, on a scaffold where the Shelby County Fair grounds are now located. King was the son of a respectable family who lived near where the execution occurred. At that time he was described as a wild, harum-scarum young fellow known as the "handsomest and also the worst" young man in Shelby County. He is said to have sold the negro whom he found on a southern tramp and compelled to follow him through the swamps; and then killed him because he threatened to tell the truth about the sale. His conviction was purely upon circumstantial evidence, but it is told that he left with Robert McGrath, the then jailer of the County, a confession, which was never made public because McGrath promised not to do so until King's mother agreed to it, and such permission was never given.

In 1842, James McLaughlin, proprietor of a coffee house and gambling house near the river front in Louisville, killed a man, under conditions that produced great indignation and because of which he was granted a change of venue to Shelby County were he was tried in March, 1843. He had influential friends and notwithstanding the bitter prosecution of the friends of William Patten, the man he had killed, was defended by prominent attorneys from both Shelbyville and Louisville. The trial began March 23, 1843, before the then circuit judge, Mason Brown, and a jury composed of J. P. Bristow, Ambrose Stone, George Milburne, Zachary Bell, John P. Balee, Daniel Johnson, Wm. Garrett, John Price, Joseph Straton, Henry Atherton, Thos. G. Morton, and John Churchill. During the trial McLaughlin became enraged with the prosecuting attorney, Nathanial Wolfe, and threw a heavy book striking him and felling him to the floor. Wolfe arose and knocked the prisoner down and gave him a thrashing before officers could interfere, and then proceeded with the prosecution. The jury was a long time arriving at a verdict. They went into court the second time and informed the judge they could not agree, but after three days agreed that the prisoner was guilty. He was sentenced to be hung on April 28. Every effort was made by him to escape and two days before the time set for the execution, word was received in Shelbyville that an effort would be made by his Louisville friends to free him. The militia was called out and guarded day and night, but on the morning of the day set for the execution while more than one hundred men had their eyes on the building, McLaughlin, rather than suffer the ignominy of hanging, cut his throat from ear to ear; and when the sheriff entered the room to escort him to the place of execution, he found him weltering in his blood and well-nigh dead. Doctors Nuckols and Knox, prominent physicians of that time, sewed up the wound, but each time they did so the prisoner tore it loose, and in spite of all efforts to get him in condition to be hanged, he died in the jail.

The laws inherited from Virginia by Kentucky, for a number of years permitted capital punishment or hanging for a number of crimes, besides murder. The records show that Caleb, a negro found guilty of stealing whiskey and money to the amount of one pound and one shilling, was hung for his crime, and his master was paid more than a hundred times over, in the way of reimbursement, the value of the goods stolen.

There seems to have been no other legal execution in Shelby County, until the Vonderheide hanging in 1881. Vonderheide was a tramp who escaped from the penitentiary and in his wanderings murdered a colored girl in the north edge of the County and hid her body in a secluded spot. There have not been in the fifty years since then, any particularly noted crimes or executions or jail deliveries in Shelby County, excepting the lynchings, to which reference has been made.

CHAPTER III

Blockhouse and Raids

Just when the blockhouse was built and which cut a considerable figure during the stirring days of the war between the States, is not definitely known. It was Shelbyville's first "center piece" and stood in the middle of the intersection of Fifth and Main Streets, equa-distant from the four little parks on which the churches, courthouse, and city hall front. For many years, the fountain now in one of these parks, stood on the same spot.

The blockhouse was about twelve by eighteen feet with loop-holes looking in four directions and was quickly manned by the townsmen, who rushed to it with their guns when an alarm was given. For two years during the Civil War, guards were posted every night and the several exciting encounters with guerrillas from both Federal and Confederate territory made up the town's chief events during said war. The killing or fatal wounding of Edward Terrill, had no connection with the blockhouse as his wounds were, as already told, received near the Armstrong Hotel, where he and his companion's encounter with the enraged citizenry occurred.

But there were exciting events when the shots rained from all sides of the little one-room fort. Next to Quantrill and Terrill, Captain David S. Martin and his band of guerrillas, who harrowed the Federal soldiers, were best known in Shelby. Captain Martin, of very dark complexion was known as "Black Dave." His most disastrous raid in Shelbyville, resulted in a battle in between the court house and the blockhouse in which three of his band lost their lives and a negro whom they compelled to hold their horses was killed. The raid was made about daybreak one morning, August, 1864, and was for the purpose of appropriating a lot of muskets which were stored in the court house. The guerrillas came from the northern part of the County over the old dirt road, now known as the Burks Branch pike, striking Main Street between Seventh and Eighth. Their presence was first known as the shouting and shooting men rode up the Main Street to the court house. Owen, a colored blacksmith, an employee of James Hickman, was on the street when the men arrived in front of the court house, and was ordered to hold their horses while they started to break into the building and to secure the guns. They expected to have no trouble doing this, but were very soon disabused of that idea. Thos. C. McGrath, a merchant doing business on the northwest corner overlooking the court house and J. H. Masonheimer, a tailor, immediately began firing on the guerrillas. Mr. McGrath was in the third story of the building, overlooking the court house yard, and Mr. Masonheimer stood on the Main Street pavement. A terrific battle was waged for some time, but the guerrillas were finally driven off, without the guns. Three of their men, Lieutenant Jo. Veatch, and two privates by the name of Dale and Smith, were killed, and the negro man, whom Mr. Masonheimer thought was one of the raiders, paid his life as a forfeit for acceding to the commands of the guerrillas to take charge of the horses. Four horses also were killed, three of them by Masonheimer, in his effort to get them out of his range during his attempt to shoot the man in charge of them. Captain Martin was present during all the trouble, but was at the rear door of the court house and consequently out of danger of being shot.

The brave men who so valiantly fought the guerrillas narrowly escaped death or serious injury from the numerous bullets fired at them. One ball plowed through Mr. McGrath's forehead and scalp making a painful, but not serious wound. Mr. Masonheimer escaped unharmed.

Martin was a resident of Louisville for a few years after the war, but, broken in health, he came back to Shelbyville and in his eightieth year or in July, 1896, died at the home of a relative five miles northeast of town and was buried in Grove Hill Cemetery.

Blockhouse and Raids

The Killing of Thomas McGrath

In May, 1865, Colonel Buckley's regiment of soldiers was encamped at the Fair Grounds and a negro company was marched into Shelbyville and quartered in the Court House. The negro soldiers were overbearing and it is charged were not disciplined by their white soldiers. On the morning of May 19, they concluded to take possession of the Market House which stood where the rear portion of the Court House now stands. Mr. Thomas A. McGrath (father of Mrs. C. M. Forcee of Washington and Mr. James McGrath of Shelbyville) was the lessee of the Market House. When he attempted to stop the negro soldiers from breaking up the machinery, doors and windows, with which to kindle fires, one of the negroes deliberately raised a gun and fired a shot into his body, killing him instantly. An open encounter between the citizens and the negro soldiers was begun, but the "bad Ed Terrill" with his band lined up on the side of the citizens. After maltreating of the officer of the negro company, Terrill returned to the third story of the jail with a rope in his hands and was in the act of taking the negro with the rope around his neck out on the balcony to hang him, when a squad of Col. Buckley's soldiers arrived and took the colored soldier in charge. He was later tried by court-martial in Louisville, and prosecuted by Gen. W. C. Whittaker and was found guilty of murder and executed. The Market House property was sold the next year, the building razed and law offices erected thereon.

CHAPTER IV

The County Press

File copies of most of the early newspapers of the County have been preserved and have been of invaluable assistance to those in search of early County history.

Probably the first paper of any pretentions made its first appearance in 1814. It was called the *Kentuckian*. Its file for that year showed among other contents the advertisement of Moses Hall, who wished to sell the land "adjoining the town lots of Shelbyville and between them (now Third Street) and the bridge across Clear Creek." In some of the same issues, Walsh, Staniford and Company advertised for first class wool for which they would pay $1.00 per pound, and John Mac Achran (great-grandfather of the Messrs. Charles, William, Richard, and Runer Randolph) advertised for an apprentice in a spinning wheel factory.

Isaac Watson kept a tavern "At the Sign of the Green Tree", charged $2.00 per week for day board and $2.50 for board and lodging, and fed horses at twelve and one-half cents a feed. John and James Bradshaw in the same paper advertised a general merchandise business and offered to pay twelve and one-half cents for lard and to sell sugar at twelve and fourteen cents per pound, salt at $1.00 per bushel and whiskey at from seventy-five to eighty-seven and one-half cents per gallon. Messrs. Bell and Burnett agreed to pay, "one cent and no thanks to the apprehender" for the return of Phillip Fitzgerald, a run-away apprentice. The *Kentuckian* file for 1816, said the Shelbyville Academy which was located where was later a graveyard and now is the front of the Carnegie Library lot, was flourishing with fifty pupils. With ambition to enlarge it, the trustees agreed upon a lottery scheme, whereby $2,000 were to be raised by the sale of 2,000 tickets at $5.00 each.

The prizes were 913 in number ranging in amount from

$1,000 down to $4.00 and aggregating the whole of $10,000 received for tickets. The twenty cents deducted from the winners made up the $2,000 sought for the use of the academy. The *Kentuckian* seems to have been succeeded in January 1818, by the *Impartial Compiler*, published by Joshua D. Grant and elsewhere referred to. Its issue of January, 1827, had an advertisement of Mrs. Julia A. Tevis' school, Science Hill, an institution whose history is contemporaneous with the town itself. In the 1827 issue, Mrs. Tevis, after thanking her friends for their patronage, announced that the "third year" of the school would begin on the first day of the succeeding March. The charges for tuition were: Reading, Writing and Arithmetic and English Grammar, five months, $10.00; History, Rhetoric, and Astronomy, additional two dollars. The extra charges were for Music, $16.00, French, $12.00, Painting, $8.00. The charge for board for the five months was $40.00.

During the early thirties, the *Examiner* and *Recorder* were published by Wm. Knight. In January, 1840, Messrs. Torr and Middleton founded the *Shelby News*, (very soon, thereafter and ever after called the *Shelby Sentinel*). The *News* was later owned entirely by Mr. Henri F. Middleton, until 1865, when he disposed of it to John T. Hearn. It had been Whig under Mr. Middleton, but under Mr. Hearn, who changed its name to *Sentinel*, it became democratic in politics, which it remains to date. Mr. Hearn was followed in the ownership and editorship by Alfred Ellis, he by Messrs. Cooper and Carpenter, *et al*, then by Poynter and Shinnick, and later by C. M. Lewis, James Guthrie and H. Barrickman, who sold the property to M. O'Sullivan and Sons, by whom it is still conducted as one of the wide-awake, patriotic home and county papers of the State.

For the last one-half century the contemporary rather than the competitor of the *Sentinel* has been the *Shelby News*, founded in 1886 by John P. Cozine and since his death in 1897, by his son, B. B. Cozine, and kept by him on a plane unexcelled

THE COUNTY PRESS

by any weekly paper of the State. Other worthy publications that survived the business vicissitudes encountered by all kinds of periodicals, only a short period, were the *Courant*, founded in 1870 by Messrs. John C. Searce and Emmett G. Logan, who, afterwards attained reputation for brilliance in larger fields of journalism; and the *Record*, founded in 1896 by T. S. Vance, now of Virginia. An even shorter lived publication was a second paper named the *Kentuckian* founded in 1923. A paper called *The Localizer* was published for several years by William Marshall.

It has been elsewhere suggested that the high standards and ideals maintained by the home, churches and schools of Shelby were exceptional. And this, too, has continued to pertain to its county press. The papers of this county have stood with the other weekly, local press of the State, a bulwark of protection against that tyranny that sometimes comes from great metropolitan journals, which under cover of "freedom of the press," once they have monopolized and are entrenched in a great field of their own, are like all man-made institutions, prone to become tyrants rather than tribunes of the people.

CHAPTER V

The "Shelby Fair"

The present Fair Association which has withstood the mutations of time for seventy years, was not the first fair in Shelby County. A fair was held somewhere in or near the town on Friday, October 1, 1842, nearly a score of years previous to the organization of the present institution.* It was given under the auspices of an association of gentlemen, who called themselves the Shelby County Agricultural and Mechanical Association— the same name adopted when the organization of the present Association took place in 1860. The officers of the Association, who gave the exhibition in 1842 were: N. Owsley, president, and H. F. Middleton, secretary. In advertising the Fair the idea of giving silver cups was deprecated, and it was proposed that "successful competitors" were to be given "standard agricultural" and other books pertaining to "agriculture and mechanical pursuits."

That the Shelby Fair or "Shelby County Agricultural and Mechanical Association" which has been in existence since 1860,* has been nationally known during its long life and was for years more a State Fair than any organization in the Commonwealth is true. During many years it was the central or official place of exhibition for Shorthorn and Jersey cattle, and for a number of years it was the swine breeders national association's official fair.

The first officials of record appear to have been A. B. Veech, president, and Adam Middelton, secretary. Other presidents of the Association have been Adam Middelton, John L. Donaldson, M. W. Huss and J. L. Zaring.

Some of the secretaries have been John Robinson, John

---
*A recent history of "Kentucky Fairs" says there were "Fairs" in Shelby County in 1838 and 1839, and a "reorganization" in 1842, but we have not found records or data to substantiate this.

131

Adam Middelton, Shannon Reed, Eugene Harbison, (treasurer), J. M. Logan, Thompson R. Webber and W. Henry Maddox.

Coming down for ten years or to the 13th annual exhibition of the organization in 1873, (no fair was held in 1862, during the Civil War), the personnel of the association had begun to change. The officers given in the catalogue of that year were:

Adam Middelton, President
W. L. Waddy, Vice President
John Robinson, Secretary
M. T. Smith, Treasurer
J. A. Payne, Marshal

Directors

C. B. Veech
M. Huffman
J. G. Byars
Henry Bird
G. A. Armstrong

William Calloway
H. G. Cardwell
J. W. Freeman
W. W. Hall
J. D. Guthrie

Samuel Kinkead

In the catalogue which was not unlike those of fifty or sixty years later, the merchants of the town and county were liberal advertisers.

Newkirk and Locke were grocers, as were J. K. Skooler, Oscar Farmer, T. J. Ramsey, Hastings & Hollenbach. Other merchants were John Ad Middelton, W. D. Middelton, J. M. Owen & Son, L. Miller, Caldwell Brothers, Layson Brothers, J. W. Hickman, William Shinnick, Ware & Rothchild, F. G. Bright, Randolph & Shea, Taylor & Burton, Ellingwood Brothers. The premiums offered for household and garden products were not unlike those of the present day, but motor vehicles were unknown, whereas the fine carriages, harness, saddles and bridles, ranked in importance with fine horses, thoroughbred cattle, sheep and swine.

CHAPTER VI

The Cemetery and Early Burial Grounds

Civilized man has made litttle progress or at least little change in his harrowing, unsatisfactory method of disposing of his dead. If all over the county in its early years will be found the black spots in the cultivated fields where cabins had stood, also, on many of the first farms were, and still are, spots where a clump of trees and a tangle of vines, old ivy and broken stone tell of a former family burying ground.

In some instances and as elsewhere mentioned in this volume, epidemics must have come along in the late years of the 18th century for there were at points where no sign of habitation or church buildings could be found, long rows of sunken spots with rude stones at head and foot that told their own story about an ancient big harvest time by the old man with the scythe. Along some of these when the big dirt roads were widened and ditched and "worked," sixty, seventy and eighty years ago, the neighborhood "road workers" would sometimes come upon strange objects which investigation proved were parts of a skeleton of some victim buried too close to what was later to become a highway. Both the present and former constitutions of Kentucky contain carefully worded inhibitions against the violation, through the right of eminent domain or otherwise, of any Kentucky cemetery or burial ground, and the mutations of time and of public and private enterprise and improvements have left most of them unscathed.

They were, however, gradually succeeded in a County like Shelby by the church yard cemeteries—little burial grounds around the primitive church buildings elsewhere told about, and in anyone of which, with their rude headstones and strange epitaphs, the greatest elegy in the world could have been written. These old churchyard cemeteries so far as the County itself is concerned are still used to some extent by the respective neighborhoods, but a growing trend toward the interment of their dead at and near the larger cemeteries began by the County people many years ago.

The first burying grounds, tradition says, in use in the town of Shelbyville, were just in the rear of and on where a hotel and laundry and shops now stand in the center of the city. The first of any considerable size was that part of what was called "the old graveyard," in front of what is Shelbyville's Carnegie Library. Up to 1853, this was in two lots. The part which corners at Eighth and Washington was the seminary lot where a school was conducted and largely attended. A little farther to the east was the lot where the library now stands and where the Presbyterian Church stood for many years, or until 1846, when it was moved a block farther to the southeast. In 1841, the seminary building was torn away, having been succeeded by the new Shelbyville College, a block farther to the northwest, later the Episcopal College, which sold the lot to the town. The vacated lot was graded and called the new graveyard and lots for burial purposes were sold—the first to Geo. W. Ramsey, father of the late J. J. and T. J. Ramsey, fifteen dollars for the lot. Others at the same price were sold to Samuel Topping, David Long, Henry C. Offutt and Samuel Glass. Before the church on the eastern lot was blown down, rebuilt and finally torn away, space about it was also used for burial lots. The old dividing fence was torn away when the church was removed, and the two lots became one and were long known as the "Shelbyville Cemetery," until it became evident that the space was inadequate.

Enterprising citizens of the town and County purchased a tract of land adjacent to and just south of the town. This was in 1854, and an Act of the Legislature had authorized them to form a co-partnership company, and by the year 1856, they had succeeded in bringing into their possession what is now "Grove Hill Cemetery," so much resembling in arrange-

The Cemetery and Early Burial Grounds

ment and topography the beautiful cemetery at Frankfort, and like it, widely known. The land was purchased of Mark Hardin, Daniel Livly and Josephus Wilson.*

The names of the men who originated the idea of a new cemetery and who successfully carried it out were Josephus H. Wilson, James L. Elingwood, Henri F. Middleton, James L. O'Neil, Thos. W. Brown, Joseph Hall, and Shelby Vannatta. Of them and of all the sixty original stockholders, none are living and most of them are buried in Grove Hill. The management of this splendidly conducted institution through its eighty years of life has been for the most part in the hands of the secretaries.

The first secretary was Henri F. Middleton, who served until his death in 1878. He was succeeded by James M. Owen, who lived for only a year, and was succeeded by G. W. Riley, who was in charge for nearly forty years and who was followed by Mr. A. M. Weber, and he by Mr. C. M. Mapes, who is still in charge.

A beautiful appropriate chapel of medieval gothic architecture was erected in the center of the beautiful grounds by the trustees in 1893, and has been much used for the funeral services, particularly of those whose remains have been brought back from distant parts, for burial in their home County.

---
*The land was originally owned by William Owen and Moses Hall.

PART V
Pioneer Personages

CHAPTER I

Explanatory Mention

Repeating the quotation from Carlyle, found in the preface, that "History is the essence of innumerable biographies," is explanatory of, and not apology for the considerable space herein devoted to sketches and biographies of, and papers by distinguished persons dead and living. Our only apology is that not more of the pioneers themselves can be sketched; and that many of equal distinction of much later years, can not be extendedly mentioned. Joseph Winlock, 1804-74, grandson of General Joseph Winlock, was, in the Navy, at Washington, in astronomical work here and in all of his activities among the greatest sons that Shelby ever produced. We hope that in a later volume about Shelby county, by whomsoever written, that his biography will appear well up toward the top of a list that will include James G. Simrall, and such distinguished descendants of these first pioneers as Lloyd Tevis, J. Franklin Bell, R. A. Long, Alice Hegan Rice, Fanny Caldwell Macauley, and others of a "Long Roll" already safely on "Fame's Eternal Camping Ground."

Squire Boone

Always in a history of pioneers of Shelby County must come first the names of Boone, Shannon, Owen, Ballard, Hall, Allen, Pope, Simpson, Logan, Knight, and on almost endlessly.

Squire Boone, a younger brother of the great pioneer, Daniel Boone, was born not far from Reading, in Berks County, Pennsylvania, about 1737, and was left an orphan when about eight years old; soon after he was taken to near Winchester, Virginia, and thence to Holeman's Ford, on the South Yadkin River, North Carolina, in what was then Rowan County, but is now Wilkes County and about eight miles from Wilkesboro, the County Seat of the latter. His youngest

History of Shelby County

sister, Hannah, was still living in 1872, in the adjoining county, Caldwell, at the ripe age of eighty-five.

Late in the fall of 1769, Squire Boone and another adventurer (name unknown), left the Yadkin in search of his brother Daniel, who with five others had gone to the wilds of Kentucky, on the first of May preceding. They stumbled upon Daniel's camp—the locality of which is unknown, but was probably on Station Camp Creek in now Estill County—shortly after his and John Stewart's seven days' captivity among Indians; during which time their companions, John Findlay, Joseph Holden, James Monay and Wm. Cool, had abandoned the camp and gone home. The joy of that meeting cannot be described. Soon after, John Stewart was killed by Indians and Squire's companion went home by himself, leaving the brothers alone in the wilderness. They "prepared a little cottage to defend them from the winter storms." On May 1, 1770, Squire "returned home to the settlement by himself, without bread, salt or sugar, without company of his fellow-creatures or even a horse or dog." On July 27, 1770, Squire met Daniel, "according to appointment, at the old camp." They soon abandoned this camp for fear of Indians, and "proceeded to Cumberland River, reconnoitering that part of the country until March, 1771, and giving names to the different waters." About April, 1771, they returned to North Carolina, to make preparations for removing to Kentucky.

On September 25, 1773, with their families, they started for their new home; and in Powell's Valley, were joined by five families and forty men; on October 10, when still a few miles east of Cumberland Gap, the rear of their company was attacked by Indians; who killed six men—among them James Boone, Daniel's eldest son; aged eighteen—and wounded one man. They retreated with their families until March, 1775. They reached Boonesborough on March 31, or April 1, of that year, and immediately began to erect the fort; and there made their home for several years. On the twenty-fifth of May ensuing, Squire Boone had his first legislative experience—taking his seat as one of the delegates from Boonsborough in the Transylvania Convention.

It appears from his and other depositions, taken in 1795, 1797, 1804, 1806, and 1808, and from other sources, that Squire Boone continued generally a resident of Boonesborough until early in 1779, when he removed to Clear Creek, in Shelby County, and erected near where Shelbyville now stands, the station known as Spire Boone's Station or the "Painted Stone." Here he made his home until 1806, except when compelled to abandon it for a short time in consequence of the exterminating Indian raids on Long Run in 1781, and to move to the station at the Falls (Louisville). He had been shot in his left shoulder at the siege of Boonesborough, was shot in his breast and in one arm in defense of his station, and again shot while removing the people to Louisville, as just stated.

While thus disabled and suffering from wounds, he was elected a representative to the Virginia Legislature; and in his own person bore to that body an appeal more eloquent and touching than his mouth could utter for assistance to the brave defenders of the frontier. To the day of his death he cherished a proud remembrance of the handsome reception and generous attentions of his brother Legislators and the people of Richmond. His plain hunter's garb, backwoods manners, and unhealed wounds seemed to be the key to their hearts and sense of justice; his appeal was not urged in vain.

In his old days he was deprived of every vestige of his property mainly, it is alleged, through the land sharks who hunted up a better title to his land—while he rested in fancied security, believing that what he had redeemed from the wilderness and shed his blood to defend from the savages, was assuredly his own. In a deposition at his own house in Shelby County, May 18, 1804, he said, "he was principled against going into the town of Shelbyville upon any business whatsoever"—the cause of which deep-seated feeling the author has not learned. It may have been because of what seemed to him the persecution of the courts. Shortly after, he was in prison bounds in Louisville for debts which he could not pay. Kind friends obtained his release. In 1806—with his sons, Isaiah, Enoch, Moses, and Jonathan, and the five sons of his nephew, Samuel Boone—he, like his great precedent and elder brother, left Kentucky with a sad heart; and forming a new settlement (called "Boone Settlement"), in the then territory of Indiana, in what is now Harrison County, about twenty-five miles northwest of Louisville, erected a small mill and laid the foundation of a flourishing and populous township, called also, "Boone Township," which is now the happy home of many worthy Kentuckians and their descendants. One of them, John Boone, a native of Shelby County, Kentucky, was a prominent member of the convention which formed the constitution of Indiana, and afterwards of the State Legislature.

Squire Boone died there, in 1815, and at his special request was buried in a cave near the summit of a lofty eminence that commanded a beautiful and extended view. He was a man of strong and earnest feelings and convictions, simple-hearted, patriotic and religious.

CHAPTER II

William Shannon*

The name Shannon, in its different forms is widely distributed throughout the United States. Although they are supposed to run back to a common ancestry in Ireland, there are several stocks in this country which seem to have no connection with one another. So far as can be discovered at the present time, the earliest member of the branch to which the subject of my sketch belonged, was Thomas Shannon, who died in Sadesbury Township, Lancaster County, Pennsylvania, in April, 1737. In his will, filed in the office of the Register of Wills, in Lancaster, he names five children, Samuel, John, Margaret, Anna and Thomas. His farm was divided between his sons, John and Samuel, with the provision that his wife, Agnes, should be supported for the remainder of her life out of the share falling to Samuel. The other children are variously provided for.

John Shannon is the only one of these children of whom any further record can be found. He was one of the executors of his father's will and presumably spent his life on the farm which he inherited. He seems to have been a man of some standing in the community, for in June, 1746, he was given a commission as captain to organize a company of men for an expedition against Canada. The company was formed and sent to Albany, New York, where they spent the winter. They were finally discharged, October 31, 1747, the attack upon Canada having been postponed.

John Shannon married Sarah Reid, the daughter of John Reid, of Delaware. He probably died in the latter part of 1767, for on January 7, 1768, his son John, appeared before

---
*This paper was read at a meeting of the Genealogical Historical Society by Miss Martha Harbison, and was prepared from data furnished her by Dr. R. S. Moore of Washington, D. C.

an orphan's court at Lancaster, and asked for a division of the estate. He was the father of eleven children, one of whom was William Shannon, whose life and adventures are the subject of this paper.

The exact date of the birth of William Shannon is not known, but he is understood to have been the oldest of the family. His sister, Agnes, was born in 1744, which would place his birth somewhere about 1740. Not much is known of his early life. He seems to have settled in Virginia, at an early age, for his name appears on a roster of the militia of Augusta County, in 1758. There is reason to believe that he was a member of Braddock's expedition against Fort Du Quesne.

During the war of the Revolution, his name appears in the records of the War Department, as ensign and lieutenant in Captain William Lewis' company of the first Virginia regiment. The company muster and payrolls carry his name until November 30, 1777, when they show that he had resigned, date not stated. He probably served again at a later period for he is called Captain Shannon, in the family traditions. There was a Captain William Shannon, who served as quartermaster under George Rogers Clarke in his western expedition, but it has not been ascertained whether it was this one or not.

There is a tradition that he was a captain in Colonel Lochry's regiment, which was sent down the Ohio River in the summer of 1781, to join General Clark, in his intended expedition against Detroit. Captain Shannon was sent ahead with seven men to carry a letter to Clark, announcing the approach of reinforcements. Near the present site of Lawrenceburg, Indiana, they were attacked by the Indians. Several men were killed, and the rest, including Captain Shannon, were made prisoners.

Lochry, unaware of their capture, was attacked at the south of Lochry's Creek, a short distance below Aurora, and defeated. Forty-two were killed, including Colonel Lochry, Shannon

WILLIAM SHANNON

was carried north some distance, but was released or made his escape.

A difficulty arises in connection with this story from the fact that in the Pennsylvania Archives, Volume XIV, Page 698, the Captain Shannon of Lochry's expedition is called Samuel. Heitman's Historical Register of the Officers of the Continental Army, speaks of a Captain Samuel Shannon, who was captured by the Indians on the Ohio, in 1781, carried north and put to death. Whether this was the same one or another is not known. It is hoped that something may be discovered which will verify the story. William Shannon is said to have been very much liked by the Indians, and they showed kindness to him on several occasions.

About the close of the Revolution, he settled in Kentucky. He was a member of the Virginia Legislature (Jefferson County), in 1790*, and of the Kentucky House of Representatives (Shelby County), in 1793. He was an engineer and surveyed his own land, which he received from Virginia while Patrick Henry was Governor. He took up large tracts of land in Kentucky—two hundred thousand, it is said. The present city of Shelbyville, Kentucky, was laid out on his farm, and he gave it a plot of ground for a public square.

He was preparing to go as an officer with Wayne on his expedition against the Indians of Ohio, in 1794, when he came to his death in a quarrel with John Felty. He was struck on the head with a stone and died the next day, July 5, 1794. He was never married. His quarrel with Felty, resulted, his descendants say, from his resentment at language used by Felty in the hotel dining room. In their difficulty he threw a dirk knife at Felty, inflicting a wound from which Felty, also, died.

---

*He accomplished as a member of that legislature, what George Rood Robertson, of Berea, shows he tried to accomplish by petition, viz., to persuade the Virginians to furnish funds with which to pay the soldiers that served under him in the George Rogers Clark expedition; on which expedition his admirers termed him the "Great Conductor" of the Illinois Division.

CHAPTER III

Bland Ballard

Captain Bland W. Ballard, was born near Fredericksburg, Virginia, October 16, 1761, and died in Shelby County, Kentucky, September 5, 1853—aged ninety-two years. He came to Kentucky in 1779, when eighteen years old; joined the militia; served in Colonel Bowman's expedition, May, 1779; in General Clark's expedition against the Pique towns, July, 1780, where he was dangerously wounded in the hip, and suffered from it until his death; in General Clark's expedition, November, 1782, against the same towns; in 1786, was a spy for General Clark, in the Wabash expedition, rendered abortive by mutiny of the soldiers; in 1791, was a guide under Generals Scott and Wilkinson; and August 20, 1794, was with General Wayne at the battle of the "Fallen Timbers."

When not engaged in regular campaigns, he served as hunter and spy for General Clark, who was stationed at Louisville, and in this service he continued for two years and a half. During this time he had several encounters with the Indians. One of these occurred just below Louisville. He had been sent in his character of spy to explore the Ohio from the mouth of Salt River to the falls, and from thence up to what is now the town of Westport. On his way down the river, when six or eight miles below the falls, he heard early one morning, a noise on the Indiana shore. He immediately concealed himself in the bushes, and when the fog had scattered sufficiently to permit him to see, he discovered a canoe filled with three Indians, approaching the Kentucky shore. When they had approached within range, he fired and killed one. The others jumped overboard, and endeavored to get their canoe into deep water, but before they succeeded, he killed a second and finally the third. Upon reporting his morning's work to General

Clark, a detachment was sent down, who found the three dead Indians and buried them. For this service, General Clark gave him a linen shirt, and some other small presents. This shirt, however, was the only one he had for several years, except those made of leather; of this shirt the pioneer hero was doubtless justly proud.

At the time of the defeat on Long Run, he was living at Lynn's Station on Beargrass and came up to assist some families in moving from Squire Boone's Station, near the present town of Shelbyville. The people of this station had become alarmed on account of the numerous Indian signs in the country and had determined to move to the stronger stations on the Beargrass. They proceeded safely until they arrived near Long Run, when they were attacked front and rear by the Indians, who fired their rifles and then rushed on them with their tomahawks. Some few of the men ran at the first fire of the others, some succeeded in saving part of their families, or died with them after a brave resistance. The subject of this sketch, after assisting several of the women on horseback who had been thrown at the first onset, during which he had one or two single handed combats with the Indians, and seeing the party about to be defeated, succeeded in getting outside of the Indian line, when he used his rifle with some effect, until he saw they were totally defeated. He then started for the station, pursued by the Indians, and on stopping at Floyd's Fork, in the bushes, on the bank, he saw an Indian on horseback pursuing the fugitives ride into the creek, and as he ascended the bank near to where Ballard stood, he shot the Indian, caught the horse and made good his escape to the station. Many were killed, the number historically indefinite, some taken prisoners, and some escaped to the station. They afterwards learned from the prisoners taken on this occasion, that the Indians who attacked them were marching to attack the station the whites had deserted, but heard of their flight at Bullskin, and marched in the direction of Long Run. The

BLAND BALLARD

news of this defeat induced Colonel Floyd to raise a party of thirty-seven men, with the intention of chastising the Indians. Floyd commanded one division and Captain Holden the other, Ballard being with the latter. They proceeded with great caution, but did not discover the Indians until they received their fire, which killed or mortally wounded sixteen (only fourteen are accounted for under the Eastwood monument) of their men. Notwithstanding the loss, the party under Floyd maintained their ground, and fought bravely until overpowered by three times their number, who appealed to the tomahawk. The retreat, however, was completed without much further loss. This occasion has been rendered memorable by the magnanimous gallantry of young Wells (afterwards the Colonel Wells of Tippecanoe), who saved the life of Floyd, his personal enemy, by the timely offer of his horse at a moment when the Indians were near to Floyd, who was retreating on foot and nearly exhausted.

In 1788, the Indians attacked the little fort at Tyler's Station on Tick Creek (a few miles east of Shelbyville), where Ballard's father resided. It happened that his father had removed a short distance out of the fort for the purpose of being convenient to the sugar camp. The first intimation they had of the Indians, was early in the morning, when his brother Benjamin, went out to get wood to make a fire. The Indians shot him and then assailed the house. The inmates barred the door and prepared for defense. His father was the only man in the house, and no man in the fort, except the subject of this sketch and one old man. As soon as he heard the guns he repaired to within shooting distance of his father's house. Here he commenced using his rifle with good effect. In the meanwhile the Indians broke open the house and killed his father, not before, however, he had killed one or two of their number. The Indians, also, killed one full sister, one half sister, his stepmother, and tomahawked the youngest sister, a child who recovered. When the Indians broke into the house, his stepmother endeavored to effect her escape by the back door, but an Indian pursued her and as he raised his tomahawk to strike her, the subject of this sketch fired at the Indian, not however, in time to prevent the fatal blow, and they both fell and expired together. The Indians were supposed to number about fifteen, and before they completed their work of death, they sustained a loss of six or seven.*

During the period he was a spy for General Clark, he was taken prisoner by five Indians on the other side of the Ohio, a few miles above Louisville, and conducted to an encampment twenty-five miles from the river. The Indians treated him comparatively well, for although they kept him with a guard they did not tie him. On the next day after his arrival at the encampment, the Indians were engaged in horse racing. In the evening, two very old warriors were to have a race, which attracted the attention of all the Indians, and his guard left him a few steps to see how the race would terminate. Near him stood a fine black horse, which the Indians had stolen recently from Beargrass, and while the attention of the Indians was attracted in a different direction, Ballard mounted this horse and had a race indeed. They pursued him nearly to the river, but he escaped though the horse died soon after he reached the station. This was the only instance with the exception of that at the River Raisin, that he was a prisoner. He was in a skirmish with the Indians near the Saline Licks, Colonel Hardin being the commander; the Colonel Hardin who fought gallantly under Morgan at the capture of Burgoyne, and who fell a sacrifice to Indian perfidy in the northwest; the father of General M. D. Hardin, and grandfather

---

*11CC297, Draper, MSS., State Historical Society of Wisconsin. (Interview with Samuel Graham.) "I came to Kentucky, perhaps in 1795. It was the same fall with Wayne's victory. When I came, there were but two or three houses in Shelbyville. Tyler's Station was on the south side of Tick creek, between that and the pike, about one-half mile from Middleton's (Cross Keys Inn). Bland Ballard's father was in a little cabin close by the creek. Bland Ballard, himself, was in the station, more on the top of the hill. When the Indians came, Bland Ballard ran out in his shirt tail; kept on till he came to a stump. The Indians were breaking into his fathers house, and B. B. fired (from behind that stump) till he had killed two or three of them. His father was killed.

of Colonel J. J. Hardin of Illinois, whose heroic death at Buena Vista was worthy of unsullied life.

In after life, Major Ballard repeatedly represented the people of Shelby County in the Legislature, and commanded a company in Colonel Allen's regiment which fought the first battle of the River Raisin—was wounded slightly on that day, and severely by a spent ball on the twenty-second of January. This wound, also continued to annoy his old age. On this disastrous occasion he was taken prisoner and suffered severely by the march through snow and ice, from Malden to Fort George.

As an evidence of the difficulties which surrounded the early pioneer in this country, it may be proper to notice an occasion in which Major Ballard was disturbed by the Indians at the spot where he then resided. They stole his only horse at night. He heard them when they took the horse from the door to which he was tied. His energy and sagacity was such that he got in advance of the Indians before they reached the Ohio, waylaid them, three in number, shot the one riding his horse and succeeded not only in escaping, but in catching the horse and riding back in safety.

"Ye Ole Stone Inn" at Simpsonville, seven miles west of Shelbyville--probably second oldest stone residence in the County. Building begun by Fleming P. Rogers, one of its first Virginia-land-grant owners, and nearly complete when sold to Isaac Greathouse, in 1827; to Philip Johnston in 1833, who sold it in 18'5, to Lindsay W. George, whose son, Captain Richard George, lived in it for nearly eighty years.

The Charles Todd residence five miles North of Shelbyville, built by Isaac Shelby, for his daughter, in imitation of the Governor's first mansion at Frankfort.

CHAPTER IV

Colonel Charles S. Todd

Colonel Charles S. Todd, a soldier and diplomatist, son of Judge Thos. Todd, of the U. S. Supreme Court, was born near Danville, Kentucky, January 22, 1791, and died at Baton Rouge, Louisiana, May 14, 1871, aged over eighty years. He was educated in the best schools of Kentucky; graduated at William and Mary College, Virginia, 1809; studied law with his father and attended the law lectures at Litchfield, Connecticut, under the celebrated Judges Gould and Reeves, 1810; practiced law at Lexington, 1811-12; volunteered June, 1812, and was made acting quartermaster of the advance of the northwestern army; was on General Wm. H. Harrison's staff, as division judge advocate of the Kentucky troops, December, 1812; bearer of instructions to General Winchester, previous to the disastrous affair of the River Basin; upon the recommendation of General Harrison, was appointed captain in the seventeenth United States infantry and soon after appointed aid to that commander, whose official report highly commended his important services in the campaign and particularly in the battle of the Thames; he subsequently acted as deputy inspector general of the eighth military district, then as adjutant general, and in March, 1815, was promoted inspector general with rank of brevet colonel of cavalry. General Harrison, in a letter subsequent to the war, to a member of President Madison's cabinet, expressed the opinion that "Colonel Todd was equal in bravery and superior in intelligence to any officer of his rank in the army."

Upon the disbandment of the army in 1815, Colonel Todd resumed the practice of law at Frankfort, and in 1816, married the youngest daughter of Governor Shelby, was secretary of State under Governor Madison, 1816; representative in the

Legislature from Franklin County, 1817 and 1818; charge d' affaires to Colombia, in South America, 1818-23; on his return, settled in Shelby County, as a farmer; was a commissioner to the Presbyterian General Assembly in Philadelphia, 1837 and 1839, when the separation was effected, he sustaining the Old School, was vice president of the Kentucky State Agricultural Society for several years, and delivered the annual address 1839; in connection with Ben Drake, prepared sketches of General Harrison, 1840, and became editor of the *Cincinnati Republican*, a Whig newspaper; accompanied General Harrison to Washington, February, 1841, having been selected by him as United States Minister to Vienna, but this appointment was prevented by the death of the president; in the summer of 1841, President Tyler appointed him to the mission of St. Petersburg, which he held until displaced by President Polk, in the fall of 1845. At St. Petersburg, and during his visits to the interior of Russia, and to the King of Sweden (Bernadotte, the only marshal of the great Napoleon who retained his crown), he was treated with most marked consideration.

After his return to Kentucky, Colonel Todd was not again prominently in public life; but was active with his pen upon the subjects of religion, agriculture, and politics, and often presided or was the leader at public meetings.

CHAPTER V

William Logan*

William Logan, was the eldest son of General Benjamin Logan. He was born at Harrodsburg, on the eighth of December, 1776. He was probably, the fifth white child born in Kentucky. In 1799, he was a member of the convention which formed the second constitution of the State, being then only twenty-three years of age. His selection to this responsible office, so early in life, evinced the high opinion entertained of his character and talents by his fellow-citizens. About the same time he commenced the practice of the law, and soon attained considerable eminence in his profession. He was frequently elected to represent his county in the legislature, and on several occasions was made speaker of the house of representatives. He was twice appointed a judge of the Court of Appeals, in which station he was noted for the propriety with which he discharged its various duties. In 1820 he was elected a Senator in the Congress of the United States. He resigned his seat in this body in 1820, for the purpose of becoming a candidate for Governor of the State, but was not elected.

He died at his residence in Shelby County, on the eighth of August, 1822, in the forty-sixth year of his age. At the time of his decease he was generally looked to by the people of the State as the candidate for Governor in 1824, and had he lived would no doubt have succeeded General Adair in that office.

---
*David Logan, grandfather of William Logan, married Betsy Briggs and was the father of Gen. Benjamine Logan, who came to Kentucky to Lincoln County, where his fort was built in 1776, and was with Boone, Briggs, Levi Todd and others. Benj. Logan moved to Shelby County and was a member of the Convention in 1792, which framed the first Constitution of the State. His wife, Ann Montgomery, was an aunt of "Mark Twain." Gen. Benj. Logan's farm in Shelby County was on Little Bullskin creek and remained in the Logan family nearly one hundred years. Benj. Logan's wife, after his death, married Col. Knox. After he died, the farm went to James Logan, his step-son. Dr. Ben Logan, his youngest son lived all his life on the farm. Married Effie Winlock, had sons and daughters. Gen. Benj. Logan had three brothers and four sisters. Polly or Mary married Abraham Smith. Lived all her life in Shelbyville, dying in her 86th year. The Benj. Logan burial ground on the farm mentioned, is of much interest and historic value.

When he was not prevented from mingling in politics by his duties as a judge, he was an active and influential member of the then republican party, and was warmly engaged in the controversy which arose on the question of a new election upon the death of Governor Madison. On this occasion he took the ground which was finally settled as the true construction of the constitution, that upon the death of the governor, the lieutenant-governor should succeed to his place, and serve out the term. He was also an active partisan on the new and old court questions, having espoused the cause of the old court. In his private and social relations he was a gentleman of great moral worth, courteous in his manners and of inflexible integrity. His early death was a loss to the State and was very generally deplored.

CHAPTER VI

Colonel John Allen

Colonel John Allen, for whom Allen County, Kentucky, was named, was born in Rockbridge County, Virginia, December, 1772. His father, James Allen, emigrated to Kentucky, in the fall of the year 1780, and settled at Dougherty's Station on Clark's Run, about one and a half miles below the present town of Danville. Here he formed an acquaintance with Joseph Daviess, the father of Colonel Joseph Hamilton Daviess. Becoming impatient of the close confinement of the station, these fearless and ardent men removed farther down the creek and erecting a small station, lived there for three years. At the expiration of this period, Mr. Daviess purchased a tract of land three or four miles west of Danville, and removed to it.

In 1784, the father of John Allen removed to Nelson County, and settled at Simpson's Creek, seven and a half miles from Bardstown. In 1786, the subject of this notice attended a school in Bardstown, kept by a Mr. Shackleford, where he acquired a slight knowledge of the classics. This school was succeeded by one under the charge of Doctor James Priestly, with whom young Allen finished his education. At this school, Joseph H. Daviess, John Rowan, Felix Grundy, Archibald Cameron, John Pope and John Allen, all distinguished in after life, formed a class.

In the year 1791, John Allen commenced the study of law in the office of Colonel Archibald Stewart, of Stanton, Virginia. He pursued his legal studies with great assiduity for about four years, and in 1795, he returned to Kentucky and settled in Shelbyville, where he continued to practice law till

1812. As a lawyer, he ranked with the first men of his profession.

On the breaking out of the war in 1812, he raised a regiment of riflemen, for the campaign under Harrison in the northwest. Part of this regiment was in the battle of Brownstown, on the eighteenth of January, 1813. In the fatal battle of the River Raisin, Colonel Allen's regiment formed the left wing of the American force. The termination of this affair is too well known to require recapitulation here; and among the many noble and chivalrous Kentuckians, who there found a bloody grave, there was none whose loss was more sensibly felt or deeply deplored than Colonel Allen's. Inflexibly just, benevolent in all his feelings, and of undaunted courage, he was a fine specimen of the Kentucky gentleman of that day, and his name will not soon pass away from the memory of his countrymen.

CHAPTER VII

*Col. Abraham Owen**

Col. Abraham Owen, in honor of whom Owen County received its name, was born in Prince Edward County, Va., in the year, 1769, and emigrated with his equally distinguished father, Brackett Owen to Shelby County, Kentucky, 1785. The particulars of his early life are not known and his first appearance on the public theatre and in the service of the county was upon Wilkinson's campaign, in the summer of 1791, on the White and Wabash Rivers. He was a lieutenant in Capt. Lemon's company in St. Clair's defeat, November 4, 1791, and received two wounds in that engagement—one on the chin, and the other in the arm. He was in the expedition led by Colonel Hardin to White River and participated in the action which routed the Indians in their hunting camps. His brother, John James Ballard and others of Shelby County, were his associates on this occasion. It is not known that he was in Wayne's campaign; but in 1799, he was surveyor of Shelby County, and afterwards a magistrate. He commanded the first militia company raised in the county, and the late Singleton Wilson of Shelbyville, brother of the late Dr. Wilson of Cincinnati, was the lieutenant. They had been associates in Wilkinson's campaign and the humane efforts of Col. Owen to provide for the wants and promote the comforts of his companions, were characteristic of his general character. Owen was soon promoted to be a major and then colonel of a regiment. Lieutenant Wilson was promoted to rank of captain,

---

*A number of worthy descendants of Colonel Owen insist that his first name should be spelled "Abram"; but diligent search has failed to discover in the archives here and at Frankfort, where he or any one else so spelled it; whereas any number of both manuscript and printed official documents spell it as we have; and in both his own and his father's will it is so spelled. Important data in this chapter was among other such furnished by Mrs. Bell Watson Boteler.

having served with distinction as a spy in the campaign led by General Wayne.

Col. Owen was, soon after, elected to the legislature by the largest vote ever before polled in the county; and, in 1799, was with Benjamin Logan chosen a member of the convention which framed the second constitution. Shortly before his death, he was a member of the Senate of Kentucky. No man in the County had a stronger hold on the affections of the people, whom he was always ready to serve in peace or in war. In 1811, he was the first to join Harrison at Vincennes, for the purpose of aiding in the effort to resist the hostile movements of the Indian bands collected by the energy and influence of Tecumseh and his brother, the prophet. He was chosen by Gen. Harrison to be one of his aids-de-camp; and at the memorable battle of Tippecanoe, fell at the side of his heroic chief, bravely fighting for his country, deeply regretted by the whole army and by his numerous friends in Kentucky. In battle he was fearless—as a citizen, mild and gentlemanly. He was esteemed an excellent officer on parade, and possessed a high order of military talent.

In the following December, the legislature of Kentucky went into mourning for the loss of Colonels Daviess and Owen, and others who had fallen at Tippecanoe; and, in 1819-20, the memory of Col. Owen was perpetuated by a county bearing his name. McAfee, in his history of the war says: "His character was that of a good citizen and a brave soldier;" which Butler, in his history of Kentucky, speaking of him, pronounces to be "no little praise in a republic and in a warlike State."

Col. Owen was married to Martha Dupuy, descendant of the celebrated Bartholomew Dupuy, one of the founders of Mannakin, Va. They left a large family to unite with their country in deploring his premature fall. His daughters intermarried with the most respectable citizens of neighboring counties, and his son, Clark, was a distinguished citizen of Texas, having won a high rank in her civil and military annals. His brothers, Robert and William, survived him, and were highly respectable

COL. ABRAHAM OWEN

citizens of Shelby County. His father, Brackett Owen** was an early settler of high standing and marked character, and as a pioneer should be mentioned with Boone, Ballard, etc. His fort, near Shelbyville, was the resort of intrepid families of that day, and may be said to have been the foundation of the capital of the flourishing county of Shelby.

The chivalric patriotism of the son, Col. Owen, in leaving a position of ease and civil distinction at home to volunteer his services against the northwestern savages, is truly illustrative of the Kentucky character; and after ages will look back upon the deeds of heroism at Tippecanoe, with the same veneration with which the present generation regards the memory of those who fought and fell at Thermopylae.

**As in the case of Benjamine and William Logan, so with Bracken and Abraham Owen. The brief sketch possible in a volume like this is devoted more to the son than the father, chiefly for the reason that the careers of the older men had been well nigh run, whereas those of the sons began and ran with the birth and life of the county whose history this is.

"Mention must be made of Col. Brackett Owen, an officer of the Revolution, who in 1785 moved to Kentucky and became a man of great prominence and influence; and of his son, Abraham Owen, born P. E. Co., who at age of 22 went with his father to Kentucky, was in service with Gen. Wilkinson, was an officer under St. Clair and was with Col. Hardin at White River; rendered valuable service in Wayne's Expedition; was a member of Kentucky Legislature of the State Senate and of the Constitutional Convention, 1799, in 1811 was first man from Kentucky to join Wm. Henry Harrison, serving as A. D. C. He was probably a classmate of Harrison's at Hampden-Sydney, and was his warm personal friend. At the Battle of Tippecanoe, Col. Owen, just before the battle, knowing that Harrison rode a spirited horse and would be singled out by the Indians, suggested that he and the general exchange horses. This was done, Harrison not realizing the purpose Owen had in view. The latter rode out and deliberately drew the fire of the Indians, who thought they were shooting Gen. Harrison. Thus ended in a great climax the life of a distinguished soldier and patriot, whose sacrifice gave to the United States one of its presidents."

From report of Dr. J. D. Eggleston, chairman of landmark committee of Prince Edward Chapter Association for Preservation Virginia Antiquities.

CHAPTER VIII

Governor John Pope

Governor John Pope, one of the most distinguished politicians and statesmen of Kentucky, and for many years a resident of Washington County, was born in Prince William County, Va., in 1770, but brought to this State when quite a boy. In early life, while attending a cornstalk mill, he had the misfortune to lose his arm—an accident which turned his attention to the profession of the law. Being a young man of great native vigor of intellect, he soon attained eminence. He settled in Shelby, which county he represented in the Kentucky legislature in 1802, then removed to Lexington and in 1806, '07, was a representative in the lower house from Fayette County, a colleague of Henry Clay and Col. Wm. Russell. Of that body his great talents rendered him an eminently conspicuous and influential member. He was U. S. Senator from Kentucky for six years, 1807-13, a colleague of Henry Clay, Buckner Thurston, and Geo. M. Bibb; and twenty-four years later, a member of the lower House of Congress from the Springfield district, for six years, 1837-43. In the meantime, he was appointed by President Jackson, Governor of the territory of Arkansas, which office he held for six years, 1829-35. He died at his residence in Washington County, July 12, 1845 aged seventy-five years. In early life, he belonged to the Federal party, but in after years to the Democratic.

CHAPTER IX

Capt. John Simpson

Capt. John Simpson, after whom Simpson County and the town of Simpsonville in Shelby County were named, migrated with his father from Virginia to Lincoln County, Ky., at an early day. His first experience in war on a large scale against the Indians, was under Gen. Wayne, at the battle of the Fallen Timbers in 1794. At the instance of the lamented Col. John Allen, he afterwards removed to Shelbyville, studied law and entered upon the practice there—rapidly attaining success and distinction. He represented Shelby County in the legislature in 1806, '09, '10 and '11 and at the last session was chosen speaker. In August, 1812, he was elected to Congress.

When the aggressions of Great Britain upon the rights and interests of the United States led to a declaration of war, Kentucky was called upon to furnish 5,500 men, as her quota of the 100,000 authorized by congress to be received into the service. Mr. Simpson raised a company of riflemen as part of the regiment of his old friend, Col. John Allen—which became part of Gen. John Payne's brigade, and marched with the first troops from Kentucky to reinforce Gen. Hull at Detroit. Capt. Simpson's company participated in the gallant but disastrous event at the River Raisin, where Allen and Simpson both sealed their devotion to their country with their blood.

CHAPTER X

Moses Hall

Moses Hall came to Kentucky about 1780. A "Treasury Warrant" was issued to Moses and Edward Hall on the third of April, 1782 for one thousand eight hundred and eighty and one-fourth acres located in Fayette County, Ky., signed by Patrick Henry. Moses Hall was in Shelby County, July 19, 1797, as court records show he bought 300 acres at that time from Edward Worthington (bearing date Feb. 24, 1796); was paying tax in Shelby County, 1792, on property in Campbell County, Ky.

In 1814, Moses Hall advertised for sale the land which he owned, adjoining the town of Shelbyville and between them and the bridge across Clear Creek. The town lots belonging to Shelbyville in the east end at that time extended to Third Street, and the property Mr. Hall wished to sell included everything on both sides of Main Street between Third Street and the creek. The first bridge built in Shelby County was across Clear Creek at the east end of Shelbyville near where Logan & Logan afterwards operated a mill. The idea of building it was suggested first at the April term of court, 1803, and Thos. Guin, Moses Hall and William I. Tunstall were appointed commissioners to view and mark the most fit and proper place to erect a bridge across Clear Creek convenient to the road leading from Shelbyville to Frankfort. Also to make out and present a plan for the bridge and report the probable cost of the same at the next term of court.

The contract was let to the lowest bidder in 1804, who was William Tunstall, but he died before beginning the work. In December, 1805, the contract was let to John Parker, who agreed to do the work for three hundred dollars.

In 1808, a committee was appointed to have pavements made "just like the one in front of Adam Steele's store." Abraham

Owen and Uriah Glovers were the contractors and received $290.50 for making the pavements, there being forty-one and a half square at seven dollars per square. Moses Hall, who as said, owned all the property then east of the town limits, which were where Third Street now is, was the man who built the first bridge across Clear Creek on what is now known as the Mt. Eden pike. He donated to the town sufficient land for a street from the bridge to the Main Street, and what he gave is now Third Street.

Moses Hall was married September 4, 1784 to Isabelle Stevenson, daughter of Thomas Stevenson of Lincoln County, Ky.

In the Presbyterian Church records at Shelbyville and at Mulberry for 1824, the following are mentioned as members: Moses Hall, Sr., Mrs. Hall, Sr., Elizabeth Hall Hardin, Moses Hall, Jr., and wife, Elizabeth P. Hall, John Hall, Allen Hall, Isabelle Hall.

CHAPTER XI

Dr. John Knight

(Philadelphia, *Saturday Courier*, April 7, 1838)

Died on the 12th ult., March, 1838, at his residence in Shelby County, Dr. John Knight, aged 87 years—Dr. Knight was born in Scotland about 1751, and arrived in Philadelphia about 1773, at the commencement of the American Revolution. He entered the regiment as surgeon's mate in the ninth Virginia regiment, and was present at the battles of Brandywine, Germantown, Monmouth, and many other minor engagements, and towards the close of the war, was attached to Col. Gibson's regiment which was stationed at Pittsburgh. When the unfortunate expedition of Col. Crawford against the Indians was in progress, Col. Crawford requested of his friend, Col. Gibson, that Dr. Knight should accompany him as surgeon, which was readily granted. His fame as surgeon rests on the fact that he performed the first successful operation for cancer. He joined Col. Crawford at the Mingo Town on the Ohio River, May, 1782. From thence the army proceeded to the disastrous plains of Sandusky, where, after a severe batttle with the Indians, the whole party were defeated and completely routed. Dr. Knight, Col. Crawford, and many others were overtaken and captured, and many of them burned at the stake. Dr. Knight was present and witnessed the cruel and agonizing death of Col. Crawford at the stake, and was shortly afterwards himself pinioned to the stake to meet the same cruel death. But Providence ordered it otherwise. A heavy rain coming on put out the fire, and it was then determined he should be removed to an Indian town some twenty-five miles distant; there to meet his fate. The Indian force preceded, leaving the doctor in charge of one Indian. They traveled but slowly, as the doctor was much injured by blows received from the Indians. At night the Indian confined the doctor, and both lay down to rest. The mosquitoes being troublesome, the doctor proposed to kindle a fire, and agreed if he would untie him he would assist in the operation. This was done, and when the Indian stooped down to blow the fire, the doctor knocked him down with a billet of wood, seized his gun to shoot him, but pulling back the cock with such force as to break the main spring, the Indian immediately made his escape. The doctor quietly pursued his way homeward, and after a march of fourteen days nearly famished, found himself at Fort McIntosh, on the Ohio River, thirty miles below Pittsburgh, once more in the midst of his friends.

At the close of the war, Dr. Knight married Miss Stevenson, niece of Col. Crawford. He removed to Kentucky about fifty years ago, and settled on the farm where he died, leaving an amiable wife and highly respectable children—among whom is Dr. Joseph W. Knight of this city.*

The writer of this became acquainted with Dr. Knight in 1794. They were both in the expedition of Gen. Wayne against the northern Indians in that year. He has known him intimately ever since, and he never knew a better man.

Louisville, March 17, 1838.

---

*Dr. John Knight's daughter, Sallie Lane Knight, married, December, 1815, Capt. John Hall, son of Moses Hall, Sr.

CHAPTER XII

Nicholas Meriwether

The ancestor of the Meriwether family in the United States of America was Nicholas Meriwether, a subject of the principality of Wales who emigrated to the then coloney of Virginia in the 17th Century during the political trouble of King Charles II, of England; he taking up land in Virginia in payment for moneys advanced to the Crown.

His son, Nicholas Meriwether II (Born Oct. 26, 1667, died Oct., 1744), was buried near Charlottsville, Va. He married Elizabeth, daughter of David Crawford, Esq., of New Kent County, Virginia. From these two people most of the Meriwethers from Colonial times to the present day are descended. Nicholas Meriwether II outlived most of his children and acquired wealth in land and slaves. In one of his tracts were 17,952 acres of land near Charlottsville, Virginia, granted by King George II, of England, in the year 1730, a portion of which is now owned by some of the descendants. Proven records show that the Meriwethers have met demands on time and means for the upbuilding of our States and Nation.

Nicholas Meriwether V (Born in Virginia, June 4, 1749, died April 28, 1828) came with his wife, Elizabeth, who was his first cousin, and children to Kentucky in 1784 by way of Redstone, Pennsylvania on a flat boat, landing from the Ohio River at Louisville, Kentucky. In the same year, while still living at Louisville near Old Fort Nelson, he had great mortality in his family. After the death of his wife, six children and several servants, he moved to Shelby County, Kentucky taking with him his daughter, Patsy and his son, Richard. They made their home near Christiansburg, Shelby County, Ky. Patsy married Martin Daniel, April 10, 1788. Mr. Daniel had come from Virginia about the time of the Meriwethers' coming. Mr. and Mrs. Daniel had five children. The descendants of some of these children still live in Shelby County. Nicholas' son, Richard (Born Oct. 10, 1777) married first, Elizabeth Thornton in 1818. After her death he married her cousin, Susannah F. Thornton in 1822. Both these young women came from Caroline County, Virginia. Richard Meriwether died in Shelby County, Kentucky, May 17, 1850. He was survived by his wife, Susannah, a daughter, Elizabeth, who died young, and three sons, Richard, Thornton and George Wood. Richard Meriweather, Jr., never married. Thornton Meriwether and George Wood Meriwether married and left children. The Meriwethers of Shelby County are descended from the above named. Wills and deeds are on file at Shelbyville, Ky.

From the coming of Nicholas Meriweather V, from Virginia to Shelby County, Kentucky, he was active with other pioneers in the building of churches, schools and roads. He married as said the second time, a sister of Martin Daniel. The children and their descendants of this marriage live in Louisiana and Mississippi. Nicholas Meriweather V, died at the home of his son, Richard Meriwether near Christiansburg, Shelby County, Ky., where he was buried.*

References:

"Colonial Virginia Register," W. G. Stanard, pp. 98, 100, 102-105, 107.

"Meriwether Family," by Hon. George R. Gilmer, Ex-Governor of the State of Georgia.

"Family Records," by the late George W. Meriwether of Louisville, Ky.

---
*Compiled by Mrs. Susan Thornton Meriwether Henning.

CHAPTER XIII

Joseph Hornsby*

The master and mistress of Mt. Vernon were no busier with, or more ambitious about the landscaping or gardening they were doing on the banks of the Potomac one hundred and forty years ago than was one of the pioneers of Shelby County. A diary written in ink between April, 1798 and August, 1804, by Joseph Hornsby at his home in Southwestern Shelby County near where Clark's Station on the Southern Railway now stands was devoted almost entirely to a record of the planting of rare flower seeds, the transplanting of valuable vines and shrubbery and to his visits and inter-relations with those who were then his relations and neighbors.

His beautiful home at that place was called, "Grasslands," and he is said to have owned eight thousand acres at the time of his death. A son of Joseph Hornsby and Hannah Linkley of Great Yarmouth, Norfolk County, England, born in 1746, he came to Williamsburg, Virginia when seventeen years of age. In about 1770, he was married to Mildred Thornton Walker, daughter of the distinguished Dr. Thomas Walker, the first Kentucky explorer, and of Mildred Thornton. Just what year they reached Shelby County is not definitely shown by the records, but his large holdings of land in the vicinity of Clark's Station and where he died when he was sixty-six years old, came to him, of course, through grants, when the property was still within the State of Virginia. He and his wife of such distinguished ancestry were the parents of five children, all born in the 1770's. They were Hannah Hornsby, who married Thomas Allen, Mildred Hornsby, who married her cousin, Nicholas Merriwether Lewis, Joseph Hornsby, who married Cynthia Allen (they had ten children) Thomas Hornsby, who married Frances Henderson and Margaret

---
*Data furnished by Mrs. Bell Watson Boteler.

Hornsby, who married John Allen. The latter couple like Joseph Hornsby and Cynthia Allen, reared a family of ten children, and all five of the children of Thomas Hornsby were the parents of families whose descendants for four and five generations have lived and died in Shelby County; or are still esteemed citizens of Shelby, or have been among those who went out into the world and helped to make Shelby County favorably known, particularly in the States out under the western skies, long years after the original Joseph Hornsby had sowed and planted and raised his flowers in the pioneer Kentucky. The Allen, Hornsby, Boteler and Lewis families are some of those whose names have been familiar in Shelby County and to Shelby countians, wherever located for more than a hundred and thirty years.

PART VI
Tradition and Reminiscences

CHAPTER I

Told by Squire Boone's Grandson

[The following letter to Hon. Thos. W. Bullitt is self-explanatory. And while the information it contains is "second-handed," it has been in the main verified by all the other procurable data on the same subject.—Author's Note.]

"Eden postoffice (Jefferson County), Ky., July 23, 1880. Mr. Thos. W. Bullitt—Dear Sir: Having made your acquaintance at the unveiling of the monument erected to the memory of the dead of Gen. John Floyd's defeat on Floyd's Fork, now in Jefferson County, you requested me to give you a narrative of what I knew of the massacre and Floyd's defeat. I am a representative of Squire Boone, being his grandson, and what I know I learned from Isaiah Boone, my uncle, a son of Squire Boone. He was at Floyd's defeat. He said that his father had built a station on Clear Creek, two miles east of where Shelbyville now stands, and that his father, with several families, left Boonesborough in 1779, settled in this, then called Boone's station. There was a station on Beargrass, three miles east of Louisville, Called Beargrass (or Floyd's Station), and one eight miles from Louisville, called Lynn's Station. Lynn's Station was on the place afterward owned by Col. R. C. Anderson. Boone's Station at that time was the only station between Harrod's and Lynn's Station. Squire Boone's station was about twenty-two miles east of Lynn's Station. Bland Ballard and Samuel Wells at that time lived in Lynn's Station, while Gen. Floyd lived in Beargrass Station.

"There were two couples to be married in Lynn's Station. Bland Ballard and a man named Carris went from Lynn's Station to Brashear's Station, near the mouth of Floyd's Fork, now Bullitt County, after a Baptist minister, John Whitaker, to marry them. This was to be the first legal marriage in this part of the country. In going over, Ballard discovered an Indian trail and was satisfied there was a large body of them. He retraced his steps to Lynn's Station, sent word to Beargrass

Station, and then went to Boone's Station that night. They held a meeting and agreed to leave the station and go to Lynn's Station. There were a large number of families in Boone's Station at this time, viz: the Hintons, Harrises, Hughses, Hansboro, Bryans, Van Cleves and many others. They could not all get ready to move the next day, but some were determined to go. Squire Boone was not ready and could not prevail on them to wait another day. So Major Ballard conducted this party, leaving Squire Boone and a few families in the station to come the next day. When Ballard's party reached Long Run he was attacked in the rear. He went back to protect the rear. He drove the Indians back and held them in check as long as he could. In going back he saw on the ground a man and his wife, by the name of Cline. He told Cline to put his wife on the horse and hurry on. They were in the bed of Long Run. Ballard returned in a short time, to find Cline and his wife still on the ground. He put her on his horse and gave the horse a tap with his wiping-stick and as he did so an Indian pulled a sack from her horse. Ballard shot the Indian and hurried to the front.

"Here he found a great many killed and the people scattered, leaving their cattle and losing their baggage and many horses. Some reached Lynn's Station that night, and a few, Boone's. Boone remained in his station for several days after that before he and his party went down to Lynn's Station. I'll give the names of a few of those that were killed on Long Run: Two Misses Hansboros, sisters of Joel Hansboro; a Mr. McCarby, a brother of Mrs. Richard Chenoweth, and a Mrs. Van Cleve, an aunt of my mother's. The next day General (then Colonel) Floyd, Colonel (then Captain) Wells, and Bland Ballard (afterward Major Ballard) and thirty-four others from Lynn and Beargrass Stations, went up to bury the dead. When they reached Floyd's Fork, Ballard said to them: 'You send a few men and ascertain where the Indians are.' He, however, was overruled and on they went. At the head of the ravine they were surrounded and sixteen of their men were shot down at the first fire. Fourteen of these were buried in one sink. They began to retreat. Isaiah Boone said that when he reached the Fork he discovered an Indian following him. He raised his gun. The Indian stepped behind a tree. Just at this time General Floyd and Colonel Wells came in sight, Floyd on foot and Wells on horseback. Wells said to Floyd: 'Take my horse.' Floyd, being large and fleshy, was much exhausted.

"They took to the bushes and reached the place selected, should they be defeated. It was near where Thos. Elder's new house now stands, on the Shelby Pike, about three miles above Middletown. For some time prior to this, General Floyd and Wells were not friendly. Isaiah Boone said: 'General, that brought you to your milk.' The General's reply was: 'You are a noble boy; we were in a tight place.' This boy was then but fourteen years of age. He was at that time visiting Lynn's Station. The occurrence took place in September, 1781. Squire Boone's wife's maiden name was Jane Van Cleve. Enoch Boone, their youngest son, was born in Boonesborough, October 16, 1777, being the first male white child born in Kentucky. He died in Meade County, Kentucky, 1861. Squire Boone died in 1815, and was by his request, buried in a cave in Harrison County, Indiana. Sarah Boone, my mother, was the only daughter of Squire Boone. She was married to John Wilcox, my father, in 1791, and he settled on and improved land, surveyed and patented in the name of Sarah Boone by her father, four miles north of Shelbyville. Dear Sir, pardon me for departing from the subject of my narrative. I am making it too long.

Yours truly,
G. T. WILCOX."

P. S.—"The information here given you was derived from conversations with Isaiah Boone; confirmed by conversations with my mother, who was in the fort with her father at the time of the massacre; also with Enoch Boone; also with my grandmother, Jane Boone, wife of Squire Boone, who lived at my father's house and died there in 1820.

"For further information on this interesting topic I would refer you to John Williamson, now living at Eden Station, in this county, and in the eighty-fifth year of his age. Squire was the Christian name, not the title, of Squire Boone. He was the youngest brother of Daniel Boone.

"G. T. WILCOX."

CHAPTER II

Older Story, Long Run Massacre

(A letter written from his home at O'Bannon Station by Mr. John W. Williamson, in 1872. Another interesting letter by Mr. Williamson, of about the same date, is published in the Statistical Division, or Part VII, of this Volume, and contains the names of many of the first settlers, professional and business men of the city and County.)*

O'Bannon's Station, Jefferson County, Kentucky,
(November 27, 1872)

Sometime in the year 1781, at Lynn's Station, there were four young persons to be married and there was no preacher to unite the parties nearer than Brashear's Station, two miles east of Shepherdsville, where lived old John Whitaker, a Baptist preacher. So the parties prevailed on Bland Ballard to go bring the preacher. He started, but before he arrived at the station, he discovered a large trail of Indians, who had gone south. He immediately returned to the station, and all the forts were notified. Immediately there was a council held and they supposed that the Indians had gone to destroy the stations on Cox's Creek in Nelson County, and all there were on Nolin in Hardin County. Their conclusions were right, for they did destroy a fort and put to death about one hundred and fifty persons; there were about two hundred persons in the fort, and but few escaped. It was always afterwards called, the Burnt Station. The general opinion was that they, on their return, would destroy Boone, and it was decided to send what men could be spared from the different stations and move Boone down to Lynn Station. When the men arrived at Boone's Station, they found that they could bring only half and that they would make two trips, so they divided the

*Contributed by Mrs. Josephine Matthews Thurman.

families into halves, and started, and just as they reached Long Run they met the Indians and were put to flight and defeated. There were a good many killed and lost. Among the number were the two Misses Hansboro's. Several days after, some women got to Lynn's Station, naked in a manner, for when they got to the station, all they could hold out as a flag was a little piece of their shirt. And Mrs. Mundle and Elizabeth Ballard, wife of Bland Ballard, took clothes and brought them in. This battle was called, Boone's Defeat, and I don't know from what cause, for Boone was not there, but his oldest son was there; he still remained at his station. The next day they raised what men they could to bury the dead. Their effective force was about sixty men under the command of Colonel Floyd and Wells. When they reached the west bank of Floyd's Fork they held a council and made that a rallying point in case they were defeated. Here Bland Ballard and Caress begged to be permitted to go and reconnoiter, for they were satisfied the Indians were there, but Floyd would not hear to it. They then marched in two companies, one in advance of the other some three hundred yards. The Indians, about seven hundred in number, formed a half-moon on each side of the road or trace. As soon as Floyd marched far enough, they closed their lines and had him surrounded. There were fourteen men shot down the first fire. Ballard and Caress stood near together; as the Indians came up each shot down an Indian and went over him and escaped down a ravine cross above Chenoworth's Run, and reached their rallying point uninjured. Part of the Indians passed Boone's Station but did not attack him. They destroyed all stock they could find outside of the fort. This was called Floyd's Defeat. Previous to this time Floyd and Wells had been at outs. Floyd was wounded and thrown from his horse and being a fat man was likely to fall into the hands of the Indians, but Wells got off his horse and put Floyd on him and both made their escape and were always fast friends afterwards.

Long Run Massacre

Here I will proceed to give an incident that took place at Tyler's Station. Old Colonel Bland Ballard and his son, Bland, had moved to Robert Tyler's fort. After remaining there for a short time; the families being very much crowded the colonel moved his family, consisting of his wife, his son John by his first wife, and three children, about two hundred yards outside of the fort. Early in the morning, just at daylight, the Indians made the attack. John had gone out to get some kindling for the fire. While he was breaking some sticks an Indian rose up behind the brush heap and shot him in the head. The old man at the firing of the gun, sprang and seized the bar of the door, got one end in, but before he could get the other end in, the Indians were against the door, but with the assistance of his wife, they succeeded in keeping the Indians out for a considerable time. While this was going on, Bland, his son, sprang out of the fort and ran about halfway and took a position behind a small tree, and whenever he could get a shot he did so to good effect. Bland's wife in the meantime got on top of one of the houses and whenever an Indian appeared she would holler to her husband to watch. One of the Indians got under the bank of the creek, crawled up to get a shot at Bland, but his wife was watching the Indian, and when he put his gun through the fence she hollered to him. He then fired and the Indian fell. The Indians finally succeeded in chopping a chunk out of the house and shot the old man, and broke his thigh. They then succeeded in getting in the house. His wife broke out at the back door and attempted to run to the fort. Bland had just discharged his gun or he would have saved her. The Indian caught and tomahawked her. The Indians tomahawked the three children and pitched them out in the yard. The youngest child, about two years old, survived and lived many years afterwards but very much disfigured. After the Indians had completed their murderous work they gathered up their dead, and packed them off up the big hill on the opposite side of the creek in full view of the fort. After they had left, one Indian came back, went into the house, and was there for some time. When he came out he went in a stooping position until he thought he was out of gun shot. As he straightened up, Bland fired and he fell. The Indians all came yelling back and they supposed the fort would be attacked, but they packed off the last Indian that was shot. The number of Indians killed by Bland and his father was eight or nine. Robert Tyler stated he counted eight others, say there were nine. After the Indians left they wanted to send an express to the different stations. Bland would go, but none was willing for him to leave the fort. Robert Tyler agreed if they would get him a horse and guard him over the hill, he would go. They were soon reinforced from Bracket Owen's, Colonel Aquilla Whitaker's, and Boone's Stations. They pursued the Indians for a while but they scattered. They thought it best to return, which they did in time to bury the dead five in one grave. It was ascertained that Colonel Ballard had fought desperately. His mouth was full of bullets. In loading he had spilt his powder all over the floor.

JOHN W. WILLIAMSON.

A late view of "Cross-Keys Inn," from a photograph by the author.

CHAPTER III
Cross-Keys Inn, up to 1891*

Shelbyville, November 20, 1891.—At the top of the hill, in the bend of the road, on the "State pike," five miles east of Shelbyville, there stands a great white house, whose walls are redolent with romance and history. It is older by half than is the historic turnpike road from Lexington to Louisville, for which it has stood a monumental half-way mile-stone for fifty years.

About it cling memories sacred to elderly people in half the States of the Union. Over its main portal ought to be swung an imperishable picture of the Kentucky coat of arms.

It has been the scene where most of four strangely beautiful lives have been spent; where incidents of keen interest to thousands have occurred, and where pictures of a homelike and a homestead happiness such as Denman Thompson might immortalize have shown in the fire-light of a hundred Christmas and Thanksgiving eves.

It is the Middleton homestead and looks to the traveler from the east just as it does in the accompanying cut, the L of it being more than a hundred years old, and the main building, a mammoth farm-house that would delight the picturing pen of an Irving or the brush of an artist bent on touching nature's heart.

The main building is now the farmhouse home of a happy

---

*This is but another "paper of the period," reproduced, personalities and all, as reflecting County conditions at and previous to its date of first publication. It is a newspaper letter written for the Louisville Times in 1891, and the occurrences then spoken of in it as "fifty" and "one hundred" years old are now nearly forty years older, in the history of the County.

(In a reminiscent mood our County's brilliant newspaper man, Mr. Geo. L. Willis, Sr., contributed to the January, 1929, *Kentucky Highways*, a magazine of which he is the editor, an article headed "Long Ago Photographs Resurrected," in which he told of the lives of those who made Cross-Keys Inn of this County famous. After its reading we were informed that this same Mr. Willis had contributed to *The Louisville Times* a former article, on the same subject, and that the story in *The Times* was more in detail. As nothing is too good for the readers of the *Sentinel* the longer story is given here, for both this story and the cuts that are interspersed through it the *Sentinel* gives due credit and its thanks to Mr. Willis.—Editor Shelby *Sentinel*.)

and prosperous big family, but the L was, back in another century, a tavern more famous than any one of the palace-like hostelries of the East today. It, too, was the home of a Middelton—the first Middelton—a name the most common now of all in Shelby County, but its fame came from another cause. It was the "Cross-Keys" tavern—the old-time stopping place of all who journeyed over the dirt road from the Bluegrass section to the banks of the Ohio, of all those who "staged" it from the even then effete East to the "barbarous" South and woolly West. Old men in New York and Philadelphia ask the Kentucky traveler of today quaint questions about the "Cross-Keys" tavern, where they once spent a night, had their horses fed, had their glass of free whiskey and bed and board, all for six bits, with a hearty God-speed next morning thrown in. Even they do not remember it in its palmiest days of a hundred years ago, when superstitious slaves and poor whites on the road hastened to spend the night there, because the house never had a tragedy or supported a ghost. It is estimated that the "Cross-Keys" Inn sheltered ten thousand travelers between the years 1800 and 1825; that they represented every State of the Union east of the Mississippi River, and sent their children's children along the same road with a recommendation to stop at the same inn up to and long after the war. Even now, though it is but the part of a farmhouse, occupied by people of affluence and lateday tastes, with no need to care for the load coachman and his lead, the old custom is kept up, and no stranger is ever turned from its doors. Two rooms in this famous "ell," though now the apartments of young and wealthy men of fashion, are still known to the household one as the "barroom," the other as the "office."

With the bookful of interesting things that could be written about the house and its occupants for the last hundred years, the chiefest interest in the place has been the singular lives two brothers led there—brothers who, for seventy years, lived in the house where they were born and died; who married sisters; who were bone of each other's bone and flesh of one another's flesh; who had but one wish, but one opinion and each of whom never in his whole life of seventy-odd years owned one iota of property, even were it horse, servant or child, in which the other had not a full and complete half interest. Living, they were as much one as if bound together as were the famous Siamese; dead their lives virtually went out together, the last of the two passing away Sunday, November 13, only a few months after the peaceful demise of his senior.

The Pioneer of the Cross-Keys Tavern

Their story, like all others, is best told by beginning at the beginning. In the year 1777, there was born in the heart of Virginia, a future Kentucky pioneer, whom they christened Adam Middelton. In 1794, he was married to Miss Mary Fulton, also of the "Old Dominion." In the year 1800, they came with the dawn of the century to Kentucky, settled in a little hut near where the house that figures herein is located, and he for a time plied his calling, that of a blacksmith. The stream of travelers who poured down the old dirt "State Road" suggested to young Middelton the idea of a tavern, and he bought the log structure that had served as such before, from a man across the road, and, because the road forked there, hung up two immense brass keys on a tree at the roadside and called his inn the "Cross-Keys" tavern. The stories of the travelers that passed and stopped there as the years passed by and they with the star of empire westward took their way, would fill a book. It was an historic inn with an historic bar, an historic table of good things, a cheerful landlord, a roomy barn and barnyard, and continued so until the "State Pike" was built and even rumors of war began, and the well-fed and good-humored guests of yore became ravaging wolves, the guerrillas of the war. But much had happened to Shelby's first Middelton before these last times referred to. In fact, he had been dead nearly fifty years when the war came on. But of those other days before even the first wars of the century; when the Nineteenth century was in its 'teens, there is much concerning him that could be told. Happiness came to him as rapidly as did prosperity and ease, though in those days he would lodge a six-horse team and driver, with a free glass of whiskey for the man, all for "six bits." Between 1800 and 1820, the last eight of ten children were born to him and the wife of his bosom. These "grew in beauty side by side," and though they were never scattered far and wide—all living and dying in the County—all left the parental rooftree for homes and farms of their own, excepting two. Two younger brothers, and it is with these twin souls and their marvelous and unexampled experience in this or any other state, I know of, that this sketch has to do.

Brothers With Twin Souls

The youngest two sons of the pioneer, Adam Middelton, were born, Adam in 1813, and Robert in 1816. They grew alike and were a veritable Damon and Pythias, when, as they reached man's estate, their father died. They were the only ones of the ten children left in and in charge of the famous old inn. It was still a valuable property, for the century itself was but thirty-odd years old, and all travel was still by stagecoach and wagon. The two brothers were inseparable, and concluded to remain so. Even then, spirited youths though they were, Adam's will was Bob's, and Bob's wish was Adam's. They put together their shares of the land about the tavern that their father left them, and agreed that so long as both should live they would be partners in everything, should be brothers indeed—an example for the whole world, a following out of the lesson taught by Him of Nazareth—and for more than fifty years they were two such brothers as even history fails to tell of and an example that the Bible itself does not record.

Both loved the same pursuits, the same companions—had the same tastes in everything—and before either was twenty-five years old he had married his sister-in-law. Both married sisters, whose difference in age was the same as between their husbands. Both wooed and won at the same fireside. Both brought to the same fireside their charming and blushing brides. And to that fireside, in all the years that followed, out of a double family of thirteen children, there never came back a sorrowing daughter or a prodigal son, and death himself once staid away for more than thirty years.

They worshipped at the same little church across the road, on their own farm, for many years, and kept green in its graveyard the same mounds.

Of these, their wives and double family of thirteen, more must be told further on. The son of each was the other's Joseph. Each mother was a Naomi, and her sister's daughter, was her Ruth. There were seven children on the one side and six on the other, and survivors of these, gathered together a few days ago, told the writer that in all the fifty years of such singular double home-life, there was never known such a thing as a family "jar." The cemented love of their families but seeded the ripening love of these sturdy brothers, who even voted the same Democratic ticket at the same voting place for fifty-odd years. So alike were they in their appearance and disposition that a neighbor born and reared near them never knew them apart to the day of their several deaths. "I never knew a difference between them in my childhood or after I became a man," was the way a son of the younger brother described the relations of the singular household. "My sisters have always been my cousins and my cousins my brothers and sisters," was the way another put it; "and the first of our two mothers or our two fathers we found was the one to whom we told our wishes or our needs."

It is told that a son of the younger, once asked if his father was at home replied: "No; neither of them." Of course, many interesting incidents could be told of the brothers themselves and the strangely attractive home life with which they surrounded themselves, but a better understanding of their relations can be had from a little biography.

Biographical and Reminiscent

In 1835, when Adam Middelton was twenty-three years old, and Robert was nineteen, the former decided to bring a bride to their double homestead. He married a near neighbor's eldest daughter, Miss Mary Willis, a few years his junior, and the child of Pearson Willis, also a Virginia pioneer to Kentucky and Shelby County. Four years later the younger brother married his brother's wife's younger sister, Miss Letitia Willis, and together, the two brothers and two sisters began the double-partnership life which continued till the fiftieth anniversary, or both their gold wedding days were passed. Each couple was blessed with children. To Adam and his wife seven children—four daughters and three sons—were born. To the other family, or half of the family, came two sons and four daughters. As the inn became more the abode of hospitality than a place of profit, and as it instead of a rambling old tavern became the big, square farm-house, surrounded by broad acres, these two sets of children who made up one family, grew to manhood's and woman's estate; but if they left the homestead, rarely left the County, and are today highly respectable and valued citizens of Shelby and adjoining counties. Of the senior couple's seven children, John T. and James D. are the principal owners and controllers of the Farmers and Traders' Bank, of Shelbyville; Price W. is connected with the wholesale firm of J. M. Robinson, of this city; Mary E. is the wife of Cal. S. Weakley, a prominent farmer of Shelby; a single daughter recently died, and the other two are unmarried, and make up a part of what is still a happy, though bereft household.

Of Robert and Letitia Middelton's six children, William R. and Wallace B., the youngest sons of all, while as much capitalists and fine horse fanciers as farmers, are in partnership charge of the old homestead; while two of their sisters married W. D. Harris and H. Thomasson, of Shelby and Henry County respectively, and the other two are living unmarried at the old home.

All but two of the six or seven unmarried live at home with the two kindly old ladies, the relicts of the dead brothers, whose pictures are given herewith, and who, while waiting to join their twin spirits under the shade of the trees on the other side, are living in the past and the memory of the happy days that came to them in such numbers. They are each near the three-score-and-ten milestone of life, and have lived to comfort each other, and to be comforted by their own and one another's children, in their long-stayed bereavements. Before the two recent deaths, and that of a daughter of the senior branch, there were fifty years of such home happiness in this family as it would be futile to attempt to describe in detail.

Domestic Happiness Doubly Beautiful

This home life was doubly happy. In the days when the thirteen children were young and some were unborn, the home with its little town of slaves and travelers from the North and East combined all the attractions of homelife in the South and in New England, too. Even after the older children went off to new homes and new pursuits and had children and homesteads of their own, there was to them but one home, and that was that found in the big house shown in the accompanying view—a house and a household regarded with respectful curiosity, if not envy, by all those who lived within a radius of a half-hundred miles. Many people came from abroad to see the house and the occupants that were pointed out and told about by every passerby. And then what reunions there were in that home. When "Thanksgiving" came, with its hallowed associations, John and Jim, from the bank, Mary and her husband from the farm, another from the store, all with their own households, came trooping back to the parent tree, festivities began which were in real life like the pictures in the "Old Homestead," Denman Thompson's masterpiece, that have been laughed over and wept over by the countrybred people in every big city of the Union. It was the same on Christmas eve and Christmas day; the same when one of the double family took unto her or himself a companion, and these happy home gatherings were but once or twice interfered with or changed by death for more than fifty years.

Such a home was naturally their all to the Middelton brothers from the time they were young inn-keepers and small farmers, until they owned the house and the landed estates that surrounded it for miles. Neither ever sought political preferment, but were in some way connected with every County enterprise Shelby ever developed. Adam, the elder, though seventy-seven years old at his death, was never out of the State, and died in the very room in which he was born. Robert, the younger, could make nearly the same boast, that he had never been farther from home than he could ride in a half day. The latter never sat for a photograph, but their marked resemblance, already referred to, makes the picture of the elder the only one necessary to an understanding of what manner of looking men they were.

Bethel Church and the Graveyard

Across the turnpike in a field, upon which the big house fronts, is the old church already referred to; and behind it is a country church graveyard. The church, a little brown brick, itself nearly a hundred years old, is almost as historic as the

CROSS-KEYS INN.

homestead. Its congregation, when the Middeltons were its ruling spirits, was of the "Anti-Missionary" Baptist faith. It was in those days the place of all places in that part of the country for big meetings, and big dinners on the ground or at the Middelton house across the road. Until after many years, when there was a "split" and the Middeltons went with the pro-missionary faction to a new church at Clayvillage, a little town farther up the road, "Bethel's May meetings" were where the wealth and fashion of the county seat and countryside gathered. But its glory has faded and its prestige has gone. Not so with the little graveyard, for graveyards never cease to flourish and grow. The one behind the little church, which partly hides it from the homestead, a stone's throw away, contains two new mounds. They are side by side and contain all that is mortal of Adam and Robert Middelton. The sun shines there when it does on the house where they were born and lived for seventy years and where they died. The birds sing there when they do in the branches of the old trees about the house. The snows and sleet patter on the old church and the graves when it does on the roof that sheltered them when alive, but in that bright land that must be beyond they are united again else it is not heaven to them.

Long Run Baptist Church. Eight feet of the front was added after the erection of this famous "meeting house" in 1796; and is supposed to be over and above the grave of Captain Abraham "Linkhorn," the grandfather of the President.

CHAPTER IV

The Lincolns and Long Run*

A student of Kentucky History recently lamented the lack of Lincoln history in Kentucky's archives. We told him that with a companion, in Washington, looking for Lincoln material, in 1909, the centennial anniversary of his birth, we discovered the fact that there were something near ten thousand different volumes and publications relating to Abraham Lincoln, in the Library of Congress alone—much more printed matter about him in one library than about the Savior of mankind—and we concluded that, sanely considered, the matter had been "a bit overdone."

We still think so. But there are some interesting facts connected with the ancestry of Abraham Lincoln, in Kentucky, that seem to have been given publicity, scant in comparison with their interest and importance. So few in Central Kentucky know that Lincoln's grandfather, Abraham "Linkhorn," lived, was killed and is buried on the western edge of Jefferson County, near the Shelby County line, not far from Oldham, and that his activities and surroundings had much to do with the life and development of that section of Kentucky, fifty years before even the birth of the "martyred President."

The illustrations herewith given are the work of the Hon. R. C. Ballard Thruston, president of the Filson Club, whose genius for detailed drawings meticulously accurate research of records, titles and legends is remarkable and whose photographic work is a pleasant side issue with him. Particular attention is called to the ingenuity with which he has pieced together the boundaries of several old surveys into an exact replica of the original four hundred acres known as the "Linkhorn Jefferson County Grant of 1780."

The use of what was then left of the former Filson Club

---
*This article, by its editor, was published in the Kentucky Highways Magazine for March, 1929.

president, Colonel Durrett's library, and the assistance rendered by Mr. Thruston, and by Mrs. Cannon, of the Kentucky Historical Society, enabled Doctor Wm. E. Barton, Oak Park, Illinois, to secure, in Kentucky, a few years ago, such intimate, complete and reliable data as make of his recently issued "Life of Lincoln" a convincingly accurate, satisfactory record of those early times. This is particularly true of the first portion of the first volume, dealing with the ancestry of Abraham Lincoln, the President.

Doctor Barton quotes Herndon's "Lincoln" as follows:

"The story of his (the grandfathers) death in the sight of his youngest son Thomas, then only six years old, is by no means a new one to the world. In fact, I have often heard the president describe the tragedy as he had inherited the story from his father. The dead pioneer had three sons, Mordecai, Josiah and Thomas, in the order named. When the father fell, Mordecai, having hastily sent Josiah to the neighboring fort after assistance, ran into the cabin, and pointing his rifle through a crack between the logs, prepared for defense. Presently an Indian came stealing up to the dead father's body. Beside the latter sat the little boy Thomas. Mordecai took deliberate aim at a silver crescent which hung suspended from the Indian's breast, and brought him to the ground. Josiah returned from the fort with the desired relief, and the savages were easily dispersed, leaving behind one dead and one wounded."

Taking up the story himself, Doctor Barton says:

"It is of interest to inquire, where did this tragedy occur? Both Washington and Jefferson Counties claim the site of Captain Abraham Lincoln's death. Washington County advances as its proof the fact that the family are found living there very soon after the pioneer's death, and also that his estate was administered in Nelson County, from which Washington was subsequently formed. But the Nelson and Wash-

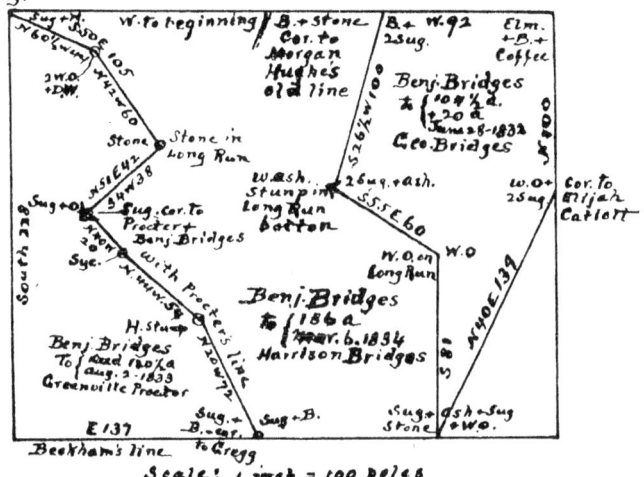

See "Lincoln Ancestors", Chapter IV, Part VI.

The Lincolns and Long Run

\ington County records contain no evidence that Abraham ever owned land or lived in that county. On the other hand, it is certain that he owned land on Long Run, with an improvement, which was almost certainly a cabin. There is not known to have been any fort near enough to the land subsequently owned by the Lincolns in Washington County to have met the requirements of the situation.

"I have been shown two additional alleged sites of the death of the pioneer Lincoln, one in Hardin County, which may be dismissed without comment, and the other in the heart of the city of Louisville. The latter calls for a moment's attention, because it appears to rest on good authority. It comes direct from Honorable J. L. Nall, of Carthage, Missouri, grandson of Nancy Lincoln and William Brumfield, and was first published over his signature in 1881. The account which he gave was specific and detailed, and claimed to have been derived from what he had heard from his mother through her grandmother, the widow of the pioneer Abraham Lincoln. But Mr. Nall was incorrect in this and in very much besides. Captain Abraham Lincoln was not killed within the corporate limits of Louisville.

"Among the papers of Colonel Durrett is a sketch of Hughes' Station made by George Rogers Clark, and bearing this note in pencil in Durrett's handwriting:

"Bland W. Ballard states that the station was erected by Morgan Hughes in 1780; that it stood on Long Run in Jefferson County not far from the Baptist meeting house; that it consisted of eight cabins and four blockhouses at the four corners and that it was a weak fort, poorly built. In 1786, a man was killed here by an Indian while he was coming to the station from his land near by on Long Run, where he had been putting in a crop. His family resided in the station, and soon after his death the widow and children moved into Nelson County."

"Colonel Durrett added to this note a penciled query whether this man killed might have been the president's grandfather, but subsequently erased it, thinking that that event could not have occurred at so late a date as 1786, since the death of Lincoln seemed to have been fixed two years earlier.

"Major Bland W. Ballard, relating his narration before the name of Lincoln had become noted or seemed significant, and thinking it unimportant even to learn the name of the man killed, or to record it if he knew, as he probably did, tells the story of the death of this unnamed man almost exactly as we know from other sources the story of the death of Captain Lincoln. It occurred in the spring, when he was putting in his crop; it was near the fort; his family removed to Nelson County, in which was included the present county of Washington. It is no wonder Colonel Durrett raised the question whether it was not the president's grandfather whose death is thus described. But Colonel Durrett believed that the death of Abraham Lincoln occurred in 1784, and Major Ballard was explicit in his affirmation that this murder occurred in 1786. If we knew that the date 1786 was not impossible, we should have no doubt this description by Major Ballard, together with the testimony of President Lincoln, fixed the place and also gave the date of the tragedy.

"The survey of the Long Run tract of May 7, 1785, showed that Abraham Lincoln was certainly alive a full year later than the Lincoln family tradition affirmed. These facts, and a careful survey of the several alleged sites of the tragedy, had convinced me that the real date of the murder of Abraham Lincoln, the pioneer, was 1786, when Reverend Louis A. Warren discovered a further confirmation in a suit of Mordecai, as heir-at-law of his father, in which Mordecai made oath that his father, Abraham Lincoln, died intestate, in May, 1786. The day of the month is not stated.

"One other interesting and highly important document may

The Lincolns and Long Run

be cited here completing the proof of the location of the home of the pioneer Abraham Lincoln, and the place of his residence at the time of his death. It is a subscription list, dated September 18, 1786, signed by Bland W. Ballard, Morgan Hughes and the other neighbors in the vicinity of Long Run, to arm and equip an expedition against the Indians, the expedition to be commanded by George Rogers Clark. Most of the subscriptions are in kind, horses, cows, blankets and provisions. Halfway down the list is a gun, appraised at eight pounds, the gift of 'the Widow Lincoln!' This document is in the Library of the University of Chicago, and it adds the last essential argument to the proof already cited. We now know where the Lincoln's made their first home on the western side of the mountains, and where the tragedy occurred which President Lincoln was accustomed to say impressed him more than any tale he heard during his boyhood. 'The Widow Lincoln' did not remove to Washington County, where she had relatives, until she had harvested the pathetic crop which her husband was sowing when he was killed; she was still living on Long Run in September, 1786.

"Further investigations in the Hughes' Station neighborhood have resulted in a practical establishment of the site of the Lincoln home upon this Long Run farm, and also of the spring which supplied the water for the family. Unexpectedly, I have discovered also a considerable body of local tradition, which the records of the Long Run Church tend to confirm, as to the probable situation of the grave of the pioneer, Captain Abraham Lincoln.

"That he was buried upon his own farm appears almost certain, and that the land now within the enclosure of the Long Run Baptist Church, located on that farm, was the community burying-ground from the beginning of the settlement, appears equally evident. The church was organized in 1797, but the place was used for worship at a date still earlier. The tradition, which is unusually clear and consistent, is to the effect that several of the oldest graves, five at least, were covered by the brick church edifice, on its enlargement in 1860, and that one of these was the grave of Captain Lincoln. It is rather more than probable that the brick building still in use as a place of regular worship by the Long Run Church covers the mortal remains of Captain Abraham Lincoln."

Doctor Barton, in this portion of the first volume of his work, disposes also of the old story that there was a Mary Shipley Lincoln, and that she was the second wife, and the grandmother of the martyred president. There was no Mary Shipley Lincoln. Bathsheba Herring Lincoln, the only wife Captain Abraham Lincoln ever had, was the grandmother of Abraham Lincoln, the president, and was the widow of Captain Abraham Lincoln, and she took his children, after his murder, into Washington County and reared them there. He shows and proves that these children, five in number, two daughters and three sons, were neither brilliant nor famous, but made up "an honest, virtuous family;" that the youngest, Thomas, only six years old when his father was killed in 1786, married Nancy Hanks on June 12, 1806, and they were the parents of the president, born three years later, and whose grandfather, for whom he was named, sleeps 'neath the flooring of the old Long Run Baptist Church, just at the forks of the creek from which it takes its name, just over the Shelby County Line, and in Shelby, on the edge of Jefferson.

4 Lincoln, 200 yds N of Baptist Ch. Br. of Long Run, June 12, 1922. S. M. Talbott, Rev. W. E. Barton, O. T. Proctor, Miss Lucie J. Kinkead, T. C. Fisher + Rev. L. A. Warren at site of old Abraham Linkhorn cabin in N.E. cor. of Jefferson Co. Ky. near Shelby Co. line.

2 Lincoln, Tree near, Barton + Proctor standing, at Abraham Linkhorn's spring, 200 yards N. of Baptist Church branch of Long Run, in Shelby Co. near Jefferson Co. Ky. line. June 12, 1922.

CHAPTER V

*Distinguished Attorney's Reminiscence**

On the twenty-fifth day of December, 1871, in the old ramshackled red brick court house in Shelbyville, Kentucky, in lawyer's parlance, I was "sworn in" before that upright and learned judge, that splendid and courteous gentleman, Confederate Congressman and Confederate Veteran, Honorable H. W. Bruce of Louisville.

The redoubtable Colonel Phil Lee was the Commonwealth's Attorney. After all these years I still believe he was the greatest and most effective advocate before a jury I ever heard. His wit and humor sparkled like old wine, his pathos touched the hearts of men like the wail of a distressed child, and his sarcasm, which he seldom used, bit like a hornet's sting.

I remember on one occasion we were leaning against one of the old stone gate posts in front of the courthouse when an ardent admirer of the old Confederate came up, greeted him affectionately and said, "Colonel Lee, I was an old Rebel too." The Colonel with beaming face immediately asked him to what company he belonged. I forget his answer, but it was either Morgan, Forest or Wheeler, and the Colonel looked him straight in the face and said, "Oh, Hell, you were not in the army, you belonged to the cavalry."

When I recall his friendship for me when a mere boy and my fondness for him I cannot forget the scene when his brave spirit passed just as the dawn was breaking cold and gray on an autumn morning with no one in the room but his wife and myself.

That inimitable wit and story teller, Dick Owen, was circuit clerk. His friends often chided him about being too fond of his cups. He would say, "I may get drunk, but my books

---
*The chapter is an extract from a talk delivered by Judge Luther Clay Willis at a home banquet to leading attorneys of the State in 1921, celebrating his fiftieth anniversary at the bar of this circuit court district, where he has long been the dean of his profession.

never do." And if you should go through Order Books, seven, eight and nine you will find that he told the truth about his books for they are models of neatness and accuracy. Dick was severely wounded in the battle of "Anteitam" and left on the field as dead, but in the darkness of the following night his gallant brother, Colonel Bob Owen of Mississippi, and a comrade crept through the dead and dying on that bloody field and at the risk of their lives, carried him to safety. Forty years afterwards when one of my daughters was at the old Mary Baldwin School in Staunton, Virginia, the president of the school, a grand and gracious old lady, when she learned I knew Dick, took me into the basement and showed me the little hidden room where he was nursed back to strength. When I came back I told Dick about it; he was overcome with memories and emotions, tears rolled down his cheeks and he said, "God bless those Virginia women."

H. C. Malone (Clint, we called him), was sheriff. He looked at that time to be a mere boy, slender and modest. A stranger would have thought him timid—yet he had the heart and courage of a "Black Prince." It was Clint Malone who met General John Morgan when escaping from the Columbus Penitentiary, conducted him to his father's home in this County which is now the family residence of the Pickett family, and afterwards, together with some friends, conducted him into Confederate lines.

Colonel T. O. Shackleford, who always maintained the reputation of being the best dressed man in Kentucky, and a Chesterfield in manner, was master commissioner, too old to be a soldier.

C. J. Hinkle, the County Attorney was a cripple, not fit for a soldier, but his handsome and dashing young brother, only a few months before the end of the war, gave his life for the South.

Across the hall was Colonel John F. Davis, then the County Clerk. He was Quarter Master in the Confederate Army, and it was said he could find food and provender for his regiment where a jackal would starve to death.

My reason for referring to the military service of these men is that the young men may understand the trend of public sentiment and sympathy in those days. There were many able and distinguished lawyers who resided here or attended the court, some of them of State and National reputation. But all officers and attorneys are gone—not one of them is alive now.

Tonight, memories of them gather thick and fast about me. I can almost see their faces and hear their voices. I feel that to me a part of this occasion is in memory of them. "Oh, for the touch of a vanished hand, and the sound of a voice that is still."

CHAPTER VI.

A Document of its Time

Know all men by these presents that John Blackbourn, Issac Rendfroe, Bland W. Ballard, James Bradshaw, William Renfroe, Chichester Benson; all of the State of Kentucky and counties of Henry, Shelby, Lincoln and Garrett and Elisha Wallin, John Wallin, and James Renfroe, all of the county of Claibourn, State of Tennessee, vein the penal sum of ten thousand dollars to each other to be levied on our goods & chattells lands & teniments if defalt be found in the condition under written. That is to say whereas the sd John Blackbourn, Issac Rendfroe, Bland W. Ballard, James Bradshaw, Chichester Benson, William Renfro, Elisha Wallin, John Wallin & James Renfro have this day a flattering prospect of obtaining & finding a silver mine sd formerly to be occupied & worked at by a Mr. John Swift together with the Hopes of finding a number of dollars & crowns sd to be Hid by the sd Swift, now if this Companey or only part of them Shall be so successful as to find the same we jointly agree and covinant to each that we will make An Equal Divide and go our Equal Shair in all Profits and Lossis that may occur by venture of the foresaid enterprise and that we will not Directly or Indirectly make known the plan (or place) to any other person or persons whatever without the Consent of three or more of the sd Companeys Consent nor take in any other Person or Persons in any wise whatever except as Shaires in the mine and not in the silver already sd to be bouried and Hid and that we will further make such exertions and no such other things as shall be only and of advantage to the Promoting the intrust and advantage of each other as a Companey in the above mentioned persuit and do further by these presents discontinue all others who have here to fore be a part of sd Companey until sutch times as satisfac-

tion be maid for their conduct in witness whereof we have here unto set our Hands and seals this second day of november 1810.
atest
  Judith Renfro
  Mary Renfro

                      John Blackbourn
                      Issac Renfro
                      Bland W. Ballard
                      James Bradshaw
                      Winchester Benson

  Note that the above named James Bradshaw and for the use of his name in the body of the within obligation is done with consent and approbation of us, the undersigned.

                      Chichester Benson
                      Bland W. Ballard
                      John Wallin
                      James Renfro

PART VII
OFFICIAL STATISTICS AND RECORDS

CHAPTER I

Shelby County Tax List—Kentucky

1792—1795

Adams, James; Allen, Robert P., 700 Hardin County, Kentucky; Allen, Montgomery; Allen, Thomas; Allen, Ann, 226 on Meadow Creek, Shelby County; Akers, Benj.; Ashby, Obediah; Ashby, Tinson; Ashby, Stephen; Akers, Thomas; Akers, Joseph; Akers, Simon; Anderson, John; Allen, Elizha; Anderson, James; Ashcraft, Elizabeth; Acher, Joseph; Anderson, Geo.; Addams, Samuel; Addams, John; Addams, William; Allen, Andrew; Allen, James; Allen, John; Addams, Hugh.

Brent, John; Brent, Matthis; Brown, Ruben; Bullock, Wingeld; Blackwell, James, 240 A. Jefferson; Brown, James; Boles, Thomas; Boles, James; Brent, Christopher; Boyd, William; Boswell, Geo., 108 Brashears Creek; Barnett, William; Butler, William, 500 on Benson, 333 on Bullskin 50 Brennon Lick; Butler, Philip; Boals, Ambrose; Best, Samuel; Ballard, James, 250 acres on Brashe, 200 Beech; Bush, John; Bradberry, William, 100 Beech (1795); Burgen, William, 78 Beech Creek; Briscon, James, 100 Beech Creek; Baskett, John; Baskett, William; Brooks, Paul; Bennet, Daniel, 50 Tick Creek; Bell, Armiger, 338 acres on the Ohio River, in Mason County, 1792; Brown, James, 100 Braeshears, 1792; Burress, Charles, under 21; Bridgewater, William; Bell, Elizabeth, 2,000 on Grave Logan County (Robt. Bell); Baggs, John; Bennett, Daniel, 100 Elk Creek, 1792; Benett, Burrel; Belderback, Jacob; Basey, Richard, 210 Nelson; Bolyles, Henery (Balyles); Bradshaw, John.

Conner, John; Clark, Everett; Compliment, William; Campbell, Geo., 97 acres Gist Creek; Conger, Moses; Clark, Zacharia; Clark, John; Conrad, Geo., 50 acres on Beech;

Cerass, Simon, 200 on Beech; Cash, Warren; Carson, William; Clark, Joseph; Comstock, Oliver; Clutter, Simon, Jr., Gipsey, 52 acres; Crawford, John; Crawford, William; Clark, Benj.; Crutchfield, William, 120 acres on Long Run; Cayse, Billey; Cayse, Charles, 60 acres; Combs, Andrew; Case, Jacob; Carlin, Matthias, 210 Buck Creek; Clark, Saml.; Cull, James; Curd, Edmond, 800 acres Brash., 2,312 Ohio River; Conley, John, 51 acres Brash.; Carris, Benj. H., 146 acres Brash.; Cook, Isaac; Crawford, John, 50 acres on Elk Creek; Combs, Thomas, 50 acres on Elk Creek; (Cunningham, Francis—Salt River (Campbell County); Cotten, William; Crist, Geo., 50 acres Elk Creek; Crawford, Nathan, 500 Clear Creek; Cox, Benj., 50 acres Wises Run; Carlin (Kirlin), John; Cyphers, Mathias.

Davidson, Gorge; Davidson, William; Dodson, John; Dooley, James; Dooley, Saml.; Dupey, John, 112 Elkhorn, Woodford County; Dupey, James; Dougherty, Thos.; Dougherty, William; Dedmore, Abram, 130 A. Beech Creek; Denbo, Thos.; Dikes, Elijah; Duncan, Marshall, Duncan, William; Dorcas, (?) John; Dorcas, William; Devore, Saml.; Dewitt, Jacob; Devore, James, Duncan, James; Dougherty, Michael; Davis, William.

Elliott, Thos.; Eaken, Alex; Ellis, John; Eaken, John; Ellison, Robt.; Evans, Robert; Evans, David; Elliott, William; Elliott, Robt., 100 A. on Brashers Creek; Elliott, John, 100 A. on Brashers Creek.

Frazier, James; Ferguson, Saml., 100 A. Elk Creek; Ferguson, William, Jr., 170 Gist; Farmer, Chas.; Frank, Elijah; Farmer, Joel; Foreman, Thos., 250 A. Phub Creek; Fullenwider, Henry.

Griffey, Thos.; Gwin, Thomas I., 230 A. Clear Creek; Graves, David, 200 Buck Creek, 1792; Graves, Edmond; Gill, Beda, (Beeda); Gill, James; Green, Richard; Gray, Robert, 150 A. on Gist Creek; Gamble, William, 100 A. on Gist Creek; Gore, Frederick; Goodvine, Thomas; Gentry, Hugh; Gregory,

First Tax List

Will; Griffin, Wm.; Glover, Jonah, 300 A. on Buck Creek; Griffith, Eli; Greggs, David.

Hill, Forges; Hansley, (Hamley), James; Hansley, John; Huff, Luke, 700 Brasheres c.; Huff, Abm.; Hall, Moses, 500 Cedar Creek, Franklin County, 490 Campbell County; Ham, Jacob; Holmes, Andrew, 286 Gipsey Creek, Shelby; Ham, Mathias; Ham, David; Hansley, Barman; Hostedler, Abram, 110 on Buck Creek (Beech); Hostedler, Christian, 287 Beech Creek; Horns, John; Holmes, James, 300 A. Clear; Honrey, James; Harbart, Josiah, 111 Gist; Harbart, Thomas; Harrison, Geo.; Hansley, Richardson; Hansley, Jonathan; Hansbrough, John, 100 A. Tick Creek; Harmon, Joesph, 100 on Beech; Hartman, Abm., 468 on Gist, 108 Snake Run, 185 Beech; Hillman, Benj.; Harter, Adam, 108 Gist Creek, 250 Corn Creek; Hartman, Anthony, 71 A. Bresheares Creek; Hart, Philip; Hicklin, Hugh, 126 A. Elk Creek; Henry, Jesse; Hantan, Darby; Humphras, Mirry; Haynes, John, 50 Elk Creek; Hornsby, Joseph, 400 Washington County, 2,400 Plumb Creek, 400 Fox Run, 400 Kentucky River.

Ingram, Archer.

Johnston, John; Johnston, John, James, Geo.; Jonkerston, Andrew; Johnson, Lanty; Johns, Henry, 100 Elk Creek; Johnson, William, 50 A. Elk; Johnston, John; Johnson, Edw.; Johnson, David; Johnson, John.

Kuykendall, Peter, 125 on Gist Creek; Kester, Paul, 50 A. Elk Creek; Kester, William, 150 Elk Creek; Kester, John, 175 Elk Creek; Knox, (?) Jacob; Knap, Joshua; Killin, Robt.; Kare, Moses, 200 A. on Salt River; Kuykendall, Mathew; Kare, Absolem, 450 Elk Creek; Kinkead, Robt., 156 A. Bresh Creek.

Logan, David; Lee, William; Lane, Craven; Lane, John; Lindsey, Vechel; Lindsey, Elisha; Lapp, John; Liston, Edmond, 50 A. Elk Creek; Lymen, David; Long, Saml.; Letherman, Peter, 150 Buck Creek; Letherman, Nancy, 370 Buck Creek; Lishy, (Lasly?), Gilliam, 100 A. Clear Creek; Linsey,

William; Logan, Alexander; Lane, Lambert; Lane, Thos.; Lane, James; Lucke, Abm.; Lukes, John; Lemmon, James; Lasly, Nancy; Legon, Wilson; Lowry, Robert; Lamb, Geo.; Lemmens, Robert.

McCarter, Robert; Morlan, John; Morrow, Philip; Morton, James, 150 Gist, 250 Beech; McCourtney, Jane, 59 Elk Creek; Maddox, Absolom; McClanon, Joseph; M i l l e r, David; Miller, Conrad; Mahuron, Silas; Mahuron, Othenal; Mahuren, Saml.; Meeks, (Muks), Priddy, 50 A. Beech; Melone, Drurey, 231 Brashears Creek; Matingly, James, 300 Gist; McMannis, John, 100 Gypsey Creek; Montgomery, Geo.; McGlachen, James, (McLaughlin); McCormack, John, 171 Beech; Meeks, Jesse; Maginnis, John, 82 on Gist; Malin, Isaac, 92 Beech Creek; McKinley, James, 77 Gist; Miller, David, 100 Breshers; Martin, Thos., 100 Breshers; Malone, Benj.; Massie, William, McClannon, William; Martin, Nimrod; McCampbell, James; McDaniel, James; McGren, Joseph; McDowell, Chas.; McDaniel, Daniel, 200 Buck Creek; Miser, John; McBride, Robert; Miller, Isaac; McMaster, Michael; McClure, John, 100 Ducks Creek, Lincoln Co.; Montgomery, John, McCourtney, John; McCampbell, Saml., 250 Bullskin; Martin, Lewis, 57 A. Tick; McKinley, John, 70 Snake Run; Martin, Saml.; McCormack, William, 80 Beech; Merriwether, Nicholas; McClain, David; McMamess, John; McClelland, Daniel; Murray, William; McNanes, John; Murray, Wm.

Newman, Henry; Neal, Wm., Beech; Nation, Geo.; Northsinger, Andrew; Nearn, Mordici; Norman, Isaac; Norris, John.

Owen, Joseph; Owen, Robert; O'Leckland, John; Outhouse, Peter, 50 Elk Creek; Osburn, Jonathan.

Paul, Priscilla, 200 A Buck Run; Price, William, 600 A. Little Beaver, Logan County; Price, Frederick; Patterson, William, 83 A. on Brasheres, 1792; Parkers, Thomas; Pulliam, Robert; Pounds, Thos., 76 A. on Elk Creek, 1792; Peeck,

First Tax List

(Puck), John; Payne, John; Perkins, John, 250 on Gist; Paddock, Jonathan, 50 on Gist; Patton, Ebenezer, 400 Brashears Creek; Pounds, Joseph, 50 A. Elk Creek; Polly, John; Polly, Peter, 150 on Buck; Prewitt, Elisha, 300 A. Wolf Run; Pennington, Isaac, 100 Elk Creek, from Frederick County, Va.; Phigley, Simon, 137½ A. on Brasherses Creek; Polk, Charles, 540 on Brasherses; Price, David, 198 on Brasherses; Parkers, Thomas.

Quirk, James, 100 acres on Gist Creek.

Roberts, Agnes, 200 A. on Roberts Run; Richardson, Ephriam; Reid, (Rud), Alexander, 200 acres on Roberts Run; Reid, James; Roberts, Henry; Reid, Barnet, 52 A. Elk Creek; Reid, Caleb, 300 A. Elk Creek; Ruble, Adam, 80 A. on Buck Creek, 1792; Robins, James; Randolph, William; Reaser, Michael; Ritchie, Thomas, 148 A. Jepsey Creek; Rodman, Thomas; Ruble, Jacob, 71 A. on Gist; Rebel, Jonathan; Ritchie, Jacob; Rosemyer, Frederick; Reid, Saml.; Roberts, George, 1,000 A. on Pitman & Roberts Creek, Green County; Rid, Joshua, 89 A. on Elk Creek; Rose, Alexander; Rose, John; Richardson, James, Sr., 100 A. on Wises Run; Richardson, James, Jr.

Shannon, James; Simpson, Agnes; Simpson, John; Simpson, Joseph; Stevenson, Robert; Still, Murphy; Sharp, Anthony; Scott, Arter, 220 A. on Brashears; Sorrels, Ellender; Spears, Joshua; Stanley, Joseph; Shafer, (?), David; Snider, Peter, 200 A. on Buck Creek; Satterley, Saml., 100 A. on Buck Creek; Spencer, Walter; Shephard, John, 100 A. on Buck Creek; Smith, John, 500 A. on Buck Creek; Shindler, Geo.; Sharp, John, 100 Gipsey; Smith, Daniel, Shelburn, Dionysius, 160 Gipsey Creek; Sutton, Ephriam; Stepleton, Andrew, 219 A. on Buck Creek; Shelburn, Augustine, 100 A. on Buck Creek; Smith, William, 25 A. on Gist; Smith, John; Smith, Nicholas, 1,500 on Drummons Lick; Smith, Jacob; Stevens, Saml.; Stone, Benj.; Silkwood, Barzella, 100 A. on Bresheres; Sturgin, John, 100 A. on Bresheres; Sturgin, John, Jr., 75 A.

on Bresheres; Sturgin, James, 50 A. on Bresheres; Sturgin, Robt., 164 A. on Bresheres; Scott, John, 190 A. on Bresheres; Stone, William; Spencer, John, 219 A. on Bresheares; Spears, Paul; Starks, Jonathan; Starks, Jonathan; Stilwell, Joseph, 50 A. on Elk Creek; Stark, Christopher, 200 A. on Elk Creek; Starks, James, 63 A. on Elk Creek; Simpson, James; Stark, Daniel, 90 A. on Elk Creek; Stark, John, 162 A. Wolf Run; Stark, Jacob, 50 A. on Elk Creek; Stark, Danl., Jr.; Shively, Henry; Shaw, Jacob, 50 A. on Brashers; Starks, James; Sutterfield, Jesse; Swann, Edw.; Stuk, James; Stice, Andrew; Steel, James; Steel, Jonah; Stark, Jonathan; Spencer, Spear, 100 A. on Brashers; Stilwell, John, 93 on Elk; Shannon, Thomas, 300 A. on Clear, 750 Six-Mile; 400 Green County; Shannon, Saml., 700 on Clear; 400 on Mulberry, 400 Meadow Run, 560 on Bullskin; 1,680 in Hardin County; Standiford, Israel; Swesey, James; Sharvis, Davis; Smith, Nicholas; Smith, Jacob.

Todd, John, 162 A. on Gist; Tesgarden, Basel, 180 on Buck Creek; Tilly, Lazarus, 100 A. on Buck; Tilly, Aaron, 100 A. on Buck; Tinsley, Saml., 250 A. Buck; Tinsley, Jonathan, 50 A. Buck; Thomson, Saml.; Taylor, Thomas; Thacher, Joseph, 100 A. on Brasheres; Thomson, John; Tichenor, Jacob, 50 A. on Brasheres; Thomas, John; Taylor, Philip, 700 A. in Hardin; Tucker, Jacob; Tuker, William; Tyler, Robert, 637 on Gist, 77 on Tick Creek, 700 on Drennons Lick; Talbet, Ezekial.

Ullery, Jacob, 100 A. on Brasheres.

Voris, Francis; Veach, Benj.; Van de Venter, Winnet.

Whitaker, Martha, 200 Clear Creek; Webb, Augustine; Whitaker, Levi; Whitaker, John, Jr.; West, Richard; Whitaker, Elijah, 300 on Buck; Whitaker, John, Sr., 300 A. on Buck Creek, 700 A. in Bullit County, 400 A. in Franklin; Whitaker, Isaac, 250 A. on Buck Creek; Whitaker, Jesse, 400 Franklin; Winlock, Joseph, 294 A. on Bullskin; Whitaker, Abm., 522 on Clear Creek; Webb, Saml., 100 on Beech Creek;

First Tax List

Washburn, Geo., 192 A. on Beech; Wyley, Henry; Waddy, Saml., 300 A. Beech Creek, 1792; Wright, Obediah; Wayman, Edmond; Wright, John, 103 Gypsey (?); Williams, Josiah, 135 Beech Creek; Woodard, Michael; Wise, Tobias; Walker, Lewis; Williams, Joshua; White, David, 100 A. on Long Run; Webb, John; Woods, Thomas; Woods, Saml.; White, Peter, Sr., 100 A. on Bullskin; White, Joseph, 300 Elk Creek; White, Sarah; Wilson, Isaac; Williams, John.

Young, John, 225 A. Clear Creek, 225 in Hardin County; Young, Edw.

Lists not given in—Graves, Edmond; Greggs, David, given in since returned; Glenn, Wm.; Adams, David; Estes, Wm.; Shaw, Jacob; Paul, John; Spender, John.

List not sworn to—Pattrick, Robert; Blackburn, Rob; Whit, Abraham; Grigery, John; Simmons, Robt.

Persons names not given in on account of their not knowing which county they belong to—Collings, Spencer; Collings, Thomas; Collings, Benj.; Bussbey, Danl.

CHAPTER II

Senators and Representatives

Shelby County Members General Assembly from 1793 to 1929.

Senate—David Standiford, 1796-1800; Jos. Winlock, 1800-1810; John Allen, 1810-1814; Jas. Simrall, 1814-1818; Jas. Ford, 1818-1822; Samuel W. White, 1822-1830; Wm. G. Boyd, 1830-1838; Geo. W. Johnston, 1838-1842; Walter C. Drake, 1842-1846; Wm. C. Bullock, 1850, 1853-1857; Martin D. McHenry, 1851-1853; Walter C. Whitaker, 1857-1861.

House of Representatives—Wm. Shannon, 1793; Benj. Logan, 1795; John Knight, T. J. Gwyer, 1796; W. Ballard, Jos. Winlock, 1799; John Allen, 1800; Bland W. Ballard, 1800, 1803, 1805; Simon Adams, 1801; Alex Reed, 1801, 1802; John Pope, 1802; Jas. Wardlaw, 1803; M. Flournoy, 1805; Alex. Reid, 1806; John Simpson, 1806, 1809, 1810, 1811; Major G. W. Ballard, 1808; Abraham Owen, Thos. Johnson, 1808, 1809, 1810; Jas. Moore, 1811; Jas. Young, 1811, 1812; Samuel Tinsley, 1812; Thos. Johnson, 1812, 1813; Major Samuel W. White, 1813, 1814, 1819, 1835; Jas. Ballard, 1813, 1814; George B. Knight, 1814, 1815, 1817, 1818; Jas. Ford, 1815, 1816, 1824, 1825, 1826, 1827, 1828, 1834, 1835, 1840, 1844; John Logan, 1815, 1816, 1817, 1818, 1825; Benj. Eggleston, 1816; Benj. F. Dupuy, 1817; Benj. Logan, 1818; Jos. W. Knight, Samuel Oglesby, 1819; Wm. G. Boyd, 1820; George Piercy, 1820, 1821; Cuthbert Bullitt, 1820, resigned November 15, succeeded by Wm. Logan, 1821; John Wells, Henry Smith, 1822; George Woolfolk, 1822, 1828; Thos. P. Wilson, 1824, 1826, 1831; Henry Crittenden, 1824, 1828, 1831; Alex. Reid, 1825, 1826, 1827; David W. Wilson, 1827; Samuel Shannon, 1829, 1836; Percival Butler, 1829, 1830, 1832; Geo. W. Johnston, 1829, 1832, 1850; Andrew White, 1830, 1833; Jas. C.

217

Sprigg, 1830, 1834, 1837, 1838, 1839, 1840, 1851-1853; Jas. M. Bullock, 1831, 1836; Isham T. Underwood, 1833; Nicholas Smith, 1837; Wm. C. Bullock, 1838; John A. Logan, 1839; Wm. Welch, Walter C. Drake, 1841; Robert Doak, Wm. S. Helm, 1842; Lloyd Tevis, Fleming L. Garnett, 1843; Martin D. McHenry, 1844, 1846; Shannon Reid, Jas. G. Bales, 1845; Wm. L. Jones, 1846, 1848; John Brower, Hartwell A. Bailey, 1847; Josiah H. Magruder, 1848; Tandy M. Allen, Gideon Mitchell, 1849; Thos. Todd, 1850; Jas. L. Caldwell, 1851-1853, 1857-1859; Marion C. Taylor, Thos. Jones, 1853-1855; Archibald C. Brown, Joshua Tevis, 1855-1857; Stephen T. Drane, 1857-1859; Henry Bohannon, 1859-1865; Fielding Neil, 1859-1861; Jos. W. Davis, 1865-1867; Culvin Sanders, 1867-1869; John F. Wight, 1869-1871; Jos. P. Foree, 1871-1873.

The Representatives from this time forward were in the order named:

Thos. W. Hinton, John F. Wight, John A. Thomas, G. N. Robinson, Harrison Bailey, J. C. Beckham, G. N. Robinson, J. J. Long, John Botts, Newton Bright, P. J. Foree, Michael O'Sullivan, S. W. Booker, J. A. Frazier, Elliott B. Beard, John W. Holland, Dr. W. R. Ray, Geo. L. Pickett, W. T. Beckham, John Edwin Brown, E. J. Doss.

Those of the Senate from 1878, who were residents of Shelby County were in the order named:

William Anderson, Newton Frazier, Philip J. Beard.

CHAPTER III

Delegates in Constitutional Convention

The State records of the compact with Virginia in 1789, and of the Constitutional Convention held in Danville in 1792, do not give the names of the representatives composing the convention.

Shelby County's delegates in the Constitutional Convention of 1799, were Benjamin Logan and Abraham Owens. In the third Constitutional Convention in 1850, Shelby was represented by Andrew S. White and John W. Johnstone; and in the fourth Constitutional Convention of 1890-91, by J. C. Beckham.

CHAPTER IV

*Shelby County Judges**

Robert Doak	1852-1856
Joseph P. Foree	1856-1860
James L. Caldwell	1860-1870
Erasmus Frazier	1870-1878
Joseph P. Foree	1878-1888
J. W. Crawford	1888-1891
W. H. Tipton	1891-1901
Edwin H. Davis	1902-1910
Ralph W. Gilbert	1910-1918
Edward T. Pollard	1918-1926
Geo. L. Willis, Jr.	1926-

Some of the earlier Justices of the Peace and Justices of the "Court of Quarterly Sessions," were: Martin Daniel, Benj. Roberts, Thomas L. Gwin, Thomas Shannon, Joseph Winlock, Daniel McClelland, Abraham Owen, David Demaree, Robert Jeffies, Obadiah Clark, Elias Cooper, Thomas Mitchell, Geo. T. Wilcox, Zach Carpenter, Peter Thurston, Peter Tichoner, J. Simrall, James Young, James C. Burnett, Samuel Ward, Robert Doak, Thos. Hornsby, Saml. Waddy, D. Shelburne, Gen. Pearcy, Wm. Shanks, Phillip W. Taylor, Frederick Dayhoff, Chas. Mitchell, Seth Cook, B. T. Dupuy, Wm. Neill, Ben Mason, Saml. Harbison, Stephen Drane, Robt. T. Robb, Wm. Kin Kerde, Josiah Magruder, Gen. Bergen, R. D. Waters, Curry White, Jesse Robinson.

---

*Under the first and second constitutions, 1792 and 1799, the county courts were constituted of, and presided over by Justices of the Peace and Presiding Justices, appointed as each new County was created, by the Governor, upon recommendation of the Representative and Senator from the District concerned. There were no County Judges until 1852, and if the County Judge of Shelby ever had the assistance of "two associate Judges," (made possible by the third constitution) the records do not so show.

CHAPTER V

County Clerks

William Shannon (Pro Tem)	1792-1793
James Craig	1793-1816
John Newland	1816-1818
James S. Whittaker	1818-1851
Hector A. Chinn	1851-1858
John T. Ballard	1858-1870
John F. Davis	1870-1882
Andrew J. Stephens	1882-1890
E. J. Doss	1890-1906
Ernest Tyler	1906-1908
Luther Black	1908-1918
Ezra Ford	1918-1926
James C. Ray	1926-

CHAPTER VI

Circuit Judges and Clerks

The first tribunals in the nature of Circuit Courts not supplied by the Presiding Justices of the Quarterly Sessions, were held until 1812, by justices appointed by the Governor. Those who served longest and up until about that date were:

Justices Alex Reid, D. Demaree, James Logan, Arthur Mac Gaughey, and Henry Davridge.

The latter became the first judge of the circuit in which Shelby was located and served for many years. James Craig (also County Clerk), being the clerk to serve the Court.

Beginning with the early 1830's, Judge Davridge was succeeded by James Pryor; he by Mason Brown, Samuel Cooper, and W. F. Bullock in turn, the latter served until after the making of the new constitution in 1850.

The clerks who succeeded Craig in those days of the first half of the century were: Robert and Samuel Tevis and William A. Jones.

Beginning under the regime in 1852, the circuit judges were: P. B. Muir, Thomas H. Throup (Pro Tem.), Geo. W. Johnstone, 1867; H. W. Bruce, 1869; W. L. Jackson, 1872; all of Louisville.

Judge S. E. DeHaven, of Oldham County succeeded Judge Jackson and he was succeeded by W. S. Carroll of Henry County, and he, after twelve years, by Judge Frank Peak, who served two years, resigning at the beginning of 1907, and was succeeded by Judge Chas. C. Marshall, who was still occupying the bench of this district in 1929.

The clerks serving under these later judges were: John Robinson, succeeded by Richard T. Owen, who served until 1884, when he was succeeded by T. C. Bailey, in 1884, he by W. M. Cardwell, in 1902, Cardwell by Frank R. Wight, in

1914, he by Rolla Tipton, in 1926, who died after a year and was temporarily succeeded by H. A. Campbell, until the election of M. A. Harbison, who took the office in 1928.

CHAPTER VII

Postmasters of Shelbyville

[Furnished by Miss Florence Ballard]

James Wardlow	1801-1802
Samuel McGaughey	1802-1804
James McGaughey	1804-1804
Winfield Bullock	1804-1813
Isaac Watkins	1813-1813
Abraham Smith	1813-1822
Robert Brenhams	1822-1830
John Lane	1830-1844
Henry Ellingwood	1844-1845
James Ellingwood	1845-1858
Randolph R. Russel	1858-1860
Pulaski Ellingwood	1860-1861
William Standeford	1861-1867
Basil H. Crapeter	1867 or 69-1881
Camden W. Ballard	1881-1886
Joseph N. Bell	1886-1890
James S. Vannalta	1890-1894
James M. Logan	1894-1898
Ludlow F. Petty	1898-1909
Mike Hughes	1909-1913
Arrin D. Todd	1913-1922
Samuel C. Hedden	1922-

CHAPTER VIII

Shelby County Marriages—1792-1800

[Copies from original bonds by Mrs. Katherine Bryant Smith.]

Ashby, Thomas—Polly Achers (Akers) ....Feb. 19, 1779
Adcock, Edmond—Mary Ford ....Nov. 28, 1794
Admire, George—Mrs. Sarah Lock ....June 2, 1800
Alexander, Benj.—Betsy Williams ....Aug. 26, 1798
Allen, John—Jean Logan ....Oct. 19, 1799
Anderson, James—Mary Montgomery ....Feb. 13, 1797
Anderson, James—Mary Whitaker ....Dec. 21, 1799
Anderson, Thomas—Sarah McCarty ....Dec. 10, 1799
Applegate, Benj.—Leasey Huss ....March 19, 1795
Ashby, Beasley (Benj.)—Polly Bradshaw ....Feb. 8, 1800
Baird, Charles—Catherine Tyler ....Jan. 22, 1798
Baker, Jesse—Betsey Weakley ....Feb. 19, 1799
Bean, Lewis—Sally Hensley ....Dec. 5, 1794
Bedwell, Thomas—Mary Holson ....April 15, 1799
Bell, John—Mary Demaree ....March 27, 1800
Bennett, Asa—Anny Wright ....Aug. 3, 1800
Best, John—Elizabeth Whitaker ....Jan. 25, 1794
Blanton, Jesse—Sarah Cozine ....Oct. 28, 1800
Boals, Ambrose—Jenny McCortney ....Jan. 2, 1796
Boiles, John—Harriet Jones ....April 16, 1799
Bols, Abraham—Geney McCortney ....Dec. 28, 1795
Bonta, Henry—Nancy Adams ....Sept. 2, 1799
Boone, Enoch—Lucy Goldman ....Jan. 29, 1797
Boone, Jonathan—Catherine Fullenwider .....April 10, 1793
Booth, John—Sallie Kinder ....
Boyd, Samuel—Agness Moore ....Dec. 21, 1797
Boyd, William—Ruthey Carr ....Dec. 28, 1798
Boyle Henry—Sarah Park ....May 22, 1797
Brackett, Jeremiah—Jesse Cardwell ....June 31, 1800
Brackett, Thomas—Polly Renshaw ....Dec. 16, 1799

Bradshaw, Thomas—Ann McGaughey ....Aug. 7, 1799
Brady, Jonathan P.—Jemima Hunter ....May 24, 1800
Brannon, Vinson—Elizabeth Arterburn ....Jan. 9, 1800
Breeden, Paul—Elizabeth Stanley ....Aug. 17, 1799
Breeden, William—Polly Breeden ....June 4, 1798
Brenton, Henry—Mrs. Hanna Gwin ....Sept. 7, 1798
Bright, Lewis—Polly Ford ....April 16, 1797
Brown, James—Isabel Brown ....Jan. 19, 1798
Brown, Robert—Margaret Johnson ....Feb. 5, 1799
Bruce, William—Sarah Polk ....Oct. 15, 1798
Buckhannon, Victor—Rebecca Tucker ....April 12, 1799
Bennett Asa—Anna Wright ....Aug. 3, 1800
Burton, Alexander—Mary Sutton ....April 16, 1799
Burton, George—Rebecca Lee ....May 7, 1797
Cain, Samuel—Sally Dugan 1799
Cameron, Robert—Mary Ann Shields ....Nov. 24, 1791
Campbell, George—Margaret Ferguson ....Sept. 29, 1796
Cardwell, Jesse—Jemimah Brackett ....June 31, 1800
Carlin, John—Francis Glover ....Oct. 3, 1800
Carr, Elijah—Seany Bean ....July 17, 1798
Carr, George—Jane Williams ....Nov. 28, 1796
Carr, Samuel—Sally Buzan ....Dec. 21, 1798
Castleman, Jacob—Sarah White ....Jan. 12, 1797
Chapman, Nathan—Jane Vancleve ....Jan. 7, 1796
Chenwith, John—Mary Buskirk ....March 11, 1793
Chenowith, Thomas—Nancy Collings ....Dec. 9, 1798
Childers, Thomas—Susanna Cobern ....April 6, 1798
Childras, Thomas—Rachel Munsey ....April 6, 1797
Clark, Jesse—Elizabeth Sullivan ....Feb. 15, 1799
Clark, John—Polly Nation ....May 25, 1799
Clark, Lewis—Polly McIntire ....Dec. 24, 1795
Clark, Ruben—Betsy Lacefield ....Dec. 27, 1794
Cline, John—Elizabeth Yunt ....Jan. 15, 1799
Cline, Nicholas—Elizabeth Favours ....March 4, 1794
Cochran, James—Catherine Casey ....Nov. 20, 1797

SHELBY COUNTY MARRIAGES

Coleman, Daniel—Elizabeth Connell .... Jan. 9, 1798
Colglazure Daniel—Mary Galbraith .... Jan. 15, 1798
Collins, Richard—Catherine Still .... Dec. 7, 1798
Collings, Spencer—Catherin Lucas .... Feb. 21, 1797
Congleton, William—Margaret Wilcox .... Jan. 11, 1800
Connelly, James—Milly Laukford .... Dec. 31, 1798
Connely, Thomas—Margaret Lowder .... Oct. 6, 1795
Cooper, Samuel—Hester Lindsey .... Jan. 9, 1795
Cox, David—Mehitable Boyd .... Dec. 5, 1798
Crawford, John—Sally Denbo .... Dec. 3, 1792
Crawford, Nathaniel—Nancy Hicks .... Nov. 3, 1797
Crawford, William—Nancy Denbou .... Sept. 22, 1796
Crockett, James—Nancy Ferguson .... Dec. 3, 1795
Crume, Jesse—Jane Cyphers .... May 4, 1795
Cull, John—Rachel McHenry .... Feb. 23, 1797
Curd, Edmund—Milly Herriford .... April 9, 1800
Cyphers, Mathias—Sarah Edwards .... July 8, 1794
Daugherty, Benj.—Miss Ralph Vancleve .... June 18, 1793
Daugherty, Thomas—Jane Smith .... Sept. 27, 1796
Davis, John—Charity Bryan .... Dec. 8, 1797
Davis, John—Rachel Munsey .... May 16, 1797
Davis, William—Charlotte Clifton .... June 1, 1798
Delaney, James—Mrs. Barsheby Coleman .... March 23, 1799
Demaree, Abraham—Nancy Stansberry .... Feb. 26, 1800
Demaree, David—Jane Kerns .... Dec. 25, 1792
Denbo, Robert—Mary Ann Crawford .... Feb. 27, 1797
Dining, Anthony—Susanna Hoke .... Dec. 12, 1796
Dennis, John—Effie Rawlings .... Jan. 7, 1796
Devore, James—Patsy Duncan .... Feb. 4, 1797
Dillon, John—Mary Mahurin .... April 15, 1798
Doyle, Farmer—Rebecca Coles .... June 15, 1799
Drake, Moses—Elizabeth Pound .... Sept. 9, 1800
Duley (Dooley), James—Betsy Denbou .... March 1, 1796
Duncan, Marshall—Sarah Johns .... April 6, 1799
Dykers, William—Susanna Carmichael .... April 2, 1799

Eakin, Alexander—Jenny Clark .... Dec. 11, 1797
Ealem, Richard—Elizabeth Sorrels .... Oct. 24, 1796
Edwards, David—Sussana Meeks .... Aug. 12, 1799
Elliott, John—Fanny Prewitt .... April 5, 1796
Favours, Thomas—Easter McNew .... May 14, 1800
Ferguson, Arthur—Sary Wilson .... March 15, 1798
Ferguson, David—Eve Kester .... Dec. 18, 1798
Ferguson, William—Easter Allison .... July 21, 1795
Field, Cane—Ann Lewis .... March 29, 1793
Fish, David—Frankey Sheppard .... Aug. 24, 1797
Fitzgarrold, Joseph—Caty Parkers .... June 18, 1799
Flemming, Enoch—Ann Cornwell .... April 30, 1799
Flude, Timothy—Mary Oliver .... May 29, 1796
Ford, Spencer—Susanna Bright .... March 14, 1796
Forgeson, Andrew—Rebecca Robins .... Oct. 21, 1800
Gallion, Elijah—Eliner Jenkins .... Nov. 19, 1799
Garret, Isaac—Elizabeth McDowell .... Dec. 8, 1794
Garrett, William—Sally Cully .... June 25, 1799
Garrett, William—Sally Gassaway .... Dec. 21, 1795
Gassaway, Nicholas—Dorothy Leatherman .... Oct. 28, 1800
Gill, George—Caty Bullard .... Aug. 8, 1800
Glass, Robert—Sally Owen .... Nov. 2, 1796
Gobin, James—Elizabeth Jacobs .... Nov. 12, 1799
Goddard, William—Winny Duree .... May 24, 1796
Gouterman, John—Anne Stark .... Dec. 4, 1800
Gott, Robert—Lydia Nichols .... Feb. 15, 1800
Graham, William—Patsy Shillady .... June 12, 1798
Graves, Dickey—Nelly Tilley .... Dec. 26, 1797
Green, Stephen—Mary Griffin .... Sept. 18, 1798
Gregory, Andrew—Mary Lunsford .... May 10, 1796
Gregory, John—Pricilla Brackett .... Sept. 20, 1796
Gregory, Joseph—Polly Kindle .... June 17, 1797
Gregory, William—Rebeckah Lane .... Jan. 17 1797
Haff, Abraham—Ann Whitaker .... Aug. 2, 1797
Halfland, Henry—Barshebah Monroe .... Dec. 11, 1800

Hall, Francis—Mrs. Elizabeth Elam ....Oct. 14, 1797
Hammond, Joseph—Esther Garrett ....May 22, 1795
Hansbrough, George—Nancy Howard ....April 27, 1799
Harris, John—Mary Carman ....April 10, 1797
Hart, Philip—Susanna Johnston ....Dec. 19, 1796
Hathaway, Philip—Nancy Miller ....Oct. 13, 1800
Hatton, John—Patsy Ellison ....Nov. 19, 1800
Hatton, Robert—Ann Harris ....Jan. 30, 1799
Hawkins, Claiborne—Mary McDowell ....Dec. 17, 1798
Hedden, Daniel—Nancy Tilly ....Dec. 1, 1798
Hedden, Gilbert—Barcella McHuren ....Nov. 19, 1799
Hedden, John—Sarah Howe ....Jan. 25, 1800
Henry, Jesse—Nelly Elliott ....March 18, 1799
Hensley, Berryman—Elizabeth Morgan ....Aug. 10, 1797
Hensley, Edmond—Polly Garrett ....Aug. 14, 1797
Hensley, Jonathan—Nancy Garrett ....Dec. 24, 1794
Hensley, Samuel—Allefer Cooper ....Dec. 31, 1794
Hickman, Daniel—Mary Dermon ....Feb. 12, 1799
Hill, Fergus—Jenny Perkins ....March 6, 1798
Hogland, Henry—Bersheba Monroe ....Dec. 8, 1800
Hogeland, Moses—Sarah Elgin ....Dec. 3, 1792
Hogland, Aaron—Elizabeth Agin ....no date on bond
Horton, Thomas—Elizabeth Hogland ....Aug. 5, 1795
Houghland, Elias—Sarah Wood ....Nov. 1, 1797
Houghstatler, Adam—Hannah Hartman ....June 20, 1797
Howard, Archabald—Clary Bean ....Jan. 29, 1799
Huckleberry, Jacob—Winney Allen ....Jan. 20, 1795
Hunter, Thomas—Percilly Milligan ....Feb. 19, 1799
Huss, Richard—Mary Sill ....Oct. 8, 1798
Infield, Thomas—Annie Fullenwider ....March 10, 1794
Ingles, John—Liddy Goben (widow) ....May 6, 1794
Irvin, Robert—Temperance Meek ....Jan. 8, 1795
Jacobs, Thomas—Elizabeth Cline ....June 28, 1796
Johns, Thomas—Sailly Reid ....April 6, 1799
Johnston, Daniel—Martha Sturgeon ....Nov. 14, 1796

Johnston, James—Jane Curry .... Jan. 31, 1797
Johnston, William—Darkus Casey .... March 11, 1799
Johnston, William—Jenny Miller .... July 3, 1798
Jones, Thomas—Polly Wood .... April 9, 1799
Jones, William—Elizabeth Metcalf .... Aug. 20, 1799
Kephart, Abraham—Rebecca Thorn .... March 18, 1796
Kennady, Samuel—Anne Evans .... Nov. 8, 1800
Kindall, Ewell—Elizab. Stephenson .... April 4, 1796
Kindell, Yelley—Nancy Clark .... Nov. 15, 1791
King, Nathaniel—Lucy Lemon .... April 23, 1800
Kulbrath, Samuel—Polly Colglazier .... March 29, 1799
Kysor, John—Catharine Forgason .... July 27, 1796
Lacefield, Jacob—Sarah Robertson .... Jan. 10, 1799
Lancaster, Jacob—Joanna Vanmeter .... Dec. 22, 1799
Landen, John—Sally Carr .... Jan. 11, 1798
Lane, Thomas—Anna Ellis .... April 10, 1799
Langford, Larkin—Rachel Tucker .... Jan. 26, 1797
Langley, Elisha—Jane Shepherd .... Feb. 11, 1797
Lasley, Robert—Hannah McCortney .... April 5, 1793
Leatherman, Christian—Barbary Hostidler ... Aug. 4, 1798
Leatherman, Frederick—Polly Lastly .... Aug. 21, 1797
Leatherman, John—Betsy Graves .... Feb. 3, 1797
Lee, Nathaniel—Isabelle Marrow .... Nov. 28, 1797
Leffear, Geo.—Mrs. Harriet Smith .... Feb. 25, 1800
Lindsey, Elisha—Sarah Holmes .... Sept. 1, 1797
Livenston, John L.—Mary Bryant .... Dec. 13, 1797
Lock, William—Elizabeth Teague .... Dec. 25, 1797
Lockhart, William—Jane Bowling .... May 5, 1796
Lockhart, Enoch—Betsy Bell .... May 18, 1798
Logan, David—Nancy McClelland .... May 28, 1800
Logan, Aaron—Matty Gill .... Aug. 15, 1797
Long, Samuel—Hannah Griffith .... July 27, 1798
Londen, John—Sally Carr .... Dec. 3, 1797
Ludwington, Esair—Betsey Dagernald .... March 25, 1800
Lyle, David—Sarah Slaughter .... Jan. 16, 1800

Shelby County Marriages

McClain, Alexander—Mary Gray .... June 12, 1800
McClain, George—Ann McHenry .... Jan. 21, 1797
McClain, John—Hephizabah Spencer .... Oct. 15, 1799
McClelland, Daniel—Mary Boyd .... March 7, 1799
McClure, Hugh—Polly Lewis .... Nov. 14, 1797
McCormack, William—Nancy Morton .... July 14, 1796
McCoy, James—Nancy Lane .... March 25, 1800
McCullough, James—Jane Perkins .... Jan. 24, 1793
McDonald, James—Jane Taylor .... March 8, 1798
McDowell, Daniel—Rhoda Stark .... July 7, 1794
McNeil, Benj.—Rachel Bryant .... June 12, 1797
McWade, Henry—Margt. Anderson .... Nov. 14, 1797
McWade, Henry—Mary Carmant .... June 12, 1797
Maddox, Daniel—Nancy Willis .... Oct. 9, 1798
Mahurin, Stephen—Sally Green .... Oct. 28, 1799
Marquiss, William—Lucy Griffin .... Aug. 28, 1797
Marshall, Robert—Elizabeth Glass .... Dec. 25, 1798
Martin, Abner—Polly White .... July 17, 1800
Martin, Lewis—Polly Wright .... Aug. 9, 1794
Martin, Wilford—Mary Winklefield .... Dec. 30, 1797
May, Francis—Mary McGren .... Dec. 20, 1796
Meek, Jeremiah—Mary Cromwell .... March 19, 1795
Meeks, John—Mary Hartman .... July 7, 1800
Meeks, William—Elizabeth Tinsley .... Aug. 27, 1799
Melone, Benjamine—Elizabeth McKinley .... Dec. 31, 1799
Metcalf, Isaac—Frances Jones .... Dec. 18, 1798
Metcalf, William—Elizabeth James .... Dec. 12, 1797
Millen, Alexander—Elinore Mayo .... Feb. 10, 1795
Miller, John—Mildred Johnston 1798
Miller, William—Melvinie Johnston .... July 26, 1798
Mitchel, Saml.—Agnes Tilley .... Dec. 4, 1798
Mitchel, Thomas—Rebecca Ketchum .... Feb. 19, 1799
Montfort, John—Nancy Mitchell .... Oct. 21, 1799
Montfort, John—Mary Saelburn .... Jan. 15, 1800
Monson, Allen—Sarah Griffin .... July 31, 1795

Montgomery, John—Lydia Lucas .... Oct. 20, 1796
Moore, William—Elizabeth Roberts .... June 28, 1799
Morris, William—Susan Courtney .... Feb. 15, 1794
Mosley, Edw.—Sarah Jones Elliott .... Nov. 21, 1791-7?
Mullikin, Burton—Jane Daugherty .... May 28, 1799
Munnet, Isaac—Hannah Carland .... May 19, 1799
Murphy, Denis—Sallie Postleweight .... Dec. 21, 1796
Neal, Archibald—Margaret Magner .... Nov. 17, 1795
Neal, Elias—Mrs. Margt Bowling .... Aug. 28, 1795
Neal, William—Sally Blackwell .... Aug. 31, 1796
Newman, Ezekil—Belsey Harrison .... April 20, 1797
Newman, Simeon—Margaret Harris .... May 2, 1797
Nicholas, William—Elizabeth Hunter .... March 27, 1800
Nichols, Reason—Elizabeth Williams .... Jan. 17, 1798
Noel, Bazel—Mary Gregg .... Oct. 8, 1794
Norris, John—Nelly McDowell .... Feb. 11, 1799
Nuttall, Price—Polly Ditto .... Dec. 22, 1797
Oliver, Joseph—Ann Blanton .... Jan. 7, 1800
Organ, John—Mrs. Elizabeth Bell .... Jan. 20, 1795
Osborne, Michael—Merry Swift .... Sept. 13, 1798
Owen, John—Patsy Talbot .... April 28, 1794
Owen, William—Susanna Cardwell .... Aug. 26, 1797
Parker, Joshua—Mary Patterson .... Aug. 7, 1800
Patterson, Arthur—Martha Allen .... May 24, 1798
Payne, Jeremiah—Sallie McCoy .... May 9, 1797
Payne, Jonathan—Elizabeth Wright .... Aug. 20, 1798
Pearce, David—Frances Pearce .... March 19, 1795
Pearcy, John—Rebeccah Radford .... Oct. 30, 1800
Pendergrass, Jesse—Betsy Moore .... April 24, 1797
Pennington, Isaac—Polly Lockheart .... Feb. 18, 1799
Perkins, Joseph—Caty Driskell .... Sept. 7, 1799
Perkins, Samuel—Polly Blake .... Dec. 29, 1797
Perkins, William—Jane Glen .... Jan. 24, 1793
Philips, John—Catharine Rible .... Aug. 11, 1800
Piles, Conradus—Nancy Baker .... Oct. 17, 1797

Shelby County Marriages

Polan, William—Polly Shuck	Oct. 23, 1798
Polly, John—Polly White	June 28, 1796
Prewitt, Joseph—Patsy Elliott	Dec. 19, 1796
Reading, William—Sarah Curd	Jan. 25, 1800
Reday, William C.—Sarah Fisher	May 25, 1796
Rees, Jacob—Betsy Gott	Feb. 21, 1800
Rees, Thomas F.—Polly Bright	June 20, 1797
Reid, Barnet—Susanna Stitlin	Dec. 10, 1792
Rhody, Chris—Isabell Busan	Dec. 20, 1797
Richardson, John—Nancy Best	Sept. 5, 1798
Ritchie, Jacob—Mary Martin	Aug. 25, 1794
Rivell, Joseph—Catharine Philips	Jan. 28, 1800
Roberts, Silvestil—Bethier Robins	Feb. 11, 1800
Robins, James—Mary Lastly	July 9, 1797
Robins, William—Rachel Hogland	Dec. 31, 1793
Ross, John—Sally Lane	Sept. 27, 1797
Ruble, Jonathan—Hanna Letherman	June 10, 1797
Sargent, Nelson—Oney Pollard	April 19, 1800
Scearce, Henry—Rebecca Weakley	Feb. 13, 1799
Scearce, Nathan—Lilly Weakley	Nov. 18, 1797
Scott, Martin—Jane Anderson	April 15, 1800
Scott, Robert—Elizabeth Kendall	Sept. 20, 1799
Scroggin, George—Anna Weakley	Feb. 12, 1800
Sebastin, Samuel—Sarah Carlin	Feb. 7, 1797
Sharp, Anthony—Rachel Ellison	March 6, 1794
Shields, James—Elizabeth Martin	Aug. 20, 1795
Shem, Cornelius—Polyn Nancy	June 12, 1798
Shipman, Stephen—Margaret Garrett	June 20, 1795
Shipman, William—Sarah Bradshaw	July 9, 1798
Sill, Adam—Ann Huss	March 26, 1797
Sill, Adam—Acenath Wright	Aug. 10, 1800
Simpson, Joseph—Elizabeth Cox	Aug. 8, 1798
Smith, Abraham—Mary Logan	Sept. 4, 1800
Smith, Adam C.—Mary Baker	April 1, 1797
Smith, Ebenezer—Betsy Graham	March 4, 1800

Smith, John—Jane Collins ....March 5, 1796
Smith, Robert—Elizabeth Nevil ....April 16, 1799
Smith, Samuel— ....Oct. 16, 1797
Smith Simon—Rebecca Wilson ....March 14, 1798
Smith, Stephen—Milly Lynch ....Dec. 18, 1798
Smock, Samuel—Rachel Robins ....Nov. 18, 1797
South, William—Nancy Mitchell ....Oct. 10, 1798
Stafford, Henry—Mrs. Mary Ritch ....July 3, 1799
Staples, Noah—Mary Mahulin ....June 21, 1796
Stark, Abraham—Sarah Stark ....June 6, 1798
Stark, Jacob—Margt. Stark ....Dec. 22, 1794
Stark, James—Rebecca Pounds ....Sept. 22, 1800
Stark, Jonathan—Rachel Devore ....Aug. 30, 1794
Steel, Charles—Polly Baker ....Feb. 19, 1799
Steel, Adam—Elizabeth B. Brook ....Dec. 12, 1799
Stephens, John—Sarah Prior ....Sept. 11, 1797
Stephens, William—Rachel McKinney ....Sept. 25, 1798
Steples, Noah—Betsy Oliver (widow) ....July 18, 1796
Stilwell, Daniel—Delilah Ashcraft ....March 26, 1798
Stout, James—Margaret Edwards ....Aug. 22, 1799
Sullivan, Dennis—Margt. Ferguson ....Oct. 12, 1799
Sut, Christ—Jenny Miller ....Nov. 11, 1797
Swayze, Samuel—Caty Campbell ....Jan. 5, 1799
Swayze, James—Elizabeth Starke ....Jan. 22, 1794
Taylor, George—Betsy Leatherman ....Feb. 4, 1797
Teague, John—Polly Harris ....Aug. 6, 1795
Teagarden, Bazel—Ann Todd ....Oct. 21, 1797
Terhune, Stephen—Mary Montfort ....Jan. 21, 1800
Theobald, Thomas—Patience Pendergrass ......Sept. 18, 1797
Thomas, William—Mary Cyphers ....Dec. 30, 1794
Thompson, Samuel—Polly Baird ....May 15, 1799
Threldkeld, Moses—Elizabeth Weakley ....Aug. 25, 1800
Townsend, Light—Betsy Duhṛoon ....June 1, 1796
Tracy, John—Catharine Fought ....Dec. 10, 1800
Trammel, John—Ellen Parris ....April 17, 1799

SHELBY COUNTY MARRIAGES

Truax, Obediah—Nelly Sturgeon ....Oct. 17, 1797
Tyler, Able—Charlotte Nevil ....Nov. 28, 1798
Tyler, Robert Jr.—Sarah Prichett ....Feb. 18, 1794
Underwood, Nathan—Betsy Wright ....April 11, 1797
Van Cleave, Benjamine—Sarah Kearns ....Dec. 30, 1800
Van Cleave, Aaron—Elizabeth Van Cleave ....March 4, 1794
Van Cleave, John—Mariah Kernes ....Nov. 8, 1794
Van Cleave, John—Eunes Van Cleave ....Sept. 22, 1794
Veech, George—Alleen Bowman ....Sept. 23, 1793
Wallace, Michael—Agnes Shannon ....May 21, 1795
Wallace, William—Sarah Shannon ....Nov. 16, 1794
Waller, Stephen—Tabitha Prewitt ....Dec. 14, 1799
Warford, Joseph—Mary Warford ....March 30, 1793
Warson, Alexander—Jane McDowell ....Oct. 14, 1797
Watson, John—Peggy Bradshaw ....Feb. 12, 1798
Watts, Mason—Deborah Ryker ....June 18, 1793
Weble, Adam—Jane Van Cleve ....Dec. 17, 1795
Wells, Edward—Phoebe Paddock ....Sept. 25, 1794
Whitaker, Acquilla—Drucey Price ....Feb. 5, 1795
Whitaker, Charles—Sarah James ....Jan. 21, 1795
White, Abraham—Abigail White ....Sept. 11, 1800
White, James—Anne Glenn ....May 2, 1797
White, John—Margaret McClelland ....Dec. 31, 1793
White, Robert—Nancy Perry ....March 17, 1800
Whitesides, Isaac—Elinor Ellis ....April 17, 1799
Wilkes, Samuel—Barbara Mattox ....Dec. 12, 1798
Williams, Bazel—Nancy Kees ....Feb. 27, 1798
Williams, Jacob—Jane Galbrath ....Dec. 16, 1795
Williams, Joseph—Easter Hambleton ....Aug. 21, 1797
Williams, Ruddy—Sarah Fisher ....May 25, 1796
Williamson, John—Charity Whitaker ....Aug. 19, 1795
Wills, John B.—Susanna Howard ....Feb. 4, 1797
Wilson, John—Prudence Munro 1793
Wise, Tobias—Mary Griggsby ....Sept. 4, 1795
Woodfield, John—Sally Sargent ....Feb. 15, 1800

Woodson, Joseph—Sarah Ford ....Sept. 18, 1798
Worthington, James—Hannah Perkins ....Dec. 8, 1797
Worthington, James—Milly Sorrels ....March 12, 1798
Wright, Asa—Phebe Martin ....Sept. 17, 1799
Young, Edward—Susanna McCartney ....April 15, 1794
Young, James—Nancy Booker ....Aug. 5, 1800
Young, Joseph—Polly Darkes ....April 4, 1798
Young, Saml.—Sophira Rollings ....Aug. 3, 1798

CHAPTER IX

Index First Will Book Shelby County, Ky.

Anderson, John
Bowling, William
Buzan, Jesse
Buchannan, Wm.
Breeding, Richard
Boyles, David
Boyd, William
Boyd, Mary
Brown, James
Boswell, George
Butlor, Eliza
Briscoe, James
Connely, John
Clarke, John
Daniel, Robert
Dorning, Oliver
Dunn, John
Elam, Richard
Fullenwider, Henry
Fetty, John
Flover, Jonah
Ford, John
Green, Johnathan
Garrett, John
Gassaway, Richard
Green, Catharine
Haneil, Philip
Hogland, Richard
Hill, Hardy
Hansbrough, Monias
Hartman, Anthony

Jacobs, Thomas
Johnson, Philip
Leatherman, John
Lemaster, Richard
Lastley, Robert
Lewis, John
Lane, Lambert
Lawrence, David
Metcalf, James
McClain, Saml.
Meeks, Jesse
McClelland, Daniel
McCampbell, James
McClure, James
McClain, John
Newland, Jacob
Newland, Isaac
Newland, Lucy
Owen, George
Owen, Brackett
Perkins, William
Pruitt, Michael
Potts, John
Pennington, Isaac
Powell, William
Robins, William
Reid, James
Redding, William
Shannon, Wm.
Smith, Jacob
Shields, Patrick

Stout, James
Sled, William
Shannon, Thomas
Shuck, Andrew
Squires, John
Thompson, Thomas
Van Cleave, Ralph
Wilson, Samuel

Warford, David
Whitaker, John
Walker, Joseph
Whitaker, Jesse
Williams, William
Williams, Elizabeth
Young, Nelson

CHAPTER X

Revolutionary Soldiers

(Pensioned Under the Act of March 18, 1818.)

Alvis, Jesse, Private, Virginia Line; September 16, 1819; June 24, 1819; $96. Age 77.

Ballew, Charles, Private, Virginia Line; September 29, 1819; May 28, 1818; $96. Age 67. Died September 13, 1818.

Callett, John, Private, Virginia Line; June 2, 1819; September 23, 1818; $96. Age 73. Died September 21, 1830.

Chapman, Amos, Sergeant, Pennsylvania Line; April 20, 1820; May 18, 1818; $96. Age 75. Died February 17, 1820.

Dougherty or Doherty, John, Private, Virginia Line; September 6, 1820; June 30, 1820. $96. Age 78.

Fitzsimmons, Thomas, Private, Virginia Line; September 24, 1819; May 23, 1818; $96. Age 61.

Hartley, Daniel, Private, Morgan's Rifle Regiment; December 24, 1819; June 25, 1818; $96. Age 80.

Johnson, 1st, James, Private, Virginia Line; January 6, 1819; May 20, 1818; $96. Age 80.

Johnson, 2nd, James, Private, Virginia Line; October 18, 1821; January 13, 1820; $96. Age 77.

Morgan, William, Private, Virginia Line; April 20, 1820; November 1, 1819; $96. Age 63.

Mullikin, John, Private, Virginia Line; June 26, 1822; May 18, 1818; $96. Age 84.

Petit, Thomas, Private, Maryland Line; November 29, 1821; April 17, 1820; $60. Age 70.

Randolph, Henry, Private, Pennsylvania Line; September 7, 1820; September 28, 1819; $96. Age 83.

Stratton, Seth, Private, Virginia Line; February 5, 1819; June 20, 1818; $96. Age 61.

Sampson, Isaac, Private, North Carolina Line; April 8, 1825; July 20, 1824; $96. Age 69. Died April 21, 1829.
Sacrey, James, Private, Virginia Line; December 8, 1830; December 7, 1830; $96. Age 79.
Wentworth, Levi, Private, Connecticut Line; October 13, 1818; May 11, 1818; $96. Age 72.
Wayland, Joshua, Private, Virginia Line; December 3, 1819; April 5, 1819; $96. Age 60.
Yager, Samuel, Private, Virginia Line; April 20, 1820; July 1, 1819; $96. Age 82.

Pensioners Under the Act of June 7, 1832

(Began March 4, 1831)

Blomkenbaker, Nicholas, Private, Virginia Line; October 24, 1832; $63.33. Age 75.
Blackmore, John, Private, Virginia Militia; November 3, 1832; $23.33. Age 72.
Brown, William, Private, Virginia Line; December 26, 1832; $31.66. Age 75.
Baskett, Martin, Private, Virginia Militia; September 23, 1832; $23.33. Age 73.
Brevard, Benjamin, Private, North Carolina Militia; November 29, 1833; $20. Age 73.
Blackwell, John, Private, Virginia Militia; January 16, 1834; $46.66. Age 76.
Bryant, Peter, Private, Virginia Line; November 29, 1833; $60. Age 73. Died December 9, 1833.
Brumback, Peter, Private, Virginia Line; June 10, 1832; $100. Age 80.
Christie, James, Private, Virginia Militia; February 11, 1833; $56. Age 76.
Carnine, Peter, Sergeant, New Jersey Line; September 24, 1833; $120. Age 82.
Casey, Charles, Private, Virginia Militia; February 7, 1834; $20. Age 85.

Revolutionary Soldiers

Conyers, Benjamin, Private, Virginia Militia; May 23, 1834; $40. Age 74.
Clark, Obadiah, Private and Corporal, North Carolina Militia; May 27, 1834; $40. Age 78.
Farra, Samuel, Private, Pennsylvania Militia; May 16, 1833; $20. Age 85.
Ford, Elisha, Private, South Carolina Line; September 23, 1833; $80. Age 76.
French, William, Private, Virginia Militia; June 6, 1834; $40. Age 73.
Franklin, James M., Private, North Carolina Line; January 9, 1834; $80. Age 71.
Force, (Foree?), Joseph, Private, Virginia Militia; May 23, 1834; $28.33. Age 92.
Gale, Robert F., Private, Virginia Militia; August 3, 1833; $60. Age 68.
Grigsby, Benjamin, Private, Pennsylvania Militia; September 23, 1833; $23.33. Age 85.
Gibson, Elisha, Private, Virginia Militia; July 10, 1834; $20. Age 86.
Graves, Edmund, Private, North Carolina Line; May 27, 1834; $40. Age 72.
Hawkins, George, Private, Virginia Line; October 26, 1832; $80. Age 84.
Holland, James M., Sergeant, Virginia Militia; $38.33. Age 78.
Higgason, Thomas, Sergeant, Virginia Militia; $55.33. Age 73.
Heppard, William, Private, New Jersey Militia; $40. Age 73.
Herring, George, Private, Virginia Militia; $20. Age 76.
Hickman, James, Private, Virginia Militia; $20. Age 73.
Johnson, Archibald, Private, Virginia Militia; $20. Age 83.
Kelso, Thomas, Private, Maryland Militia; $30. Age 70.
Kendricks, William, Sergeant, Virginia Militia; $35. Age 87.

Knox, John, Private, Delaware Militia; February 11, 1832; $100. Age 75.
Lemaster, Hugh, Private, Virginia Line; February 7, 1834; $30. Age 83.
Maddox, Wilson, Private, Virginia Militia; February 11, 1833; $80. Age 79.
McCalister, Daniel, Private, Virginia Militia; May 29, 1833; $36.66. Age 74.
McCleland, Daniel, Captain, North Carolina Line; July 15, 1833; $480. Age 82.
Moore, Abraham, Private, Virginia Militia; September 28, 1833; $51.33. Age 77.
Mitchell, Charles, Private, Virginia Militia; January 20, 1834; $23.33. Age 75.
Morse, Alexander, Private, Virginia Militia; April 25, 1834; $30.22. Age —.
Neal, Micajah, Private, Virginia Line; January 21, 1843; $80. Age 81.
Paris, Robert, Private, Virginia Line; January 4, 1834; $80. Age 84.
Rowe, James, Private or Artillery, Virginia Line; October 21, 1832; $100. Age 75.
Riley, John, Private, Lieutenant and Ensign, Virginia Line; October 26, 1832; $26.66. Age 78.
Roberts, Benjamin, Captain, Virginia Line; November 3, 1832; $480. Age 84.
Ragsdale, Godfrey, Sergeant of Cavalry, Virginia Line; January 22, 1833; $180. Age 72.
Richards, Joshua, Private, Virginia Militia; December 2, 1833; $25. Age 71.
Rayzor, Paul, Private, Virginia State Troops, $20. Age 83.
Stout, Reuben, Private, Virginia Line; March 18, 1833; $60. Age 73.
Sanders, Reuben, Private, Virginia Militia; September 23, 1833; $30. Age 75.

Revolutionary Soldiers

Smith, Henry, Private, Maryland Militia; July 21, 1834; $20. Age 75.

Thompson, Evan, Sergeant, South Carolina Line; April 25, 1833; $45. Age 71.

Tinsley, William, Private, Virginia Militia; October 21, 1833; $20. Age 71.

Thompson, Joseph, Private, Virginia Militia; January 4, 1834; $20. Age 71.

Thompson, John, Private, North Carolina Militia; January 7, 1834; $52.50. Age 79.

Travis, James, Private, Virginia Militia; June 18, 1834; $80. Age —.

Van Swearingen, ———, Lieutenant, Pennsylvania Line; October 26, 1832; $80. Age 80.

Watts, Peter, Private, North Carolina Line; August 21, 1833; $40. Age 78.

Washburn, Benjamin, Private, Virginia Line; January 21, 1833; $80. Age —.

Woolfolk, Robert, Private, Virginia Line; January 19, 1833; $60. Age —.

Wilcoxzen, Daniel, Lieutenant, North Carolina Line; March 2, 1833; $120. Age —.

Wiley, Henry, Private, North Carolina Militia; May 26, 1834; $40. Age 80.

Pensioners Under the Act of May 15, 1828

(Began March 3, 1826)

Holley, Samuel, Private Second Regiment, New York Line; September 1, 1828; $80.

Jones, Thomas, Dragoon, White's Dragoons; September 5, 1828; $100.

Knight, John, Surgeon Second Regiment, Virginia Line; December 18, 1828; $480.

Long, William, Corporal Tenth Regiment, North Carolina Line; $88.

Rucker, Elliott, Lieutenant, Gibson's Virginia Regiment; December 11, 1830; $320.

Winlock, Joseph, Lieutenant, Gibson's Virginia Regiment; July 25, 1828; $320.

Revolutionary Pensioners Living in the County in 1840

(Collins, Vol. 1, P. 9)

Ballard, Bland W., age 81
Blankenbaker, Nicholas, age 82
Burke, Samuel, age 84.
Wm. Crawford
David Harbison
Fearson, Meshack, age 86
Reeves, Joseph, age 73
Reily, John, age 79
Davis, Nancy (widow), age 81

Total for the County, 93.

Thirteen miles East of Shelbyville at about where two trails over which the pioneers came now meet.

The Floyd Monument, fifteen miles West of Shelbyville, marking where John Floyd's brave soldiers were ambushed the day following the Long Run Massacre.

CHAPTER XI

*First Citizens**

G. H. Society Lawyers

John Allen
John Simpson
William Logan

John Logan
Isham Talbott
Blackburn & Roberts

First Physicians

Doctor John Knight and Doctor Penndigrass, 1796, they were succeeded by Doctor Wardlow, Doctor Moore, and Doctor Willett, 1800.

Tanners

The first brick house was built by Bruner who established the first tannery and brewery. The next tannery was built by George Lease, his yard after him was occupied by Gibbs & Harbison. Goore established a tannery on the north side of Main Street, about three squares from the courthouse after the War of 1812 and '15.

Carpenters

James White
James Blake
Col. Tunstall
Sam'l Carson

Miller Ashby
Lyon & Britton
Jno. and Robt. Logan
McIntosh

Blacksmiths

John Shannon
Singleton Wilson
M. Collier
McEltree & Shipman
Wm. Smith

Price Willis
John Willis
Lewis Crainshaw
John Scott

*Copied from a letter from John W. Williamson, of O'Bannon Station, Jefferson County, Ky., to Mr. Absalom Matthews, of Shelby County, Ky., December 7, 1872.

Tailors

Daniel, Colgan, who settled the farm now owned by the Tevis family, was the first tailor; he employed five or six hands in dressing deer skins, which he manufactured into hunting shirts and pantaloons, short pants with knee buckles, which cost about $5.00.

Enoch Hansborough
Hance McClelland, 1803
R. McGrath, 1812
Bullock & Waters, 1820
Laws W. Cannon, 1822

Isaac Heaton, 1823
J. Churchill, 1826
Yates & Vandyke, 1830 up to 1833

Hatters

Sam'l Perkins, 1799
Robert Todd, 1809
Natt Porter, 1812
Pogue & Lattimoore, 1820

Zach Bell, 1820
Topping & Redford, 1829
H. Frazier, 1834

Silversmiths

Scotthorn, 1799
Silas Tonkrey, 1812

Anthony Veeter, 1825
Blackburn, 1812

Cabinet Makers

Wm. Neal, 1799, two and one-half miles west
I. Stout, 1800
Charles Dorsey, 1802
V. Lindsey, 1820
Benjamin White, 1820

Henry Brunett, 1820
Overstreet & Kitely, 1818
Wm. Kinkade, 1820
Wm. D. Bowling, 1820
Benjamin Ashby, 1825

Brick Makers

I. Clarkes, 1800
William Rolling, 1800
Thomas Reynolds, 1818

Bridgewater, 1818
John Mintor & Richard Mintor, 1820

FIRST IN PROFESSIONS, BUSINESS AND TRADES

Stone Masons

Francis Henothorny, 1799
Jacob Martin, 1800
I. Scroggans, 1812

Wm. & John Borotins, 1819
Wm. Welch, 1819

Merchants

Butler, 1799
Adam Steele, 1799
James & John Bradshaw, 1799
Samuel Dupuy, 1818
Benjamin Dupuy, 1820
John Hall, 1820
John Graham, 1820
Wm. & Robt. Jarvis, 1820
Neal & Davis, 1821

Rouse & Co., 1821
James Simrall, 1816
Robertson & Bailey, 1818
Bell & Logan, 1820
Josiah & Frank Jackson, 1816
Waller & Bolling Holmes, 1816
Alfred G. Mounts, 1816
J. & Robt. Bull, 1828

Chair Makers

James Denny, 1800
Wm. Rankin, 1820
Joseph Mills, 1820

I. Holmes, 1819
Dutton & Hor, 1820

Wheelwrights

John McCachron, 1799
George Cardwell, 1800

I. Holmes, 1819
Dutton & Hor, 1820

Saddlers

Benjamin Perry, 1800
John McGaughey, 1820
Daniel Leach, 1820

John Fisher, 1821
A. W. Hickman, 1825

Carriage Makers

Wm. Keassey, 1820

W. Dutton & Randolph, 1821

Shoe Makers

Sturman & Waters, 1800
Timothy Redding, 1799
W. & H. Atherton, 1800

Wm. Grooms, 1806
Gilbert, 1812
Charles Green, 1820

Tinners

Postelwait, 1800

Jack, 1830

Sickle Makers

Wilson & Authur McGaughey Wm. Boyd

Bakery

Mrs. Carson, 1800
Speck, 1808
Fisher, 1818

A. Clay, 1821
J. & Nar Garrison, 1830

CHAPTER XII

Officials—Branch Bank of Kentucky
(July 1, 1816)

W. Bullock .... *President*

Directors

Mark Hardin	Geo. Waller
B. F. Dupuy	Isaac Watkins
John Newland	John Willett
Jacob Castleman	James Moore

Subscribers Names   No. Shares

Benj. F. Dupuy	160
Samuel Dupuy	30
Benj. R. Pollard	15
John Newland	55
James Moore	35
Mark Hardin	20
Daniel Leach	5
Luke Haff	10
Samuel Harbison	18
Isaac Watkins	50
John Willett	40
John W. Rankin	10
John McGaughey	10
Edward Boone	5
Thomas P. Coates	10
John Logan, Jr.	5
Rowland Thomas	10
James Briston	20
Judith Venable	10

David Harbison 15
N. Peay & I. Nabb 10
Martin D. Hardin 10
John F. Graham 10
John Hall 10
James Knox 50
Steele & Luckett 60
George Robinson 5
Francis Jackson 5

693

William Taylor 20
Philip Johnston 5
Edward Talbott 10
Philip W. Taylor 5
Isaac Greathouse 10
William & Lee White 20
John Shannon, Jr. 8
William G. Boyd 5
Andrew Holmes 5
Cuthbert Bullitt 30
George Waller 5
John Hunt 15
W. Bullock & Co. 20
John Brandshaw 15
Nathaniel P. Porter 3
Francis Davis 5
John Gwathmey 50
Gwathmey & Beamon 20
Richard Waller 10
Martha Owen (Guardns) 15
James Moore .....
Joseph L. Fore 10
Josiah Jackson 5

Early Bank Officials

J. & F. Jackson 10
Robert P. Allen 6
                                                                    ———
                                                                    307

CHAPTER XIII

Pioneer Grist Mills

Permission of the Justices of the "Quarter Sessions," at the sessions of 1709, was granted William Helm, to locate a Grist Mill just north of where the three mile bridge on the State Pike is now located, and not far west of the original Tyler Station.

The second mill was built by Robert Tyler and on the Leonard Scarce farm in much the same locality and near the site of the old Helm permit. The latter became the site of the old Carding Mill remembered by some of the older members of the last generation.

Another new mill was built by Benjamine Logan on Bull Skin, and a second by Robert Tyler, on what was known as the Miss Miller place. Another by Col. Whitaker just south of Shelbyville, another by Elija Carr on Mulberry Creek, and still another by Samuel Shannon, which was afterwards known as the Old Caldwell Mill, near where the Shelbyville Water Works stand.

A deed shows about the same time that Moses Hall, a sketch of whose life is given in Part V, gave to his son, David Stevenson Hall, a tract of land lying on the west side of Guists Creek, adjoining land belonging to the heirs of Andrew Holmes, and another tract containing two hundred and fifteen acres—"also one-half of Grist and Saw Mills upon Guists Creek with one-half of land attached thereto."

CHAPTER XIV

Interesting Weather Records

Kentucky weather, declared by the United States Bureau, to be "on the whole, about the best the country affords," has variety for its most attractive characteristic. Occasionally the variety is severe.

The United States Weather Bureau and its branch offices, do not and cannot tell all that is to be known about this—if not the most interesting—the most general theme of conversation under the shining sun. They are not old enough. But the everywhere published, "signs of hard winter" has sent us back to some older records of severe weather, to be found in a record kept by the late John W. Adams and his son E. L. Adams, of Shelby County, beginning with the last half of the last century. The years and dates on which the thermometer was below zero are those given, the records begin seventy-five years ago, but the coldest weather recorded during the seventy-five years was in February, 1899, or only thirty years ago.*

The figures copied from the Messrs. Adams records are:

1852—Jan. 19, 13°; Jan. 20, 11°.
1856—Jan. 9, 20°; Jan. 10, 23°; Feb. 3, 12°; Feb. 4, 16°; Feb. 5, 13°.
1859—Dec. 23, 15°.
1864—Jan. 1, 16° "and wind blowing a gale. Many people were badly frozen."
1871—Dec. 21, 15°.
1876—Dec. 31, 21°.
1877—Jan. 4, 14°; Jan. 9, 28°.

---

*The worst storm that visited Shelby County during the first half of the century was that on March 20, (the equinox) 1849, which was central over Nelson, Shelby, Mercer, Woodford, Jessamine and Fayette. In Shelbyville it unroofed or blew down the walls of the Masonic Building, colored Baptist Church, rope walks, mechanic shops, dwellings, stables, carriage houses and other buildings.

1878—Jan. 5, 14°; Jan. 7, 22°; Jan. 8, 12°.
1879—Jan. 3, 18°; Jan. 4, 19°; Jan. 5, 22°; Jan. 10, 25°.
1880—Nov. 19, 11°; Dec. 30, 12°; Dec. 31, 14°.
1881—Jan. 1, 17°.
1884—Jan. 5, 23°; Jan. 6, 16°; Jan. 25, 20°.
1885—Jan. 22, 12°.
1886—Jan. 10, 12°; Jan. 11, 16°; Jan. 12, 22°; Feb. 5, 21°.
1893—Jan. 11, 15°; Jan. 15, 13°; Jan. 17, 18°; Jan. 20, 13°.
1895—Jan. 12, 12°; Jan. 14, 12°; Feb. 8, 13°.
1899—Feb. 8, 13°; Feb. 9, 14°; Feb. 10, 15°; Feb. 13, 30°.

Only four times within the fifty years was the zero weather prior to Christmas or New Year's, but two winters of severe weather in the history of the country are not referred to. There is not before us the record of the "cold year" of the fifties or of the great drought, floods and wet years between 1800 and 1900, but all records seem to agree that the winters of 1779-80 and 1917-18, one hundred and thirty-six years apart, were the severest since the settlement of Kentucky by the whites; and all remember the awful winter in the last year of the World War and its world of woes.

CHAPTER XV

Shelby County Masons

While other such orders as the Odd Fellows, Knights of Pythias, et al, have been perhaps as much agencies for the upbuilding of the community, none of them are anything like as old or as distinctively a part of the pioneer history of the County as the old lodge of Masons elsewhere referred to. And no distinctively pioneer history of either the County or whole State would be complete without reference to "Solomon Lodge No. 5, F. & A. M.", Shelbyville, Kentucky.

There are only four older lodges west of the Alleghenies. The rank it always took in State lodge affairs and the part it has taken in the organization and support of smaller lodges of the County of nearly equal age and importance, had doubtless much to do with the location in this County of the fine home for aged Masons, from the State at large.

A number of the first settlers were already members of the Masonic order, and early in 1800 it was determined to organize a lodge at Shelbyville, and steps to that end were taken by members of the order who lived in the town and surrounding county; and on July 10 of that year, a dispensation was obtained from the Grand Lodge of Virginia. Simon Adams was appointed master; James Wardlow, Senior Warden; William Tunstall, Junior Warden. They met at the home of Robert Moore, where the lodge was organized and at first named "Abraham Lodge."

There were at that time four other lodges in the State, the lodge at Lexington having received its dispensation in 1788, that at Paris in 1791; at Georgetown in 1796, and at Frankfort in 1799. Immediately after the organization of the Shelbyville lodge, the five met in convention and organized the Grand Lodge of Kentucky.

Lexington changed from No. 35, under the Virginia dispensation, to No. 1; Paris became No. 2, Georgetown No. 3, Frankfort No. 4, and Shelbyville changed from Abraham to Solomon No. 5. These five lodges were not only the original organizers of the State Grand Lodge, but Simon Adams of the Shelbyville Lodge was the first Senior Grand Warden.

Many of the first lodges of Indiana, Ohio, Illinois, Mississippi, Missouri, Louisiana and Tennessee obtained their chapters from the Grand Lodge of Kentucky.

One of the first applicants for membership in the Shelbyville Lodge was John Pope, prominent attorney and land owner. One corner of his land on Clear Creek has been known as Pope's Corner for many years, and was established by Daniel and Squire Boone, in the survey that they made for John Pope. He became a member of the Lodge by special dispensation from the Grand Lodge in 1801. He afterward represented his district in Congress, and among his living direct descendants in Shelby are Messrs. Pope and Prather Nicholas and Mrs. T. E. Bland.

The first lodge hall in Shelbyville, elsewhere referred to, was built in 1884 on Washington Street between Fifth and Sixth on a lot donated by John McGaughey, one of the enthusiastic first members. In 1839 the property on the south of the public square was acquired, and the Lodge has had its home there now for 90 years. Dr. James Moore who conducted the dedicatory exercises of the first lodge building in 1805, was a distinguished scholar and author. He and the noted Carey L. Clark wrote the first Masonic manual west of the Alleghenies. The original charter of Solomon Lodge No. 5, is still in existence, but badly mutilated.

The membership of the Lodge in its first years contained names of many distinguished Kentucky families, including Knight, Owen, McClelland, Pope, Simpson, Allen, Bullock,

Rowan, Floyd, Boone, Bell, Castleman, Logan, Todd, Tevis, et al.

The complete list of members for the years from 1800 to 1830 was as follows:

John Willitt, David Blackwell, Joseph W. Knight, B. F. Dupuy, Nicholas Peay, William G. Boyd, Robert Owen, James B. McClelland, George Gill, Wm. Rowland, John McGaughey, Charles Henderson, Robert King, Daniel Jennings, Nathaniel Zoursen, Benjamin Roberts, George Clifton, Thomas Johnston, Drury Melone, William Bridgewater, Warden Pope, John Romgue, James Wardlaw, John Simpson, Edward Evans, John Allen, Johannes Goodman, William J. Turnstall, Joseph Simpson, William Roberts, Samuel Waddy, Abraham Owen, John Bullock, Matthew Flournoy, James McDavitt, John Rowan, George R. C. Floyd, James McConnell, Nathaniel Crawford, Luke Happ, Abraham King, John H. Bullock, Charles Allen, Edward Boone, Zachariah Bell, David Owen, W. Bullock, George B. Knight, James Castleman, Wingfield Bullock, William Shipman, John G. Matheney, Joseph Allen, Edmond Curd, John Simpson, Edmond Blanton, Abraham Smith, Joseph M. Payne, James Craig, Montgomery Allen, Richard Stephens, Joseph Ficklin, Simon Adams, Isaac Watkins, James Moore, Adam Guthrie, Daniel L. Morrison, James L. Henderson, Peter Hansbrough, John Bradshaw, George I. Johnston, James Cox, Adam Steele, James Blair, Obediah Clark, William Wardlaw, John Pope, C. Allen, James Reynolds, Charles Adams.

CHAPTER XVI

Gallant First Sons of Shelby

(The names given below are from an article written recently by Mr. F. M. Ballard of Cincinnati, concerning his distinguished ancestor General Joseph Winlock, and the part he and other Shelby County soldiers took in nipping the conspiracy of Aaron Burr.)

On December 23rd, 1806, the Legislature passed an act to prevent unlawful enterprises; and under this law measures were immediately taken to order out portions of the militia. Before the militia could be assembled at their posts, all the boats of Burr, not intercepted by the authorities of Ohio, effected a passage to the mouth of the Cumberland.

It is the intent of this notice to present here the muster rolls of the two companies of militia which were under the command of General Joseph Winlock, of Shelby County, Ky., assembled upon the banks of the Ohio at Louisville in December, 1806, pursuant to the instructions of Governor Christopher Greenup.

Jonathan Taylor, captain; Frances Taylor, lieutenant; Samuel Washburn, ensign; John Lang, sergeant; John Hollingsworth, sergeant; James B. Washburn, sergeant; John Panabaker, corporal; William Newland, corporal; John Millar, corporal; William Jetter, bugler. Privates: James Bridgeford, George Bridgman, Thomas Buckner, James Chenoweth, William Clayton, Robert Dunbar, George Durment, Henry Dougherty, William Daniel, James Elliott, John Eadlin, Robert Ewing, John Evans, Jr., John Fenley, Jacob Fine, James Fontaine, John Ferguson, Edekiel Glover, Isaac Hawes, Abraham Hite, Elijah Jeter, John Kirkpatrick, Jesse Murray, Joseph Pomeroy, David Richie, George Rudy, John Redd, Hugh Scott, Zachary Taylor, John G. Taylor, Roger Taylor, William Wallace, John Young.

Muster Roll of a Company of Militia of Kentucky, commanded by Captain Jesse Holmes, called into actual service under the command of Brigadier General Joseph Winlock, December 25, 1806, to January 25, 1807:

Jesse Holmes, captain; Samuel Vancleve, lieutenant; James Holmes, ensign; Thomas Gates, sergeant; James Barbee, sergeant; Joseph Love, sergeant; William Swearengen, sergeant; James Mitchell, corporal; Samuel Shanks, corporal; William Pusey, corporal; William Ewing, corporal; Samuel Jacob, fifer; Martin Jacob, drummer. Privates: William Ashby, Thomas Baskett, Jacob Bucey, Bland W. Ballard, Samuel Bucey, Charles Bucey, John G. Barnett, Cornelius Bice, Thomas Bedwell, Felty Bargo, William Boyd, Charles Baird, Elijah Creed, Thomas Cooper, Daniel Colgan, George Churchill, John Demaree, Samuel Demaree, Elijah Deadman, William Gillespie, Thomas Hinton, Evan Hinton, Thomas Hankins, Archibald Howard, Bennett Jacobs, William Jones, David Johnson, John Ketcham, George Kinder, Cornelius Lester, Charles Marshall, John Milner, William Mitchell, Stephen Milan, Charles Neale, William Nicholas, John Potts, Bailey Romaine, John Robinson, Thomas Reynolds, Robert Shanks, Sterling Shackelford, Jacob Smock, James Standiford, Micajah Sharp, Samuel Samples, David Taylor, George Thomas, Benjamin Vancleve, Levi Whitaker, Aquilla Whitaker, Benjamin White, Elisha Whitaker, Robert White, Samuel Watson, John Weaver, John Weatherford, William Yunt.

CHAPTER XVII

Noted Burial Grounds

Like those mentioned under head of "Cemetery" in Chapter VI, Part IV, and in the sketches of the County churches and churchyards, the Logan family burial grounds in the southwestern portion of the County furnish truly pioneer history. The inscriptions on the tombs and headstones not only give much added information to the otherwise meagre sketches of the lives of Benjamin Logan and his son William, but they are typical of the epitaphs and sentiments of that day in the churchyards of the County at large; and have therefore been copied verbatim, as follows:

In Memory of our Mother and Father: William Logan, Priscilla Logan. William was born December, 1776; died August, 1822. Priscilla was born March, 1784; died June, 1833.

Mary Logan Smith died October 22, 1867, aged 86 years.

Benjamin L. Smith, born August 28, 1801; died October 5, 1804.

Dr. Benjamin Logan, born January 3, 1789; died March 19, 1873.

Col. James Knox was born in Ireland. Came to America at the age of 14 years. Served in the Revolutionary War. Died December 24, 1822, at an advanced age.

Robert Logan, born November 7, 1829. Died June 27, 1833.

John K. Logan, born December 20, 1830; died July 31, 1833.

In Memory of Jane Logan, wife of John T. Parker, and daughter of Col. John Allen who was killed at the River Raisin in 1813—and Jane Logan Allen, who died February 28, 1821. Born September 24, 1808—Died September 12, 1844.

Benjamin Logan, died December, 1802, in his 60th year. A name so engraven in the history of his country, and the affections of posterity—the highest monument of fame—Married Ann Montgomery, who nobly shared with him in the many perils of their wilderness home.

Ann Logan, died October 18, 1825, in her 73rd year.

James K. Logan, born November 13, 1820; died October 19, 1867.

Judge Z. Wheat, born July 26, 1806; died April 26, 1877. "Blessed are the dead who die in the Lord."

Ann M. Wheat, born April 22, 1823; died September 23, 1885.

William P. Monroe, born September 15, 1825; died July 19, 1851.

Elizabeth S. Logan, born January 8, 1793; died March 3, 1862. Wife, Mother, Christian, Friend. "Blessed are the pure in heart, for they shall see God."

Dr. Robert W. Glass, born August 21, 1821; died July 10, 1854. "Let me die the death of the righteous, and let my last end be like his."

These two graves were just outside of the enclosure, and there were evidences of other graves, but no stones.

In memory of John W. Storts, who was born May 16, 1831, and died March 2, 1833. "Of such is the kingdom of Heaven."

In memory of Albert C. Storts, who was born December 24, 1833—died January 17, 1835. "Suffer little children to come unto me, for of such is the kingdom of Heaven."

FULLNAME INDEX

----, Old Hickory 36 Rebecca 96
ACHER, Joseph 209
ACHERS, Polly 229
ADAIR, Gen 155
ADAMS, Charles 263 David 215 E L 259 Frances M 91 James 209 John W 109 259 Louisa 108 108 Nancy 229 Simon 104 217 261-263
ADCOCK, Edmond 229 Mary 229
ADDAMS, Hugh 209 John 209 Samuel 209 William 209
ADMIRE, George 229 Sarah 229
AGIN, Elizabeth 233
AHSBY, William 266
AKERS, Benj 209 Joseph 209 Polly 229 Simon 209 Thomas 209
ALEXANDER, Benj 229 Betsy 229
ALEXANDRIA, Dr 87
ALLEN, 109 139 262 Andrew 209 Ann 209 Anne 96 Benj 77 C 263 Charles 263 Col 151 158 Cynthia 173-174 Deborah 96 Elizha 209 Frances M 71 Hannah 173 James 98 157 209 Jane 96 267 Jane Logan 267 Jean 229 John 104 113-114 157 165 174 209 217 229 249 263 267 Joseph 263 Margaret

ALLEN (cont.)
174 Martha 236 Montgomery 209 263 Robert 96 115 Robert P 209 255 Tandy M 218 Thomas 173 209 Winney 233 Wm 96
ALLISON, 80 Easter 232
ALVIS, Jesse 243
ANDERSON, Elizabeth 108 Geo 209 James 209 229 Jane 237 John 209 241 Lawrence 35 Margt 235 Mary 229 R C 177 Sarah 229 Thomas 229 William 218
APPLEGATE, Benj 229 Leasey 229
ARMSTRONG, G A 100 132
ARTERBURN, Elizabeth 230
ASHBY, Beasley 229 Benj 229 Benjamin 250 Miller 249 Obediah 209 Polly 229 229 Stephen 209 Susan 108 Thomas 229 Tinson 209
ASHCRAFT, Delilah 238 Elizabeth 209
ATHERTON, H 252 Henry 120 W 252
BADEN, Mr 99
BAGGS, John 209
BAILEY, 251 Harrison 218 Hartwell A 218 T C 225
BAIRD, 81 Catherine 229 Caty 96 Charles 96 229 266 Polly 238
BAKER, 118 Betsey 229 J 90 90-91 Jesse 229 Mary 237 Nancy 236 Polly 238
BALEE, John P 120

BALES, Jas G 218
BALL, W D 66
BALLARD, 139 148-150 161
  Benjamin 149 Bland 36 45-47 54 103-104 150 177-178 181-184 Bland W 147 197-199 205-206 217 248 266
  Camden W 117 227
  Elizabeth 182 F M 265
  Florence 227 G W 217 James 66 209 Jas 217 John 183
  John James 159 John T 48 90 115 223 Maj 151 178 W 217
BALLEW, Charles 243
BALYLES, Henery 209
BANK, David 51
BANTA, 50 Abraham 51-52 Albert 51 Cornelius 51-52 David 51 Henry 51 Jacob 51 John 51 Peter 51 97 Samuel 51
BARBEE, James 266
BARGO, Felty 266
BARKER, T W 87
BARNETT, John G 266 William 209
BARNWELL, Middleton 91
BARRICKMAN, H 128
BARRIGER, Mrs 86
BARTON, Wm E 196
BASEY, Richard 209
BASKET, Martin 67-68 Thos Sr 68
BASKETT, James 73 John 209 Martin 244 Thomas 266 William 209
BAX, Lawrence 101
BEAMON, 254
BEAN, Betty 119 Clary 233 Joany 108 Lewis 229 Sally 229 Seany 230

BEARD, 81 Elliott B 218 Philip J 218
BEAVER, 118
BECKHAM, J C 218-219 Nimrod 67 W T 218
BECKLEY, John R 85
BEDWELL, Mary 229 Thomas 229 266
BEKKERS, Father 101 John H 100
BELDERBACK, Jacob 209
BELIA, Peter 54
BELL, 105 127 251 263 Armiger 209 Betsy 234 Elizabeth 209 236 J Franklin 139 John 229 Joseph N 227 Mary 229 Robt 209 Selia A 109 Zach 250 Zachariah 263 Zachary 120
BENETT, Burrel 209
BENNET, Daniel 209
BENNETT, Anna 230 Anny 229 Asa 229-230 Daniel 209
BENSON, Chichester 205-206 Winchester 206
BENTON, M M 91
BERGEN, 50 Gen 221 George 52
BERNADOTTE, 154
BERRY, Gardner 73
BEST, Elizabeth 229 John 229 Nancy 237 Samuel 209
BIBB, Geo M 163
BICE, Cornelius 266
BIP, Polly 97
BIRD, Henry 132
BLACK, Dave 123 Luther 223
BLACKBOURN, John 205-206
BLACKBURN, 114 249-250 Rob 215
BLACKMORE, John 244
BLACKWELL, David 263 James 209 John 244 Sally 236
BLAIR, James 263
BLAKE, James 249 Polly 236
BLAND, T E 262

INDEX

BLANKENBAKER, Dr 87
  Nicholas 248
BLANTON, Ann 236 Edmond
  263 Jesse 229 Sarah 229
BLOMKENBAKER, Nicholas
  244
BOALS, Ambrose 209 229
  Jenny 229
BOHANNON, Henry 218
BOILES, Harriet 229 John 229
BOLES, James 209 Thomas 209
BOLS, Abraham 229 Geney 229
BOLYLES, Henery 209
BONNEY, Julia 89 91
BONTA, Henry 229 Nancy 229
BOOEN, Enoch 179
BOOKER, Nancy 240 S W 218
BOONE, 23 155 161 181-182
  184 263 Catherine 229
  Daniel 21-22 47 139-140 180
  262 Edward 253 263 Enoch
  142 180 229 Hannah 140
  Isaiah 142 177 179 James
  140 Jane 179-180 John 142
  Jonathan 142 229 Lucy 229
  Moses 142 Samuel 142
  Sarah 179 Squire 22 24 30
  45-47 50 65 139-142 148
  177-180 262
BOOTH, John 229 Sallie 229
BOROTINS, John 251 Wm 251
BOSWELL, 86 Chas 86 Dr 87
  Everett 86 Geo 209 Geo W
  86 George 241 George G 87
  James 87 Jennie 87 John 87
  Madison T 87 Taylor 86
BOTELER, 174 Bell W 36
BOTTS, 110 John 218
BOWEN, Mrs 97
BOWLING, Jane 234 Margt 236
  William 241 Wm D 250

BOWMAN, Alleen 239 Col 147
BOYD, 103 Agness 229 Benj 68
  Mary 235 241 Mehitable 231
  Ruthey 229 Samuel 229 W 96
  William 209 229 241 266 William
  G 254 263 Wm 252 Wm G 217
  217
BOYLE, David 101 Henry 229 Sarah
  229
BOYLES, David 241
BRACKETT, Jemimah 230 Jeremiah
  229 Jesse 229 Polly 229 Pricilla
  232 Thomas 229
BRADBERRY, William 209
BRADDOCK, 144
BRADSHAW, 55 Agnes 108 108
  Ann 230 James 127 205-206 251
  John 55 84-85 127 209 251 263
  Peggy 239 Polly 229 Sarah 237
  Thomas 230
BRADY, Ed 100 Jemima 230 John
  100 Jonathan P 230
BRANDSHAW, John 254
BRANNON, Elizabeth 230 Vinson
  230
BRASHEAR, Camilla 108
BREEDEN, Elizabeth 230 Paul 230
  Polly 230 William 230
BREEDING, Richard 241
BREEDON, Elizabeth 69
BRENHAMS, Robert 227
BRENT, Christopher 209 John 209
  Matthis 209
BRENTON, Hanna 230 Henry 230
BREVARD, Benjamin 244
BREWER, Abraham 51
BRIDGEFORD, James 265
BRIDGEWATER, 250 William 209
  263 Wm 61
BRIDGMAN, George 265
BRIGGS, 155 Betsy 155

HISTORY OF SHELBY COUNTY

BRIGHT, 79-80 Emma 79 F G 132 G M 90 George 91 Graham 91 Hannah 91 Horatio 91 Jeptha 79 Lewis 230 Minnie 91 Newton 218 Polly 230 237 Susanna 232
BRISCOE, James 241
BRISCON, James 209
BRISTO, Geo 66
BRISTOL, Geo 67
BRISTON, James 253
BRISTOW, J P 120
BRITTON, 249
BROADDUS, Dr 106
BROOK, Elizabeth B 238
BROOKS, Paul 209
BROOKY, Robert 96
BROTHERS, Mcdonald 119
BROWER, John 218
BROWN, Archibald C 218 Isabel 230 James 209 230 241 John Edwin 218 Kate 101 Margaret 230 Mason 120 225 Michael 101 Nancy 80 Robert 230 Ruben 209 Thos W 135 William 244
BRUCE, H W 201 225 Sarah 230 William 230
BRUMBACK, Peter 244
BRUMFIELD, Nancy 197 William 197
BRUNER, 103 249 A 55
BRUNETT, Henry 250
BRYAN, 178 Alex 45 Charity 231
BRYANT, Mary 234 Peter 244 Rachel 235 Simon 118
BUCEY, Charles 266 Jacob 266 Samuel 266
BUCHANNAN, Wm 241
BUCKHANNON, Rebecca 230

BUCKHANNON (cont.) Victor 230
BUCKLES, John 45
BUCKLEY, Col 125
BUCKNER, Thomas 265
BULL, J 251 Robert 85 Robt 251
BULLARD, Caty 232
BULLITT, Cuthbert 217 254 Thos W 177
BULLOCK, 103 250 262 Eliza 59 J M 90 James M 91 Jas M 218 John 263 John H 263 Josiah 114 Mrs 96 W 253-254 263 W F 225 Winfield 227 Wingeld 209 Wingfield 114 263 Wm C 217-218
BURGEN, William 209
BURGOYNE, 150
BURKE, Samuel 248
BURNETT, 127 Jas C 221 Polly 67
BURR, Aaron 265
BURRESS, Charles 209
BURTON, 132 Alexander 230 George 230 Mary 230 Rebecca 230
BUSAN, Isabell 237
BUSH, John 209
BUSKIRK, Mary 230
BUSSBEY, Danl 215
BUTLER, 55 160 251 Percival 217 Philip 209 William 209
BUTLOR, Eliza 241
BUZAN, Eliza 71 Jesse 71 241 Sally 230
BYARS, J G 132
CAIN, Sally 230 Samuel 230
CALDWELL, 132 James L 221 Jas L 218 Thomas B 78
CALLETT, John 243
CALLOWAY, William 132
CAMERON, A 98 Archibald 93-95 157 Mary Ann 230 Mrs 97 Robert 230

INDEX

CAMPBELL, 80 Absolom 87 Alexander 77 Caty 238 Elder 78 Geo 209 George 230 H A 226 Jane 100 Margaret 230 Sallie 87 William F 100
CAMPION, 101
CANNON, Laws W 250 Mrs 196
CARDING, 257
CARDWELL, G 55 George 251 H G 132 Jacob 85 Jemimah 230 Jesse 229-230 Susanna 236 W M 225 William 85
CARESS, 182
CARLAND, Hannah 236
CARLIN, Francis 230 John 210 230 Matthias 210 Sarah 237
CARLISLE, 35
CARMAN, Mary 233
CARMANT, Mary 235
CARMICHAEL, Susanna 231
CARNINE, Andrew 97 Mip 97 Peter 244
CARPENTER, Mr 128 Zach 221 Zachius 77
CARR, Elija 257 Elijah 230 George 103 230 Jane 230 Polly 115 Ruthey 229 Sally 230 234 234 Samuel 230 Seany 230
CARRIS, 177 Benj H 210
CARROLL, W S 225
CARSON, 103 Mrs 55 252 Sam'l 249 William 210
CASE, Jacob 210
CASEY, Catherine 230 Charles 244 Darkus 234
CASH, Warren 66 72 210
CASTLEMAN, 263 Jacob 230 253 James 263 Sarah 230
CASWELL, C H 87

CATES, Richard 45
CAYSE, Billey 210 Charles 210
CERASS, Simon 210
CHANDLER, T 87
CHAPMAN, Amos 243 Dr 91 Jane 230 Nathan 230
CHARLES, Ii King Of England 171
CHEEK, Pamelia 108
CHENOWETH, James 265 Richard 178
CHENOWITH, Nancy 230 Thomas 230
CHENWITH, John 230 Mary 230
CHILDERS, Susanna 230 Thomas 230
CHILDRAS, Rachel 230 Thomas 230
CHILES, Thomas 78
CHINER, Martinette 105
CHINN, Achilles 78 Hector A 223
CHRISTIE, James 244
CHURCHILL, George 266 J 250 John 120
CLARK, Bell 87 Benj 210 Betsy 230 Carey L 262 Elizabeth 230 Everett 209 Gen 144 147-148 150 George Rogers 145 197 199 Jenny 232 Jesse 230 John 87 209 230 Joseph 210 Lewis 230 Nancy 234 Obadiah 221 245 Obediah 263 Polly 230 Ruben 230 Saml 210 Zacharia 209
CLARKE, George Rogers 144 John 241
CLARKES, I 250
CLAY, A 252 Henry 36 61 163
CLAYTON, William 265
CLIFTON, Charlotte 231 George 263
CLINE, 178 Elizabeth 230 233 John 230 Nicholas 230
CLUTTER, Simon Jr 210
COATES, Thomas P 253

COBERN, Susanna 230
COCHRAN, Catherine 230
  James 230 Julia Owen 36 T
  B 85
COLEMAN, Daniel 231
  Elizabeth 231 Mrs Barsheby
  231
COLES, Rebecca 231
COLGAN, Dan 103 Daniel 250
  266
COLGLAZIER, Polly 234
COLGLAZURE, Daniel 231
  Mary 231
COLLIER, 103 M 249
COLLINGS, Benj 215 Catherin
  231 Nancy 230 Spencer 215
  231 Thomas 215
COLLINS, 110 Catherine 231
  Jane 238 Lydia 67 Mary 67
  Richard 231 William 67
COLORED, Woman Rebecca 66
COMBS, Andrew 210 Thomas
  210
COMINGORE, Jno 51
COMPLIMENT, William 209
COMSTOCK, Oliver 210
CONGER, Moses 209
CONGLETON, Margaret 231
  William 231
CONLEY, John 210
CONNELL, Elizabeth 231
CONNELLY, James 231 Milly
  231
CONNELY, John 241 Margaret
  231 Thomas 231
CONNER, John 209
CONRAD, Geo 209
CONYERS, Benjamin 245
COOK, Abraham 66 Isaac 210
  Moses 103 Seth 221
COOKE, T B 87

COOL, Wm 140
COOMES, Mrs 99 William 99
COON, Cleo Clark 109
COOPER, Allefer 233 D B 87 Elias
  221 Hester 231 Mr 128 Samuel
  225 231 Thomas 266
CORN, George 115
CORNWELL, Ann 232
CORWINE, Richard 84
COSART, Francis 51
COTTEN, William 210
COURTNEY, Robert 48 Susan 236
COWHERD, 109 Ann Lucinda 70 D
  C 70 Douglas 70 Gertrude 70
  Lucinda 70 M M 70 Mariah 70
  Mattie 70 Sarah Catherine 70
  Waller 70
COX, Benj 210 David 231 Elizabeth
  237 James 263 Mehitable 231
COZINE, B B 128 Heirs Cornelius 51
  John P 128 Sarah 229
CRAIG, 103 Anna 108 James 114 223
  225 263 Louis 65 Mr 96 Mrs 96
CRAINSHAW, Lewis 249
CRANE, D F 101
CRAPETER, Basil H 227
CRAPSTER, Jane 100 Peter 100
CRAVINSTON, George 61
CRAWFORD, "billy" 79 Col 169-170
  David 171 Elizabeth 171 J W 221
  John 210 231 Juliet 108 Margaret
  98 Mary Ann 231 Nancy 231 231
  Nathan 114 210 Nathaniel 231 263
  Pauline 79 Sally 231 Sarah 108
  William 79 98 210 231 Wm 248
CREED, Elijah 266
CRIST, Geo 210
CRITTENDEN, Henry 217 John
  Jordan 36
CROCKETT, James 231 Nancy 231
CROMWELL, Mary 235

INDEX

CROSBY, John 80
CROW, John F 98
CRUME, Jane 231 Jesse 231
CRUTCHFIELD, William 210
CULL, 103 James 210 John 231
   Mr 96 Rachel 231 Singleton
   96 Wilson 96
CULLY, Sally 232
CUNNINGHAM, Francis 210 J
   W 85
CURD, Edmond 210 263
   Edmund 231 Milly 231
   Sarah 237
CURRETT, Col 197
CURRY, Jane 234
CYPHERS, Jane 231 Mary 238
   Mathias 210 231 Sarah 231
DAGERNALD, Betsey 234
DALE, 124 V A 109
DALTON, Eliza 108
DANIEL, Martin 113-114 171-
   172 221 Patsy 171 Robert
   241 Walker 84 William 265
DARKES, Polly 240
DAUGHERTY, Benj 231 Jane
   231 236 Miss Ralph 231
   Thomas 231
DAVAGE, Judge 114
DAVIDGE, Judge 225
DAVIDSON, Gorge 210
   William 210
DAVIESS, Col 160 Joseph 157
   Joseph Hamilton 157
DAVIS, 251 Charity 231
   Charlotte 231 Edwin H 221
   Francis 254 Geo 69 H C 67
   John 231 John F 115 202 223
   Jos W 218 Nancy 248 Rachel
   231 Sarah Ann 108 Theodore
   69 William 210 231
DAVRIDGE, Henry 225

DAWSON, Jeremiah 83
DAYHOFF, Frederick 221
DEADMAN, Elijah 266
DEAN, Margaret 98
DEDMAN, 109
DEDMORE, Abram 210
DEHAVEN, S E 225
DEISS, Herman 79 101 Lizzie 101
DELANEY, James 231 Mrs Barsheby
   231
DEMAREE, Abraham 231 D 225
   David 221 231 Jane 231 John 96
   266 Mary 229 Nancy 96 231
   Rachel 97 Sam 97 Samuel 51 266
DENBO, Mary Ann 231 Robert 231
   Sally 231 Thos 210
DENBOU, Betsy 231 Nancy 231
DENNIS, Effie 231 John 231
DENNY, 55 James 251 Thomas 73
DENSMORE, James H 98
DERMON, Mary 233
DEVORE, James 210 231 Patsy 231
   Rachel 238 Saml 210
DEWITT, Jacob 210
DIEHL, Patricia S 13
DIKES, Elijah 210
DILLO, 119
DILLON, 103 John 231 Mary 231
DINING, Anthony 231 Susanna 231
DITTO, Polly 236
DOAK, Robert 218 221
DODD, J W 85 Professor 109
DODSON, John 210
DOHERTY, John 243
DOLEMAN, Chas 45
DONALDSON, 80 John 79 John L
   131
DOOLEY, Betsy 231 James 210 231
   Saml 210
DORCAS, John 210 William 210
DORNING, Oliver 241

HISTORY OF SHELBY COUNTY

DORSEY, Charles 250 E V 87 Edwin 87 Eliza 87
DOSS, E J 218 223
DOUGHERTY, Henry 265 John 243 Michael 210 Thos 210 William 210
DOW, George 91
DOWDEN, Nathaniel 73
DOYLE, Farmer 231 Georgia 87 Rebecca 231
DRAKE, Ben 154 Elizabeth 231 Moses 231 Walter C 217-218
DRANE, 80 James H 79 Nancy 79 R B 104 Stephen 221 Stephen T 218
DRISKELL, Caty 236
DUBOURG, Alyce 101
DUGAN, 110 Sally 230 Sarah 67
DUHROON, Betsy 238
DULEY, Betsy 231 James 231
DUNBAR, Robert 265
DUNCAN, James 210 Marshall 210 231 Patsy 231 Sarah 231 William 210
DUNN, John 241
DUPEY, James 210 John 210
DUPUY, B F 253 263 B T 221 Bartholomew 160 Benj F 217 253 Benjamin 251 James 74 Martha 160 Samuel 251 253
DUREE, Winny 232
DURMENT, George 265
DURRETT, Col 196 198
DUTTON, 251 W 251
DYKERS, Susanna 231 William 231
EADLIN, John 265
EAKEN, Alex 210 John 210
EAKIN, Alex'der 232 Jenny 232

EALEM, Elizabeth 232 Richard 232
EASTWOOD, John 46 Joseph 46
EDWARDS, David 232 Margaret 238 Martha Jane 108 Sarah 231 Sussana 232
EGGLESTON, Benj 217
ELAM, 103 Elizabeth 233 Richard 241
ELDER, Thos 179
ELGIN, Sarah 233
ELINGWOOD, James L 135
ELKIN, Robert 80
ELLENWOOD, S H 90 S H Jr 90 Sam H 91
ELLINGWOOD, 132 Henry 227 James 227 Pulaski 227
ELLIOTT, Dr 103 Fanny 232 James 265 John 210 232 Nelly 233 Patsy 237 Robt 210 Sarah Jones 236 Thos 210 William 210
ELLIS, Alfred 128 Anna 234 Elinor 239 John 210
ELLISON, Patsy 233 Rachel 237 Robt 210
ERVIN, Joseph 71 Margaret 71
ESTES, Wm 215
EVANS, Anne 234 David 210 Edward 263 John Jr 265 Robert 210
EWING, Miss 109 Robert 265 William 266
FALL, Phillip 77
FALLENWIDER, Annie 233
FARMER, Chas 210 Joel 210 Oscar 132
FARRA, Samuel 245
FAVOURS, Easter 232 Elizabeth 230 Thomas 232
FEARSON, Meshack 248
FELTY, John 55-56 145
FENFROE, James 205

INDEX

FENLEY, John 265
FERGUSON, Arthur 232 David 232 Easter 232 Eve 232 John 265 Margaret 230 Margt 238 Nancy 231 Saml 210 Sary 232 William 232 William Jr 210
FERMONT, Polydore 101
FERRIS, Mary L 109
FETTY, John 241
FICKLIN, Joseph 263
FIELD, Ann 232 Cane 232
FIELDS, Miss 108
FIGG, 86 Bushrod 87 James 83 87 Lucinda 86-87 Margaret 87 Marvin 87 Susan 83 Warren 87 Warren T 86-87
FINDLAY, John 140
FINE, Jacob 265
FINLEY, 23 110 John 21
FIRGUSON, Mary 67
FISH, David 232 Frankey 232
FISHER, 110 252 Angeline 87 D O 87 John 251 Sarah 237 239
FITZGARROLD, Caty 232 Joseph 232
FITZGERALD, Phillip 127
FITZSIMMONS, Thomas 243
FLEMMING, Ann 232 Enoch 232
FLOURNOY, M 217 Matthew 263
FLOVER, Jonah 241
FLOWERS, Dr 91
FLOYD, 263 Col 30 149 182 Gen 178-179 George R C 263 John 46 177
FLUDE, Mary 232 Timothy 232
FONTAINE, James 265
FORCE, Joseph 245

FORCEE, C M 125
FORD, 80 Elisha 245 Ezra 223 Jas 217 217 John 86 241 Mary 229 Polly 230 Sarah 240 Spencer 232 Susanna 232 William 49 72 Younger 86
FORE, Culvin 100 Joseph L 78 254 Lud 100
FOREE, Jos P 218 Joseph 245 Joseph P 221 P J 218 W W 73
FOREMAN, Thos 210
FOREST, 201
FORGASON, Catharine 234
FORGESON, Andrew 232 Rebecca 232
FOSTER, A J 67
FOUGHT, Catharine 238
FOX, Thomas 101 Tom 118
FRANK, Elijah 210
FRANKLIN, James M 245
FRAZIER, Erasmus 221 H 250 Hamilton 78 J A 218 James 210 Newton 218
FREE, Negro Ned 119
FREEMAN, A F 89 91 J W 132 John 73
FRENCH, William 245
FROK, George 87
FULLENWIDER, Catherine 229 Elizabeth 108 Henry 210 241 Jacob 98 Lucinda 108
FULTON, Mary 187 Professor 109
GALBRAITH, Mary 231
GALBRATH, Jane 239
GALE, Robert F 245
GALLION, Elijah 232 Eliner 232
GAMBLE, William 210
GARNETT, Fleming L 218
GARRET, Elizabeth 232 Isaac 232
GARRETT, Esther 233 John 241 Margaret 237 Nancy 233

GARRETT (cont.)
Polly 233 Sally 232 William 232 Wm 120
GARRISON, J 252 Nar 252
GARROT, Nathan 66 Peggy 66
GASSAWAY, Dorothy 232 Nicholas 232 Richard 241 Sally 232
GATES, Thomas 266
GENT, Isaac Ellis 61
GENTRY, Hugh 210
GEORGE, Ii King Of England 171
GERNERT, Thos 101
GIBBS, 249
GIBSON, 248 Col 169 Elisha 245
GILBERT, 252 Ralph W 221
GILL, Beda 210 Beeda 210 Caty 232 George 232 263 James 210 Matty 234
GILLESPIE, William 266
GLASS, Elizabeth 235 Robert 232 Robert W 268 Sally 232 Samuel 134
GLEN, Jane 236
GLENN, 103 Anne 239 Joseph 55 William 55 Wm 215
GLOVER, Edekiel 265 Francis 230 Jonah 211
GLOVERS, Uriah 168
GOBEN, Liddy 233
GOBIN, Elizabeth 232 James 232
GODBEY, T J 87
GODDARD, William 232 Winny 232
GOLDMAN, Lucy 229
GOOD, Maria 108
GOODMAN, J W 48 Johannes 263
GOODVINE, Thomas 210
GOORE, 249
GORE, Frederick 210
GORLEY, Margaret 108
GOTT, Betsy 237 Lydia 232 Robert 232
GOULD, Judge 153
GOUTERMAN, Anne 232 John 232
GRAHAM, Betsy 237 James 96 John 251 John F 254 Mrs 97 Patsy 96 232 Sam 96 Samuel 150 William 96 232
GRANT, Joshua D 58 128
GRAVES, Betsy 67 234 David 210 Dickey 232 Edmon 67 Edmond 210 215 245 Jane 67 John 67 Nelly 232
GRAY, Catharine 67 Mary 235 Robert 210 Samuel 67
GREATHOUSE, America 108 Isaac 254
GREEN, Catharine 241 Charles 252 Jonathan 241 Mary 232 Richard 210 Sally 235 Stephen 232
GREENUP, Christopher 265
GREGG, Mary 236
GREGGS, David 211 215
GREGORY, Andrew 232 John 232 Joseph 232 Mary 232 Polly 232 Pricilla 232 Rebeckah 232 Will 210 William 232
GRIFFEY, Thos 210
GRIFFIN, Lucy 235 Mary 232 Sarah 235 Wm 211
GRIFFITH, Eli 211 Hannah 234
GRIGERY, John 215
GRIGGSBY, Mary 239
GRIGSBY, Benjamin 245
GRINSTEAD, W S 87
GROOMS, Wm 252
GRUNDY, Felix 157

INDEX

GUIN, Thos 104 167
GUINN, 103
GUTHRIE, Adam 263 Caleb 66 73 J D 132 James 128
GWATHMEY, John 254
GWIN, Hanna 230 Thomas I 210 Thomas L 221
GWYER, T J 217
HAFF, Abraham 232 Ann 232 Luke 253
HALEY, O L 67
HALFLAND, Barshebah 232 Henry 232
HALL, 103 139 Allen 168 David Stevenson 257 Edward 167 Elizabeth 108 233 Elizabeth P 168 Francis 233 Isabelle 168 John 168 170 251 254 Joseph 135 Margaret 108 Moses 55 55-56 96-97 127 135 167-168 211 257 Moses Jr 168 Moses Sr 168 170 Sallie Lane 170 W W 132
HAM, David 211 Jacob 211 Mathias 211
HAMBLETON, Easter 239
HAMLEY, James 211
HAMMOND, Esther 233 Joesph 233
HANEIL, Philip 241
HANKINS, Thomas 266
HANKS, Nancy 200
HANNAH, Martha I 108
HANSBORO, 178 Joel 178 Miss 178 182
HANSBOROUGH, Enoch 250 George 56
HANSBROUGH, Geo 55 George 233 John 211 Marius 60 Monias 241 Nancy 233

HANSBROUGH (cont.) Peter 263 Rodman 60
HANSLEY, Barman 211 James 211 John 211 Jonathan 211 Richardson 211
HANTAN, Darby 211
HAPP, Luke 263
HARBART, Josiah 211 Thomas 211
HARBISON, 249 David 96 248 254 Eugene 132 M A 226 Patsy 97 Sam 96 Saml 221 Samuel 253
HARDESTY, J W 66
HARDIN, 105 Betsy 96 Col 150 159 161 Elizabeth Hall 168 J J 151 Jane 59 M D 150 Mark 135 253 Martin D 254 Mary 108
HARMON, Joseph 211
HARRIS, 178 Ann 233 Jere 46 John 101 233 Margaret 236 Mary 233 Michael 101 Polly 238 W D 191
HARRISON, 36 158 160 Belsey 236 Eleanor 87 Gen 154 160 Geo 211 James 87 Wm H 153 Wm Henry 161
HART, Dr 99 Philip 211 233 Susanna 233
HARTER, Adam 211
HARTLEY, Daniel 243
HARTMAN, Abm 211 Anthony 211 241 Hannah 233 Mary 235
HARWOOD, Chas 101
HASTINGS, 132
HATE, Betsy 97
HATHAWAY, Nancy 233 Philip 233
HATTON, Ann 233 John 233 Patsy 233 Robert 233
HAWES, Isaac 265
HAWKINS, Claiborne 233 George 245 Mary 233
HAYNES, John 211
HEARN, John T 128

HISTORY OF SHELBY COUNTY

HEATON, Isaac 250
HEDDEN, Barcella 233 Daniel 233 Gilbert 233 John 67 233 Nancy 233 Samuel C 227 Sarah 233
HELM, 79 William 257 Wm S 218
HENDERSON, Charles 263 Frances 173 J A 87 James L 263 Samuel 103
HENOTHORNY, Francis 251
HENRY, Jesse 211 233 Nelly 233 Patrick 145 167
HENSLEY, Allefer 233 Berryman 233 Edmond 233 Elizabeth 233 Jonathan 233 Nancy 233 Polly 233 Sally 229 Samuel 233
HEPPARD, William 245
HERNDON, 196 James 103
HERRIFORD, Milly 231
HERRING, George 245
HICKLIN, Hugh 211
HICKMAN, A W 251 Daniel 233 J W 132 James 124 245 Mary 233 William 66
HICKS, Nancy 231
HIGGASON, Thomas 245
HIGGINS, Pat 100
HILL, Dr 106 Fergus 233 Forges 211 Hardy 241 Jenny 233 Professor 105
HILLMAN, Benj 211
HINER, Robert 87
HINKLE, C J 202
HINTON, 178 Evan 45 266 John 46 Thomas 266 Thos W 218
HITE, Abraham 265 Joseph 83
HOBBS, W G 67
HOGELAND, Moses 233 Sarah 233

HOGLAND, Aaron 233 Bersheba 233 Elizabeth 233 Henry 233 James 71 71 Mary 71 Rachel 237 Richd 241
HOKE, Susanna 231
HOLDEN, Capt 149 Joseph 140
HOLLAND, Ann 67 James M 245 John 66-67 John W 218 Mary P 67 Rev 74
HOLLENBACH, 132 Albert 91
HOLLENBACK, A 90
HOLLEY, Samuel 247
HOLLINGSWORTH, John 265
HOLMES, Andrew 211 254 257 Bolling 251 I 251 James 211 266 Jesse 265-266 Sarah 234 Waller 251
HOLSON, Mary 229
HOLT, Abraham 46
HONREY, James 211
HOPE, 110
HOPKINS, 80 Horace 74
HOR, 251
HORNS, John 211
HORNSBY, Cynthia 173-174 Frances 173 Hannah 173 173 Joseph 104 173-174 211 Margaret 174 Mildred 173 Mildred Thornton 173 Thomas 173-174 Thos 221
HORTON, Elizabeth 233 Thomas 233
HOSTEDLER, Abram 211 Christian 211
HOSTIDLER, Barbary 234
HOUGHLAND, Elias 233 Sarah 233
HOUGHSTATLER, Adam 233 Hannah 233
HOWARD, Archabald 233 Archibald 266 Clary 233 Nancy 233 Susanna 239
HOWE, Sarah 233
HUCKLEBERRY, Jacob 233 Winney 233

INDEX

HUFF, Abm 211 Luke 211
HUFFMAN, M 132
HUGHES, Mike 227 Morgan 46 197 199
HUGHS, 178
HULL, Gen 165
HUME, John 49
HUMPHRAS, Mirry 211
HUMSTON, N A 66
HUNGERFORD, V M 67
HUNT, Geo 46 John 254
HUNTER, Elizabeth 236 Jemima 230 Mr 113 Percilly 233 Thomas 233
HUSS, Ann 237 Leasey 229 M W 131 Mary 233 Richard 233
INDIAN, Tecumseh 160
INFIELD, Annie 233 Thomas 233
INGLES, John 233 Liddy 233
INGRAM, Archer 211
IRVIN, Robert 233 Temperance 233
JACK, 252
JACKSON, F 255 Francis 254 Frank 251 J 255 Josiah 251 254 President 163 W L 225
JACOB, Martin 266 Samuel 266
JACOBS, Bennett 266 Elizabeth 232-233 Thomas 233 241
JAMES, Elizabeth 235 Geo 211 Sarah 239
JARVIS, Gilbert 80 Robt 251 Wm 251
JEFFIES, Robert 221
JEFFRIES, Robert 61
JENKINS, Eliner 232
JENNINGS, Daniel 263
JESSIE, Bettie 87
JETER, Elijah 265
JETTER, William 265
JILLSON, Dr 19
JOHNS, Henry 211 Sailly 233 Sarah 231 Thomas 233
JOHNSON, Archibald 245 Daniel 120 David 211 266 Edw 211 J J 87 James 1st 243 James 2nd 243 John 211 Lanty 211 Lucinda 108 108 Margaret 230 Mrs 96 Philip 241 Thos 217 William 211
JOHNSTON, 118 Daniel 233 Darkus 234 Geo W 217 217 George I 263 James 234 Jane 234 Jenny 234 John 211 John F 66 Martha 233 Melvinie 235 Mildred 235 Philip 254 Susanna 233 Thomas 263 William 234
JOHNSTONE, Geo W 225 John W 219 Wm 96
JONES, 80 Elizabeth 234 Frances 235 Harriet 229 Polly 234 Thomas 234 247 Thos 218 William 234 266 William A 225 Wm L 218
JONKERSTON, Andrew 211
JUDITH, James M 67
KALTENBACHER, W S 101
KARE, Absolem 211 Moses 211
KAVANAUGH, Bishop 83 William 83
KEARNS, Sarah 239
KEASSEY, Wm 251
KEES, Nancy 239
KELSO, Thomas 245
KENDALL, Elizabeth 237
KENDRICKS, William 245
KENNADY, Anne 234 Samuel 234
KENNEY, Ann J 70 Geo W 70
KEPHART, Abraham 234 Rebecca 234
KERDE, Wm Kin 221
KERNES, Mariah 239

KERNS, Jane 231
KESTER, Eve 232 John 211 Paul 211 William 211
KETCHAM, John 266
KETCHUM, Rebecca 235
KILLIN, Robt 211
KILLPATRICK, Mrs 96
KINDALL, Elizab 234 Ewell 234
KINDELL, Nancy 234 Yelly 234
KINDER, George 266 Sallie 229
KINDLE, Polly 232
KING, 120 Abraham 263 Ann 96 Annie 96 George 97 Jeff 119 Lucy 234 Nathaniel 234 Nelly 97 Robrt 263 Thom 96
KINKADE, Wm 250
KINKEAD, Allen 73 Robt 211 Samuel 132
KINKLE, Charles 91
KIRK, 110
KIRKPATRICK, John 265
KIRLIN, John 210
KITELY, 250
KNAP, Joshua 211
KNIGHT, 139 262 Doctor 56 Dr 170 George B 217 263 John 66 169-170 217 247 249 Jos W 217 Joseph W 170 263 Sallie Lane 170 William 60 Wm 128
KNOSE, Mrs 96
KNOTT, Professor 105
KNOX, Ann 155 Col 155 Dr 121 Jacob 211 James 254 267 John 246
KULBRATH, Polly 234 Samuel 234
KUYKENDALL, Mathew 211 Peter 211

KYSOR, Catharine 234 John 234
LACEFIELD, Betsy 230 Jacob 234 Sarah 234
LAFAYETTE, Gen 59
LAMB, Geo 212
LANCASTER, Jacob 234 Joanna 234
LANDEN, John 234 Sally 234
LANE, Anna 234 Craven 211 James 212 John 211 227 Lambert 212 241 Nancy 235 Rebeckah 232 Sally 237 Thomas 234 Thos 212
LANG, John 265
LANGFORD, Larkin 234 Rachel 234
LANGLEY, Elisha 234 Jane 234
LAPP, John 211
LASLEY, Hannah 234 Robert 234
LASLY, Gilliam 211 Nancy 212
LASTLEY, Robert 241
LASTLY, Mary 237 Polly 234
LATTIMOORE, 250
LAUKFORD, Milly 231
LAWLER, M D 101
LAWRENCE, David 241
LAWSON, Robert Sr 58 Stokeley 87
LAYSON, 132 Jeptha 79 R M 79
LEACH, Daniel 251 253
LEASE, George 249
LEATHERMAN, Barbary 234 Betsy 234 238 Christian 234 Dorothy 232 Frederick 234 John 234 241 Polly 234
LEE, Isabelle 234 Nathaniel 234 Peter 101 Phil 201 Rebecca 230 Tarlton 67 William 211
LEFFEAR, Geo 234 Harriet 234
LEGON, Wilson 212
LEMAM, Mr 96
LEMASTER, Hugh 246 Richard 241
LEMMENS, Robert 212
LEMMON, James 212
LEMON, Capt 159 Lucy 234

INDEX

LEODOCY, James M 67
LESTER, Cornelius 266
LETHERMAN, Hanna 237
  Nancy 211 Peter 211
LEWIS, 174 Ann 232 C M 128
  John 241 Mildred 173
  Nicholas Merriwether 173
  Polly 235 William 144
LIGHT, George C 85
LINCOLN, 29 Abraham 49 195-200 Bathsheba Herring 200 Capt 198 Josiah 196 Mary Shipley 200 Mordecai 196 198 Nancy 197 200 Pres 25 Thomas 196 200 Widow 199
LINDSAY, 35
LINDSEY, Elisha 211 234 Hester 231 Sarah 234 V 250 Vechel 211
LINKHORN, Abraham 195
LINKLEY, Hannah 173
LINSEY, William 212
LISHY, Gilliam 211
LISTON, Edmond 211
LIVELY, 103
LIVENSTON, John L 234 Mary 234
LIVLY, Daniel 135
LOCHRY, 145 Col 144 144
LOCK, 55 David 103 Elizabeth 234 Sarah 229 William 234
LOCKE, 132
LOCKHART, Betsy 234 Enoch 234 Jane 234 William 234
LOCKHEART, Polly 236
LOGAN, 139 167 251 263
  Aaron 234 Alex 98
  Alexander 96 212 Ann 155 268 Ben 155 Benj 103-105 217 Benjamin 113 155 160 219 267-268

LOGAN(cont.)
  Benjamine 155 161 257 Betsy 155
  David 155 211 234 Effie 155
  Elizabeth S 268 Emmett G 129 J A 93 J M 132 James 104 114 155 225 James K 268 James M 59 227 Jane 59 267 Jane A 108 Jean 229 Jno 249 John 114 217 249 John A 218 John Jr 253 John K 267 Mary 155 237 Matty 234 Nancy 96 234 Polly 155 Priscilla 108 267 Priscilla Jane 108 Robert 267 Robt 249 William 105 114 155 161 249 267 Wm 217
LONDEN, John 234 Sally 234
LONDON, Jane 71 Robert 71
LONG, David 134 Hannah 234 J J 218 J L 80 James L 80 Margaret 80 Mary J 80 Milly 71 Mr 96 R A 139 Robert 80 Robert A 80 S C 80 Saml 80 211 Samuel 234 William 247
LOVE, Joseph 266
LOWDER, Margaret 231
LOWRY, Robert 212
LUCAS, Catherin 231 Lydia 236
LUCKE, Abm 212
LUCKETT, 254
LUDWINGTON, Betsey 234 Esair 234
LUKES, John 212
LUNSFORD, Mary 232
LYLE, David 234 Sarah 234
LYMEN, David 211
LYNCH, Col 46 Margt 108 Milly 238
LYON, 249
LYONS, John 101
LYST, George 97
MACACHRAN, John 127
MACAULEY, 45 Fanny Caldwell 139

MACGAUGHEY, Arthur 225
MADDOX, 79 103 Absolom 212 Daniel 235 Nancy 235 W Henry 132 Wilson 246
MADISON, Gov 153 156 President 153
MAGINNIS, John 212
MAGNER, Margaret 236
MAGRUDER, Hardin 85 Josiah 221 Josiah H 218
MAHULIN, Mary 238
MAHUREN, Saml 212
MAHURIN, Mary 231 Sally 235 Stephen 235
MAHURON, Othenal 212 Silas 212
MALIN, Isaac 212
MALONE, Benj 212 Clint 202 Emma Bonney 91 H C 91 202 H H 90
MAPES, C M 135
MARQUISS, Lucy 235 William 235
MARROW, Isabelle 234
MARSHALL, Charles 266 Chas C 225 Elizabeth 235 James L 98 Robert 235 William 71 129
MARTIN, Abner 235 David S 123 Elizabeth 237 Jacob 251 Lewis 212 235 Mary 235 237 Nimrod 212 Phebe 240 Polly 235 Saml 212 Thomas 67 Thos 212 Wilford 235
MASON, Ben 221
MASONHEIMER, J H 124
MASSIE, William 212
MATHENEY, John G 263
MATINGLY, James 212
MATTHEWS, Absalom 249
MATTOX, Barbara 239

MAY, Francis 235 Mary 235 Priscella 69
MAYO, Elinore 235
MCAFEE, 160
MCALLISTER, Edw C 91
MCBRIDE, Robert 212
MCCACHRON, John 251
MCCALISTER, Daniel 246
MCCAMPBELL, James 212 241 John 96 Saml 212
MCCARBY, Mr 178
MCCARM, 80
MCCARTER, Robert 212
MCCARTHY, James 79 101
MCCARTNEY, Susanna 240
MCCARTY, Sarah 229
MCCLAIN, Alexander 235 Ann 235 David 212 George 235 Hephizabah 235 John 235 241 Mary 235 Saml 241
MCCLANNON, William 212
MCCLANON, Joseph 212
MCCLELAND, Daniel 246
MCCLELLAND, 262 Dan 104 Daniel 56 212 221 235 241 H 55 Hance 250 James B 263 Margaret 239 Mary 235 Nancy 234
MCCLURE, Hugh 235 James 241 John 212 Polly 235
MCCOCHRAN, John 55
MCCONNELL, James 263
MCCORMACK, John 212 Nancy 235 William 212 235
MCCORMICK, John 83 Lemuel 83 Lizzie 109 Sarah 83
MCCORTNEY, Geney 229 Hannah 234 Jenny 229
MCCOURTNEY, Jane 212 John 212
MCCOY, James 235 Nancy 235 Sallie 236
MCCREADY, George 91

INDEX

MCCREARY, Russell B 109
MCCULLOUGH, James 235 Jane 235
MCCURHAM, 103
MCDANIEL, Daniel 212
MCDAVID, Mrs 96
MCDAVITT, James 263
MCDONALD, James 235 Jane 235
MCDOWELL, Daniel 235 Elizabeth 232 Jane 239 Mary 233 Nelly 236 Rhoda 235
MCELTREE, 249
MCFADDEN, John 46 Will 101
MCGANN, Joseph 101
MCGAUGHEY, 103 Amanda 108 Ann 230 Authur 114 252 James 227 John 56 251 253 262-263 Samuel 227 Wilson 252
MCGAUHEY, J 55
MCGLACHEN, James 212
MCGLAUGHLIN, 117
MCGRATH, James 125 R 250 Robert 85 120 Thomas A 125 Thos C 124
MCGREN, Mary 235
MCHENRY, Ann 235 Barnabas 85 Barnabus 83 Martin D 85 217-218 Rachel 231
MCHUREN, Barcella 233
MCINTIRE, Polly 230
MCINTOSH, 249
MCINTYRE, T J 87
MCKENDREE, Bishop 84
MCKINLEY, Elizabeth 235 James 212 John 212
MCKINNEY, Rachel 238
MCLAUGHLIN, 121 James 100 120 212
MCMAHON, "big Frank" 79

MCMAMESS, John 212
MCMANNIS, John 212
MCMASTER, Michael 212
MCMILLAN, J P 98
MCNANES, John 212
MCNEIL, Benj 235 Rachel 235
MCNEW, Easter 232
MCQUADE, James 66-67 James Sr 66
MCQUILLAN, Maggie 101
MCWADE, Henry 235 Margt 235 Mary 235
MEADE, Mary 101
MEEK, Jeremiah 235 Mary 235 Temperance 233
MEEKS, Elizabeth 235 Jesse 212 241 John 235 Mary 235 Priddy 212 Sussana 232 William 235
MELONE, 110 Benjamine 235 Drurey 212 Drury 263 Elizabeth 235 Hiram 71
MERIWEATHER, Nicholas V 172 Richard Jr 172
MERIWETHER, Elizabeth 171-172 George Wood 172 Nicholas 171-172 Nicholas Ii 171 Nicholas V 171 Patsy 171 Richard 171-172 Susannah F 172 Thornton 172
MERRIWEATHER, Nicholas 104
MERRIWETHER, Nicholas 212
METCALF, Elizabeth 234-235 Frances 235 Isaac 235 James 241 William 235
METCALFE, Hester 71 James 71 Thomas 71 William 71
MICHEL, Chas 68
MIDDELTON, 185-186 188 Adam 131-132 187-188 190 192-193 James D 190 Jim 192 John 192 John Ad 132 John Adam 132 John T 190 Letitia 190-191

MIDDELTON (cont.)
  Mary 187 190 192 Mary E
  191 Price W 190 Robert 188
  190-193 W D 132 Wallace B
  191 William R 191
MIDDLETON, Adam 27 H F
  131 Henri F 128 135 Mr 128
  Mrs 96
MILAN, Stephen 266
MILBURNE, George 120
MILES, Mr 96
MILLAR, John 265
MILLEN, Alexander 235
  Elinore 235
MILLER, Conrad 212 David
  212 212 Isaac 212 Jenny 234
  238 John 235 L 132 Melvinie
  235 Mildred 235 Miss 257
  Nancy 233 William 235
MILLIGAN, Percilly 233
MILLS, Joseph 251
MILNER, John 266
MINOR, Rev 87
MINTOR, John 250 Richard 250
MISER, John 212
MITCHEL, Agnes 235 Rebecca
  235 Saml 235 Thomas 235
MITCHELL, Charles 246 Chas
  221 Gideon 218 James 266
  Mrs 97 Nancy 235 238
  Thomas 221 Thos 115 115
  William 266
MOCENSEN, William 69
MONAY, James 140
MONROE, Barshebah 232
  Bersheba 233 William P 268
MONSON, Allen 235 Sarah 235
MONTFORT, Aaron Jno 51
  Bennett 51 John 235 Mary
  235 238 Nancy 235
MONTGOMERY, Ann 155 268

MONTGOMERY (cont.)
  Geo 212 John 212 236 Lydia 236
  Mary 229 Mr 96
MOORE, Abraham 246 Agness 229
  Betsy 236 Doctor 56 Dr 249
  Elizabeth 236 James 89 253-254
  262-263 Jas 217 Mary L 60 Mr 97
  Robert 261 William 236
MORGAN, 150 201 243 Elizabeth
  233 John 202 William 243
MORLAN, John 212
MORRIS, Joshua 66 71 74 Susan 236
  William 236
MORRISON, Daniel L 263
MORROW, Philip 212
MORSE, Alexander 246
MORTON, Hiram 73 James 212
  Nancy 235 Thos G 120
MOSLEY, Edw 236 Sarah Jones 236
MOUNTS, Alfred G 251
MUELIN, Mr 97
MUIR, P B 225
MUKS, Priddy 212
MULLIKIN, Barton 236 Jane 236
  John 243
MUNDLE, Mrs 182
MUNNET, Hannah 236 Isaac 236
MUNRO, Prudence 239
MUNSEY, Rachel 230-231
MURPHY, Denis 236 Sallie 236
MURRAY, Jesse 265 William 212
  Wm 212
NABB, I 254
NALL, J L 197
NANCY, Polyn 237
NAPOLEON, 154
NATION, Geo 212 Polly 230
NEAL, 251 Archibald 236 Elias 236
  Margaret 236 Margt 236 Micajah
  246 Richard 85 Sally 236 William
  236 Wm 212 250

INDEX

NEALE, Charles 266
NEARN, Mordici 212
NEEL, Fielding 83 85
NEGRO, Caleb 121
NEIL, Fielding 218
NEILL, Wm 221
NEVIL, Charlotte 239 Elizabeth 238
NEWKIRK, 132 James E 66
NEWLAND, 110 Isaac 241 Jack 115 Jacob 241 John 223 253 Lucy 241 William 265
NEWMAN, Belsey 236 Ezekil 236 Henry 212 Margaret 236 Simeon 236
NICHOLAS, Elizabeth 236 Prather 262 William 236 266
NICHOLS, Elizabeth 236 John 46 Lydia 232 Reason 236
NOEL, Bazel 236 Mary 236
NOLAN, 101
NOLAND, Pierce 91
NORMAN, Isaac 212
NORRIS, John 212 236 Nelly 236
NORTHSINGER, Andrew 212
NUCHOLS, G W 78
NUCKOLS, Dr 121
NUNN, J E 106
NUTTALL, Polly 236 Price 236
O'CONNOR, Kate 101
O'HARA, Theodore 109
O'LECKLAND, John 212
O'NEIL, James L 135
O'SULLIVAN, M 128 Micheal 218
OFFUTT, Henry C 134
OGLESBY, Samuel 217
OLIVER, Ann 236 Betsy 238 Joseph 236 Mary 232
ORGAN, Elizbeth 236 John 236

OSBORNE, Merry 236 Michael 236
OSBURN, Jonathan 212
OUTHOUSE, Peter 212
OVERSTREET, 250
OWEN, 124 139 262 A 55 Abraham 47 53-54 159 161 168 217 221 263 Abram 159 Bob 202 Bracken 161 Bracket 113 117 184 Brackett 36 47-48 53 114 159 161 241 Clark 160 Col 160-161 David 263 Dick 201-202 George 241 J M 60 132 Jacob 85 James M 135 John 236 Joseph 212 Martha 160 254 Patsy 236 Richard T 225 Robert 160 212 263 Sally 232 Susanna 236 William 85 135 160 236
OWENS, A 103 Abraham 219 Joseph 103
OWSLEY, N 131
PADDOCK, Jonathan 213 Phoebe 239
PANABAKER, John 265
PARIS, Robert 246
PARK, Sarah 229
PARKER, 103 Jane 267 John 167 John T 267 Joshua 236 Mary 236
PARKERS, Caty 232 Thos 212-213
PARRIS, Ellen 238
PATERSON, Arthur 96 Polly 96
PATTEN, William 120
PATTERSON, Arthur 236 John 69 Johnston 69 Martha 236 Mary 236 Sarah 69 William 212
PATTON, Ebenezer 213
PATTRICK, Robert 215
PAUL, John 215 Peter 45 Priscilla 212
PAYNE, Elizabeth 236 J A 132 Jeremiah 236 John 165 213 Jonathan 236 Joseph M 263 Sallie 236

PEAK, Frank 225
PEARCE, 110 David 236
  Frances 236
PEARCY, Gen 221 George 96
  John 236 Rebeccah 236
PEAY, N 254 Nicholas 263
PEECK, John 213
PEMBERTON, 110
PENDERGRASS, Betsy 236
  Jesse 236 Patience 238
PENDIGRASS, Doctor 56
PENNDIGRASS, Dr 249
PENNINGTON, Isaac 213 236
  241 Polly 236
PENNY, John 66 72
PERKINS, 103 Caty 236
  Hannah 240 Jane 235-236
  Jenny 233 John 213 Joseph
  236 Polly 236 Sam'l 250
  Samuel 236 William 236 241
PERRY, B 55 Benjamin 251
  Nancy 239 Roderick 68
PETIT, Thomas 243
PETTIT, Eliza 59
PETTY, Ludlow F 227
PHIGLEY, Simon 213
PHILIPS, Catharine 236-237
  John 236
PICKETT, 202 Geo L 218
PIERCY, George 217
PIKE, E K 87
PILES, Conradus 236 Nancy
  236
POGUE, 250
POLAN, Polly 237 William 237
POLK, 36 Charles 213 Daniel
  85 President 154 Sarah 230
POLLARD, Benj R 253 Edward
  T 221 Oney 237
POLLY, John 213 237 Peter 213
  Polly 237

POLYNE, Mr 97 Poly 97
POMEROY, America 108 Isaac 85
  Joseph 265
POPE, 139 John 104 157 163 217
  262-263 Warden 263
PORTER, I N 73 Nathaniel P 254
  Natt 250
POSTELWAIT, 252
POSTLEWEIGHT, Sallie 236
POTTS, John 241 266
POUND, Elizabeth 231
POUNDS, Joseph 213 Rebecca 238
  Thos 212
POWELL, William 241
POYNTER, 128 Clara M 107 Harriett
  107 Julia 107 W T 107
PREWITT, Elisha 61 213 Fanny 232
  Joseph 237 Patsy 237 Tabitha 239
PRICE, David 213 Drucey 239
  Frederick 212 Henry L 98 John
  120 William 212
PRICHETT, Sarah 239
PRIESTLY, James 157
PRIOR, Sarah 238
PRUITT, Michael 241
PRYOR, James 225
PUCK, John 213
PULLIAM, Robert 212
PUSEY, William 266
QUANTRILL, 123
QUINN, Clinton 91 James 99
QUIRK, James 213
RADCLIFF, James 67
RADFORD, Rebeccah 236
RAGSDALE, Godfrey 103 246
RAMSEY, Geo W 134 J J 134 T J
  132 134
RANDOLPH, 132 251 Charles 127
  Henry 243 Richard 127 Runer 127
  William 127 213

INDEX

RANKIN, Carolina 108 John W 253 Wm 251
RATCLIFFE, Samuel 83 Susan 83
RAWLINGS, Effie 231
RAY, James C 223 W R 218
RAYZOR, Paul 246
READING, Sarah 237 William 237
REASER, Michael 213
REBEL, Jonathan 213
REDAY, Sarah 237 William C 237
REDD, John 265
REDDING, Merritt 118 T 55 Timothy 252 William 241
REDFORD, 250
REED, Alex 217 Shannon 132
REES, Betsy 237 Jacob 237 Polly 237 Thomas F 237
REEVES, Joseph 248 Judge 153
REID, Alex 217 225 Alexander 114 213 Barnet 213 237 Caleb 213 G L 98 James 213 241 John 143 Sailly 233 Saml 213 Sarah 143 Shannon 218 Susanna 237
REILY, John 96 248
RENDFROE, Isaac 205
RENFRO, Isaac 206 James 205-206 Judith 206 Mary 206 William 205
RENFROE, William 205
RENSHAW, Polly 229
REYNOLDS, James 263 Thomas 250 266
RHODY, Chris 237 Isabell 237
RIBLE, Catharine 236
RICE, Alice Hegan 139 John 67 Robert 79
RICHARDS, Joshua 246

RICHARDSON, Ephriam 213 James Jr 213 James Sr 213 John 237 Nancy 237
RICHIE, David 265
RID, Joshua 213
RILEY, G W 135 John 246
RITCH, Mary 238
RITCHIE, Jacob 213 237 Mary 237 Thomas 213
RIVELL, Catharine 237 Joseph 237
ROBB, Robt T 221
ROBERTS, 114 249 Agnes 213 Ben 104 Benj 221 Benjamin 246 263 Benjamine 114 Bethier 237 Bishop 84 Elizabeth 236 George 213 Henry 213 Silvestil 237 William 263
ROBERTSON, 251 George Rood 145 Sarah 234
ROBINS, Bethier 237 James 213 237 Mary 237 Rachel 237-238 Rebecca 232 William 237 241
ROBINSON, G N 218 George 85 254 J M 191 Jesse 221 John 73 85 131-132 225 266
RODMAN, Thomas 213
ROE, W F 104
ROGAN, 118
ROGERS, 104 Bob 79
ROLLING, William 250
ROLLINGS, Sophira 240
ROMAINE, Bailey 266
ROMGUE, John 263
ROSE, Alexander 213 John 213 R R 87
ROSEMYER, Frederick 213
ROSS, B B 55 John 237 P J 87 Sally 237
ROTHCHILD, 132
ROUSE, 251 Maria 108 108
ROWAN, 263 John 157 263

ROWDEN, Geo 90 George 91
ROWE, James 246
ROWLAND, Wm 263
ROYSTER, William 73
RUBLE, Adam 213 Hanna 237 Jacob 213 Jonathan 237
RUCKER, Elliott 248 Miss 109
RUD, Alexander 213
RUDY, George 265
RUSSEL, Randolph R 227
RUSSELL, D S 98 Wm 163
RYKER, Deborah 239
SACREY, James 244
SADLER, 80
SAELBURN, Mary 235
SAIN, Edward 117
SAINTCLAIR, 159 161
SAMPLES, Samuel 266
SAMPSON, Geo 109 Isaac 244
SANDERS, Culvin 218 Reuben 246
SARGENT, Nelson 237 Oney 237 Sally 239
SATTERLEY, Saml 213
SAWIN, P W 66
SCEARCE, Geo 109 Henry 237 Lilly 237 Nathan 237 Rebecca 237
SCOTT, 103 Arter 213 Elizabeth 237 Gen 147 Hugh 265 Jane 237 John 109 214 249 Martin 237 Moses 66-67 Mrs 96 Robert 237 Selia A 109
SCOTTHORN, 250
SCROGGANS, I 251
SCROGGIN, Anna 237 George 237
SEARCE, John C 129
SEBASTIN, Samuel 237 Sarah 237
SHACKELFORD, Sterling 266
SHACKLEFORD, Mr 157 T O 202
SHAFER, David 213
SHANKS, Robert 266 Samuel 266 Wm 221
SHANNON, 139 Agnes 143-144 239 Anna 143 Capt 144 James 103 213 John 55 143 249 John Jr 254 Margaret 143 Mr 54 Saml 214 Samuel 103 143 145 217 257 Sarah 143 239 Thomas 143 214 221 242 William 25 53 56 103 113 143-145 223 Wm 217 241
SHARP, Anthony 213 237 John 213 Micajah 266 Rachel 237
SHARVIS, Davis 214
SHAW, Jacob 214-215
SHEA, 132
SHELBURN, Augustine 213 Dionysius 213 Lucinda 108
SHELBURNE, D 221
SHELBY, Gov 153 Isaac 23
SHEM, Cornelius 237 Polyn 237
SHEPHARD, John 213
SHEPHERD, Jane 234
SHEPPARD, Frankey 232
SHIELDS, Elizabeth 237 James 237 Mary Ann 230 Patrick 241
SHILIDAY, Caty 96
SHILIDRAY, Caleb 96
SHILLADY, Patsy 232
SHINDLER, Geo 213
SHINNICK, 128 E D 117 Ed 101 Mary 101 William 132 Wm 100
SHIPMAN, 103 249 Margaret 237 Sarah 237 Stephen 237 William 237 263
SHIVELY, Henry 214
SHOUSE, 110
SHUCK, 50 Andrew 51 242 Polly 237 Wm 51
SHUGH, Mr 97 Poly 97

INDEX

SILKWOOD, Barzella 213
SILL, Acenath 237 Adam 237
   Ann 237 Mary 233
SIMMONS, Robt 215
SIMPSON, 139 262 Agnes 213
   Elizabeth 237 J W 87 James
   214 John 60 114 165 213
   217 249 263 263 Joseph 213
   237 263
SIMRALL, J 221 James 251
   James G 139 Jas 217 Joseph
   115
SKOOLER, J K 132
SLAUGHTER, 67 Sarah 234
SLED, William 242
SMITH, 124 Abraham 78 155
   227 237 263 Adam C 237
   Benjamin L 267 Betsy 237
   Bettie 87 Bishop 89 Daniel
   213 Ebenezer 237 Edward 96
   Elizabeth 238 George 96
   Harriet 234 Henry 217 247
   Jacob 213-214 241 Jane 231
   238 John 213 213 238 M T
   132 Margaret 96 108 Mary
   155 237 Mary Logan 267
   Matilda 108 Milly 238 Mr 79
   Nicholas 213-214 218 Polly
   155 Rebecca 238 Robert 238
   Samuel 238 Simon 238
   Stanley 87 Stephen 238
   Thomas 87 William 78 213
   Wm 249
SMOCK, Jacob 51 266 Rachel
   238 Samuel 238
SNIDER, Peter 213
SNYDER, Sarah 87
SORRELS, Elizabeth 232
   Ellender 213 Milly 240
SOUTH, Nancy 238 William
   238

SPADE, Ben 51
SPANGLER, John 87
SPAULDING, Bishop 100 M J 101
SPEARS, Joshua 213 Paul 214
SPECK, 252
SPENCER, Hephizabah 235 J H 89
   99 John 214 Spear 214 Walter 213
SPENDER, John 215
SPRIGG, Jas C 218
SPROOLE, Margaret 108
SQUIRES, John 242
STAFFORD, Henry 238 Mary 238
STAMPER, Jonathan 85
STANDEFORD, William 227
STANDIFORD, David 23 25 53-54
   117 217 Israel 214 James 266 Mrs
   91 William 78
STANIFORD, 127
STANLEY, Elizabeth 230 Joseph 213
STANSBERRY, Nancy 231
STAPLES, Mary 238 Noah 238
STAPLETON, John 46
STARK, Abraham 238 Anne 232
   Christopher 214 Daniel 214 Danl
   Jr 214 Jacob 214 238 James 238
   John 214 Jonathan 214 238 Margt
   238 Rachel 238 Rebecca 238
   Rhoda 235 Sarah 238
STARKE, Elizabeth 238
STARKS, James 214 214 Jonathan
   214
STEEL, Adam 238 Charles 238
   Elizabeth B 238 James 214 Jonah
   214 Polly 238
STEELE, 55 103 254 Adam 113 167
   251 263 Hannah 97 Mrs 96
STEPHENS, Andrew J 223 John 238
   Rachel 238 Richard 263 Sarah 238
   William 238
STEPHENSON, Elizab 234
STEPLES, Betsy 238 Noah 238

STEPLETON, Andrew 213
STEVENS, Saml 213
STEVENSON, Edward 85
  Isabelle 168 Miss 170 Robert 213 Thomas 168
STEWART, Archibald 157 John 140
STICE, Andrew 214
STILL, Catherine 231 Murphy 213
STILWELL, Daniel 238 Delilah 238 John 214 Joseph 214
STITLIN, Susanna 237
STONE, Ambrose 120 Benj 213 Harvey 79 William 214
STORTS, Albert C 268 John W 268
STOUT, 55 110 I 250 James 238 242 Margaret 238 Reuben 246
STRATON, Joseph 120
STRATTON, Seth 243
STROTHER, J E 87
STUART, D T 98 David Todd 105 Winchester Hall 105
STUK, James 214
STURGEON, Martha 233 Nelly 239
STURGIN, James 214 John 213 John Jr 213 Robt 214
STURMAN, 252
SULLIVAN, Dennis 238 Elizabeth 230 Margt 238
SUT, Christ 238 Jenny 238
SUTTERFIELD, Jesse 214
SUTTON, Ephriam 213 Mary 230
SWANN, Edw 214
SWAYZE, Caty 238 Elizabeth 238 James 238 Samuel 238
SWEARENGEN, William 266
SWEARNGER, D 96
SWEET, Joseph 104
SWESEY, James 214
SWIFT, John 205 Merry 236
TALBERT, Rev 119
TALBET, Ezekial 214
TALBOT, Edward 85 Isham 113-114 Nathaniel 85 Patsy 236
TALBOTT, Edward 254 Isham 249
TAYLOR, 61 86 132 Betsy 238 David 266 Dr 86 Frances 265 George 238 James 86 Jane 235 John G 265 Jonathan 265 Lucinda 86 M C 90-91 Marion C 100 218 Martha 86 Mary 86 Mary Jr 86 Philip 214 Philip W 254 Phillip W 221 Richard 61 Roger 265 Susan 108 108 Thomas 214 W T 85 William 65 86 254 Zachary 265 Zurilduer 86
TEAGARDEN, Ann 238 Bazel 238
TEAGUE, Elizabeth 234 John 238 Mary 71 Polly 238
TENNISON, Harriett Ann 108
TERHUNE, Mary 238 Stephen 238
TERRILL, Ed 125 Edward 118 123
TESGARDEN, Basel 214
TEVIS, 250 263 B P 85 John 85 100 107-108 Joshua 218 Julia A 107 128 Lloyd 139 218 Mrs 108 Robert 225 Samuel 225
THACHER, Joseph 214
THARPE, J B 67
THEOBALD, Patience 238 Thomas 238
THOMAS, George 266 John 79 214 John A 218 Lindsay 79 Mary 79 238 Oswald 79 Pauline 79 Preston 79 Rowland 253 W S 67 William 238 Wilson 79
THOMASON, Saml 214

INDEX

THOMASSON, H 191
THOMPSON, Denman 185 192 Evan 247 Harry 118 John 247 Joseph 247 Polly 238 Samuel 238 Thomas 242
THOMSON, John 214 Mrs 97
THORN, Rebecca 234
THORNTON, Elizabeth 172 Mildred 173 Susannah F 172
THRELDKELD, Elizabeth 238 Moses 238
THROUP, Thomas H 225
THRUSBY, 103
THRUSTON, Mr 196 R C Ballard 49 195
THURSTON, Buckner 163 Peter 221 Plumer 115
TICHENOR, Jacob 214
TICHONER, Peter 221
TILLEY, Agnes 235 Nelly 232
TILLY, Aaron 214 Lazarus 214 Nancy 233
TINSLEY, Dr 73 Elizabeth 235 John 73 Jonathan 214 Saml 214 Samuel 217 William 247
TIPTON, Rolla 226 W H 221
TODD, 263 Ann 238 Arrin D 227 Charles S 153 Col 154 John 214 Levi 155 Robert 250 Thos 91 153 218
TONKREY, Silas 250
TOPPING, 250 Samuel 134
TORR, Mr 128
TOWNSEND, Betsy 238 Light 238
TRACY, Catharine 238 John 238
TRAMMEL, Ellen 238 John 238
TRAVIS, James 247
TRUAX, Nelly 239 Obediah 239
TRUDLE, 103

TUBMAN, E H 90-91 Emily H 91
TUCKER, Jacob 214 Rachel 234 Rebecca 230
TUKER, William 214
TUNSTALL, Col 56 249 William 261 William I 167
TURCHUM, Polly 97
TURNSTALL, William J 263
TWAIN, Mark 155
TYLER, Able 239 Catherine 229 Charlotte 239 Ernest 223 President 154 Robert 46-47 183-184 214 257 Robert Jr 239 Sarah 239
ULLERY, Jacob 214
UNDERWOOD, Betsy 239 I 68 Isham T 218 Nathan 239
VANBUREN, 36
VANCE, T S 129
VANCLEAVE, Aaron 98 239 Benjamine 239 David 97 Elizabeth 239 Eunes 239 John 98 239 Mariah 239 Rachel 97 Ralph 242 Sarah 239
VANCLEVE, 178 Benjamin 266 Jane 179 230 239 Miss Ralph 231 Mrs 178 Samuel 266
VANDEVENTER, Winnet 214
VANDYKE, 250
VANISDAL, Simon 51
VANMETER, Abraham 46 Joanna 234
VANNALTA, James S 227
VANNATTA, Shelby 135
VANOSDAL, Lucas 51
VANSWEARINGEN, 247
VAUGHAN, T M 67
VAUGHN, W F 87
VEACH, Benj 214
VEATCH, Jo 124
VEECH, A B 131 Alleen 239 C B 132 George 239

VEETER, Anthony 250
VENABLE, Betsy 96 J 96 James 96 Judith 253
VETCH, Betsy 97
VONDERHEIDE, 121
VORAS, Albert 51 Blue John 51
VORIES, Big John 51 David 51
VORIS, Coptrea 51 Francis 214
VOZ-HIS, Albert 97 Anne 97 Caty 97 Isaac 97 Leah 97 Massy 97 Tunis 97
WADDY, Saml 215 221 Samuel 263 W L 132
WALKER, Dr 21 Joseph 242 Lewis 215 Mildred 173 Mildred Thornton 173 Thomas 173
WALLACE, Agnes 239 Michael 239 Sarah 239 William 239 265
WALLER, 110 A D 70-71 A D Sr 71 Belle R 70 Catherine 71 G 70-71 Geo 69 74 253 George 70 254 John Overton 70 Kate A 71 Mary 69 Mary A 70 Mary G 71 Polly 70 Rev 69 Richard 254 Sarah D 70 Stephen 239 Tabitha 239 William Edmund 68 Wm E 70
WALLIN, Elisha 205 Garrett 205 John 205-206
WALSH, 127
WARD, Samuel 221
WARDLAW, James 263 Jas 217 William 263
WARDLOW, Doctor 56 Dr 249 James 227 261
WARE, 132 Mary 69 Ruben 69
WARFORD, David 242 Joseph 239 Mary 239

WARREN, Louis A 198
WARSON, Alexander 239 Jane 239
WASHBURN, Benjamin 247 Geo 215 James B 265 Samuel 265
WATERS, 250 252 Margaret 108 R D 221 Richard 85
WATKINS, Isaac 227 253 263
WATSON, Isaac 127 John 239 Peggy 239 Samuel 266
WATTS, 101 Deborah 239 Mason 239 Peter 247
WAYLAND, Joshua 244
WAYMAN, Edmond 215
WAYNE, 145 150 159 Gen 147 160 165 170
WEAKLEY, Anna 237 Betsey 229 Cal S 191 Elizabeth 238 Lilly 237 Mary E 191 Rebecca 237
WEATHERFORD, John 266
WEAVER, John 266
WEBB, 110 Augustine 214 G A 109 John 215 Leonidus 109 Saml 214
WEBBER, Thompson R 132
WEBER, A M 135 Phillip 68
WEBLE, Adam 239 Jane 239
WELCH, Wm 218 251
WELL, Samuel 48
WELLS, 101 103 182 Col 149 178-179 Edward 239 John 217 Phoebe 239 Samuel 177 Thos 115
WENTWORTH, Levi 244
WEST, Richard 214
WHEAT, Ann M 268 Z 268
WHEELER, 201
WHELAN, Mr 99
WHIT, Abraham 215
WHITAKER, Abm 214 Acquilla 239 Ann 232 Aquila 66 Aquila 103-104 184 266 Charity 239 Charles 239 Col 257 Drucey 239 Elijah 214 Elisha 266 Elizabeth 229

INDEX

WHITAKER (cont.)
  Isaac 214 James 48 78-79
  Jesse 214 242 John 48 65 71
  177 181 242 John Jr 214
  John Sr 214 Levi 214 266
  Martha 66 214 Mary 66 229
  Mrs 91 Phillip 54 Rev 49
  Richard 79 Sarah 239 Walter
  C 217
WHITE, 247 Abigail 239
  Abraham 239 Andrew 217
  Andrew S 219 Anne 239
  Benjamin 250 266 Curry 221
  David 215 James 55 98 239
  249 John 239 Joseph 215 Lee
  254 Margaret 239 Nancy 239
  Peter Sr 215 Polly 235 237
  Robert 239 266 Samuel 115
  Samuel W 217 Sarah 215
  230 Sarah Brashears 71
  William 254
WHITESIDES, Elinor 239 Isaac
  239
WHITINGTON, Frances 80
WHITTAKER, James S 115 223
  W C 125
WICKERSHAM, Adam 46
  Jacob 46 Peter 46
WICKLIFFE, Lydia A E 108
WIGHT, Frank R 225 John F
  218 218
WILCOX, 45 G T 179-180 Geo
  T 221 John 179 Margaret
  231 Sarah 179
WILCOXZEN, Daniel 247
WILEY, Henry 247
WILHOIT, Miller 80
WILKES, Barbara 239 Saml 239
WILKINSON, 159 Gen 147 161
WILLETT, Dr 249 John 253 Jos
  84
WILLIAM, Garland 66
WILLIAMS, Bazel 239 Betsy 229
  Easter 239 Elizabeth 236 242
  Garland 73 Henry 73 Jacob 239
  Jane 73 230 239 John 215 Joseph
  239 Joshua 215 Josiah 215 Martha
  73 Micajah 73 Nancy 239 Ruddy
  239 Sarah 239 Tommie 73
  William 242
WILLIAMSON, 103 Charity 239
  John 45 103 180 239 John W 181
  184 249
WILLIS, Elder 81 Geo L Jr 221 J S
  80 John 249 Judge 116 L C 35 106
  Letitia 190 Mary 190 Mary J 80
  Nancy 235 Pearson 190 Price 249
  Reverend 81
WILLIT, A R 67
WILLITT, Doctor 56 John 263
WILLS, John B 239 Susanna 239
WILSON, 103 110 David W 217 Dr
  159 Elson 96 Isaac 215 J S 67
  John 239 Josephus H 135 Lieut
  159 Prudence 239 Rebecca 238 S
  55 Samuel 242 Sary 232 Singleton
  159 249 Thomas 85 Thos P 217
  Travis 78 William 87
WINCHESTER, Gen 153
WINKLEFIELD, Mary 235
WINLOCK, Adam 85 Effie 155 Jos
  104 217 Joseph 53-54 117 139
  214 221 248 265-266 Robt 85
  William 85
WINTER, W H 87
WISE, Mary 239 Tobias 215 239
WOLFE, Nathanial 120
WOMACK, Samuel V 105
WOOD, Polly 234 Sarah 233
WOODARD, Michael 215
WOODFIELD, John 239 Sally 239

WOODS, Elijah 73 Jonathan 73 Saml 215 Thomas 215
WOODSON, Joseph 240 Sarah 240
WOOLFOLK, George 217 Robert 247
WORSHAM, Milton 91
WORTHINGTON, Edward 167 Hannah 240 James 240 Milly 240
WRIGHT, Acenath 237 Anna 230 Anny 229 Asa 240 Betsy 239 Elizabeth 236 J E 87 James 46 John 215
WRIGHT (cont.) Obediah 215 Phebe 240 Polly 235 Sarah Mccormick 83
WYLEY, Henry 215
YAGER, Samuel 244
YATES, 80 250 Gilson 73
YOUNG, 110 Edw 215 Edward 240 James 80 115 221 240 Jas 217 John 215 265 Joseph 240 Nancy 240 Nelson 242 Polly 240 Saml 240 Sophira 240 Susanna 240
YOUNT, John 68
YUNT, Elizabeth 230 William 266
ZARING, J L 131
ZOURSEN, Nathaniel 263

www.ingramcontent.com/pod-product-compliance
Lightning Source LLC
Chambersburg PA
CBHW071958220426
43662CB00009B/1183